Markets and Other Social Structures

Markets and Other Social Structures

Analyzing Moral Ecologies in Christian Ethics

EDITED BY
DAVID CLOUTIER
CHRISTINA McRORIE

☙PICKWICK *Publications* · Eugene, Oregon

MARKETS AND OTHER SOCIAL STRUCTURES
Analyzing Moral Ecologies in Christian Ethics

Copyright © 2025 Wipf and Stock Publishers. All rights reserved. Except for brief quotations in critical publications or reviews, no part of this book may be reproduced in any manner without prior written permission from the publisher. Write: Permissions, Wipf and Stock Publishers, 199 W. 8th Ave., Suite 3, Eugene, OR 97401.

Pickwick Publications
An Imprint of Wipf and Stock Publishers
199 W. 8th Ave., Suite 3
Eugene, OR 97401

www.wipfandstock.com

PAPERBACK ISBN: 979-8-3852-5106-3
HARDCOVER ISBN: 979-8-3852-5107-0
EBOOK ISBN: 979-8-3852-5108-7

Cataloguing-in-Publication data:

Names: Cloutier, David, editor. | McRorie, Christina, editor.

Title: Markets and other social structures : analyzing moral ecologies in Christian ethics / edited by David Cloutier and Christina McRorie.

Description: Eugene, OR : Pickwick Publications, 2025 | Includes bibliographical references.

Identifiers: ISBN 979-8-3852-5106-3 (paperback) | ISBN 979-8-3852-5107-0 (hardcover) | ISBN 979-8-3852-5108-7 (ebook)

Subjects: LCSH: Finn, Daniel K., 1947-. | Economics—Religious aspects—Christianity. | Economics—Moral and ethical aspects. | Christian ethics.

Classification: BR115.E3 .M35 2025 (paperback) | BR115.E3 (ebook)

11/20/25

To Daniel K. Finn—scholar, mentor, friend, Christian

Contents

List of Contributors	ix
Acknowledgments	xi
Moral Ecologies and Social Structures: Daniel Finn's Essential Contributions to Christian Ethics DAVID CLOUTIER AND CHRISTINA MCRORIE	1
Reaching Out and Circling Back: Reconsidering Solidarity and Transformative Action in Daniel Finn's Catholic Social Ethics CHRISTINE FIRER HINZE	23
The Unbearable Lightness of Work in an Affluent World MARY HIRSCHFELD	45
Economic Analogies for the Sacraments in the Middle Ages MATTHEW SHADLE	61
The Advancement and Economic Empowerment of Women: How Far Have We Come? REGINA WENTZEL WOLFE	77
Reflecting on Finn's "Altruism and Self-Interest" and the Need for Humility Ten Years Later JOSEPH KABOSKI	101
Analysis and Practical Dialogue: The Moral Ecology of Markets ANDREW M. YUENGERT	118

The Social Teaching of the Church in the Last Quarter of a Century   139
   STEFANO ZAMAGNI

Catholicism, Economics, and the Critical Realist Connection   156
   DOUGLAS V. PORPORA

Emergents and the Problem of Collective Economic Responsibility   170
   ALBINO BARRERA, OP

Collective Action and Agency in Christian Ethics   185
   DANIEL J. DALY

Sinful Social Structures and Political Polarization
in the United States   203
   CONOR KELLY

Daniel Finn: An Engaged Catholic Intellectual   219
   JAMES L. HEFT, SM

List of Contributors

ALBINO BARRERA, OP, professor of economics and theology at Providence College

DAVID CLOUTIER, professor of theology and academic director of the Business, Ethics, and Society Program at the Mendoza College of Business at the University of Notre Dame

DANIEL J. DALY, associate professor of moral theology at the Clough School of Theology and Ministry at Boston College and executive director of the Catholic Health Association of the United States Theology and Ethics Center

CHRISTINE FIRER HINZE, professor and chair of the Department of Theology at Fordham University

JAMES L. HEFT, SM, James Alton Brooks Professor of Religion and founder and president emeritus of the Institute for Advanced Catholic Studies at the University of Southern California and scholar in residence at the University of Dayton

MARY HIRSCHFELD, John T. Ryan Jr. Associate Professor of Theology and Business Ethics at the University of Notre Dame

JOSEPH KABOSKI, David F. and Erin M. Seng Foundation Professor of Economics at the University of Notre Dame

CONOR KELLY, associate professor of theology at Marquette University

CHRISTINA MCRORIE, associate professor of moral theology at the Clough School of Theology and Ministry at Boston College

DOUGLAS V. PORPORA, professor of sociology at Drexel University

MATTHEW SHADLE, independent scholar and author of *Interrupting Capitalism* (Oxford University Press)

REGINA WENTZEL WOLFE, professor emerita at the Catholic Theological Union

ANDREW M. YUENGERT, Blanche Seaver Chair of Social Science and Professor of Economics at Pepperdine University

STEFANO ZAMAGNI, professor of economics at the University of Bologna and past president of the Pontifical Academy of Social Sciences

Acknowledgments

THIS LABOR OF LOVE could not have happened without the help of many hands. First and foremost, the editors are appreciative of the decision by the Catholic Theological Society of America to award its John Courtney Murray award to Dan in Atlanta in 2022. It was as guests at his banquet table at that joyful occasion when we conceived this project, knowing how much Dan had meant to us and to the profession. We also are so grateful to the wonderful response we got to our initial invitations to contribute to this volume. The ready acceptances of so many scholars attest to the importance of Dan's work and to the strong bonds he has formed within multiple fields. So do the fine essays they produced in his honor!

We are grateful to the editors at Wipf and Stock, especially Rodney Clapp and Charlie Collier, who supported the proposal and moved it forward to publication. We are also grateful to Boston College for additional support for this volume, and to Alexis Larios for superb assistance with the final editing and formatting of the essays here.

Moral Ecologies and Social Structures
Daniel Finn's Essential Contributions to Christian Ethics

DAVID CLOUTIER AND CHRISTINA MCRORIE

IN *THE RESPONSIBLE SELF*, H. Richard Niebuhr argued that the normative question at the heart of ethics—"What shall I do?"—itself necessarily rests on a descriptive question: "What is going on?"[1] To respond to a situation, Niebuhr held, we must first understand that situation, which inevitably entails interpreting the meaning of the events and phenomena we encounter. As a result, one of the central responsibilities of the moral life is not merely abstract knowledge of what is good and bad, but also that of critical attention: to both the world around us and to the interpretive lenses we use to make sense of that world.

If this is true of the moral life overall, it is even more true for the discipline of social ethics, where the question "What is going on?" is much easier to pose than to answer. Alongside the ever-increasing complexity of the ethical issues arising in our globalized and socially connected world, there is also the problem of abstraction, given that social realities are not available for empirical observation in the way that physical realities are. As Andrew Yuengert puts it, "No one has direct perceptual access to these [social] structures": we do not "see" them in the way that medieval princes could see their subjects' support, or as a parent can notice their child struggling with homework, or even as a passerby can see (or choose not to see!) someone suffering by the side of the road.[2] As a result, ethicists must turn to the social sciences for assistance—but, of course,

---

1. Niebuhr, *Responsible Self*, 63.
2. Yuengert, *Catholic Social Teaching in Practice*, 266.

none of these provides perfectly objective windows onto social realities, either; they each come laden with their own presuppositions, methodologies, and languages, and bring some aspects of social life into focus while obscuring others. Here the question of interpretation is especially crucial: how will we choose to represent and analyze the social structures, institutions, and dynamics we encounter? Making moral judgments about social life is, it turns out, a complex and multilayered process.

In one form or another, this complexity has been the subject of Daniel Finn's scholarship over the past nearly fifty years. From the start, Finn has eschewed easy and facile answers when reasoning about our social responsibilities, precisely because he has been committed to reckoning with the true ambiguity and complicated nature of social life—yet without ever losing sight of the urgency of answering, "What shall I do?" Over the course of his career, these commitments have led him to make a number of essential contributions to the field of Christian ethics that have significantly advanced our ability to answer both of Niebuhr's questions well.

In this essay we outline these contributions, starting by highlighting what he has sometimes informally referred to as his "two big ideas": first, the "moral ecology of markets," a conceptual framework for economic ethics that directs attention to the background conditions shaping economic outcomes; and second, the application in all areas of Christian ethics of a more sophisticated account of the relationship between individual agency and social structures via critical realist sociology. Given that both of these move our field beyond a number of existing impasses, these are very "big" ideas indeed! Here we explain how Finn's thinking developed over time to generate these and identify some of the new lines of theological and ethical inquiry opened by his work in unpacking them. We follow this by suggesting that equally as important for Christian social ethics (and perhaps a third "big idea") is Finn's legacy of thinking with—and critically about—multiple academic disciplines when seeking to understand social reality. Alongside the many substantive contributions he has made, we think that Finn's methodological example of *how* to attend to the interpretive dimension of the task of social ethics will also stand as a gift to our field for years to come.

THE MORAL ECOLOGY OF MARKETS: MARKETS AS SOCIAL STRUCTURES SHAPED BY BACKGROUND CONDITIONS

Finn's commitment to carefully understanding social phenomena first resulted in his critique of the terms of the debate concerning the morality of markets that had been dominant near the end of the twentieth century. At the time, the discourse on economic ethics was blandly pro- versus anti-market, and significantly shaped by the larger debate over the relative merits of capitalism and socialism. Perhaps unsurprisingly, these debates did not tend to host sophisticated reflection on the contingency and social construction of markets; rather, they tended to construe markets in monolithic terms, for better or worse, and to speak as if there were simply one "market system."

Further complicating the conversation at that time was the fact that Catholic theological discourse in particular was also divided on the question of social sin, with conservative and magisterial scholarship emphasizing the personal nature of sin, and liberationists emphasizing its structural dimensions. When applied to economic injustice, the resulting conversation was often confused and confusing. It was hard to know how to deal with the impasse between prominent Catholic thinkers as disparate as liberationists such as Gustavo Gutiérrez and neoconservatives such as Michael Novak.

As early as his first book in 1985, Finn (with co-author Prentiss Pemberton) argues that while debates between these disparate positions were "crucially important," they rest on a deeper question about whether existing market institutions are "fundamentally sound" or need "some basic change."[3] Using the good Samaritan as a foil, the book insists that the fundamental move forward necessary—for scholars and activists alike—is to attend to structures. But how? Finn sees in all his work that the temptation is always to answer this question in an either/or way—that we must talk about sin and justice *either* in terms of structures *or* in terms of individual actions. It is this either/or that he has resisted from the beginning, and in developing the moral ecology framework, he sought to offer something that spoke to those on both left and right. How might

---

3. Pemberton and Finn, *Toward a Christian Economic Ethic*, 5. Christine Firer Hinze's essay in this collection identifies how that early volume should still hold great interest for Christian ethics.

one navigate the evaluation of what terms like "fundamentally" sound or "basic" change mean?

The notion of a "moral ecology" first emerged explicitly from Finn's deep engagement with *Centesimus Annus*. In a 1998 *Theological Studies* article, he suggests that the encyclical's approach to the economy is "helpful but incomplete" and proposes the need for an "institutional analysis" that would "complement" the "personalist" analysis. There Finn asked, "Under what conditions could a Christian give moral approval to the market system?"[4] By the time of *The Moral Ecology of Markets*, he had refined this question somewhat, to "Under what conditions are the outcomes of markets just?"[5] As he explained there, the yes/no framing of the question "Are markets just?" had "generated simplicities on all sides that have undercut a real dialogue" on economic justice, and ultimately "hurt our ability to evaluate markets from a moral perspective."[6]

Moving away from such dichotomous thinking, Finn's intervention was to direct our attention to the background social conditions that shape how markets function and that thus shape their outcomes. Markets always operate within moral ecologies, he argued, which are composed of at least four elements. The first of these are the legal "fences" placed around exchange, and which designate some forms of economic activity licit and others illicit—by forbidding fraud and theft, for example, and regulating the sale of certain goods and services. The second is how a society chooses to provision essential goods and services, addressing communally the distributional challenges that arise in markets. Even for the most libertarian, public police and courts must be made available to everyone. But beyond this, no society exists without an implied minimum of goods and services that must be provided by some means, often mixing markets and governments. One can see examples of these first two elements in all eras, from the extensive regulations (and debates over them) on the price of bread in premodern Europe to contemporary debates over how to provide health care.[7]

The third element in Finn's moral ecology is the morality of individuals and groups. In another essay that leads up to the book, Finn notes that while economist James Buchanan is typical in finding personal moral behavior "analytically uninteresting," it is economically significant that

---

4. Finn, "John Paul II," 663.
5. Finn, *Moral Ecology*, 108.
6. Finn, *Moral Ecology*, 103.
7. On the history of bread regulation, see De Vries, *Price of Bread*.

"most of us, most of the time, can count on our neighbors, co-workers and friends to be generally truthful, to offer help when needed, and to show the ordinary signs of civility and cooperation—and at times real kindness."[8] Surely these behaviors, which are not legally enforceable, are important in a host of ways for making markets work well. As he notes, "There would be a tremendous loss of economic efficiency if the moral convictions of people evaporated."[9] Fourth, the ecology includes the presence and activity of the institutions of civil society. Drawing on thinkers across the ideological spectrum, Finn argues that such institutions "are critically important for the appropriate resolution of the first three elements of the moral ecology," while also supplying "an essential training ground for an effective democratic process" by which people learn the skills of reasoning and civility necessary for the reproduction of the moral ecology on which market functionality depends.[10]

In part, *Moral Ecology* advanced a normative argument for getting these four elements *right*; as Finn put it, when these "are properly defined and structured, then one can trust that voluntary interaction of individuals within markets will result in just outcomes."[11] This is an important point to counter totalizing critiques of markets. Ethicists need to pay at least as much critical attention to the "ecology" within which exchange occurs as they do to the transactions themselves.

Even more than this, however, at the core of his proposal was a *descriptive* claim about how markets already work in the first place: by nature of being social institutions, all markets operate within moral ecologies, and thus all are shaped by these four elements. Whether they realize it or not, all societies—whether socialist or the most libertarian—make important decisions about all four elements of the supporting ecology. Moreover, these decisions are inevitably shaped by normative claims about human nature and the common good, even if these are never acknowledged as such. With this last claim, Finn in particular pushed back against libertarian descriptions of markets as arenas of pure freedom and claims that markets could thus be defended "without recourse to moral argument."[12] This, he argued, was effectively a rhetorical sleight of hand. Instead, "all perspectives on economic systems, from left to right, address

8. Finn, "Moral Ecology," 158.
9. Finn, *Moral Ecology*, 135.
10. Finn, *Moral Ecology*, 139.
11. Finn, *Moral Ecology*, 6.
12. Finn, *Moral Ecology*, 5.

several common basic issues, and each, out of necessity, resorts to moral argument at least implicitly."[13]

For conversations about economic justice to be productive, participants must be reflexive and forthright about their deeper normative commitments. Whereas appeals to efficiency or some other technocratic standard threaten to distract and stymie dialogue, transparency about the basic anthropologies and social visions animating our thinking at least gives us a shot at agreement—or, barring that, at reaching respectful disagreement. Indeed, *Moral Ecology* can be read in no small part as a plea for both greater clarity and civility in economic debates.

Thus, it offered a theoretical framework in which to collaboratively search for that clarity. Finn's move to identify and evaluate the background conditions of markets moved the discussion to higher conceptual grounds, where more of our social terrain could come into view. Without itself determining policy outcomes, an ecological approach encourages and enables us to ask: how are markets themselves socially structured, and what are the practical consequences of this structuring? Following this, how should this institutional variability shape our ethical reflections on their functioning? Such questions provide a framework within which economic/empirical and theological/ethical knowledge can interact, and each play their role. Rather than separating ethics into parallel discussions of personal and policy choices, these begin to illustrate their integral interrelation.

This was especially visible in Finn's insight that self-interest and love of neighbor are not intrinsically opposed but may even be aligned in markets that are "properly defined and structured." In an article titled "Nine Libertarian Heresies," Finn begins by praising neoconservative Catholic economic thinkers for (rightly) seeing that the Catholic social teaching (CST) tradition has neglected this point. Rather than simply accepting or rejecting self-interested behavior in markets, Finn's analytical framework asks the "conditions" question: how does a given market's ecology shape the outcomes of our reasonably self-interested behavior within that market? In so doing, Finn's approach overcomes overly simple anthropological critiques of *homo economicus*, which so often allege that markets are problematic simply because they host self-interested, utility-maximizing activity. Without defending all forms of self-interest, an ecological approach directs the ethicist to consider how the collective

---

13. Finn, "Moral Ecology," 137.

outcomes generated by individual behavior will depend in large part upon institutional structures. To aid with this analysis, in *Moral Ecology* Finn also provided theological readers with a primer on how different processes within the economy interrelate—with growth often being useful for improving distributive efforts and so forth.

As a result, one of the most significant contributions of the moral ecology approach is its ability to help ethicists make more effective policy recommendations. Because the Christian social tradition seeks concrete change in the world, helping the poor cannot simply be a matter of asserting moral positions or taking actions that merely make the giver feel better; at times it will also require technical insight into how to achieve objective goals. With Finn's characteristic gift for crafting clear and memorable illustrations, *Moral Ecology* offers a range of concrete examples illuminating how shifts in institutional settings impact the consequences generated by voluntary exchange.

Even so, this framework also resists any temptation to imagine that ethics can become a matter of value-free economic calculations, by reminding us that no economy exists in a moral vacuum. In this sense, Finn's moral ecology follows and brings more clarity to Pope Pius XI's original warning in *Quadragesimo Anno* against any divorce of economics and morality. Pius writes:

> Even though economics and moral science employs each its own principles in its own sphere, it is, nevertheless, an error to say that the economic and moral orders are so distinct from and alien to each other that the former depends in no way on the latter.... It is reason itself that clearly shows, on the basis of the individual and social nature of things and of men, the purpose which God ordained for all economic life. But it is only the moral law which, just as it commands us to seek our supreme and last end in the whole scheme of our activity, so likewise commands us to seek directly in each kind of activity those purposes which we know that nature, or rather God the Author of nature, established for that kind of action, and in orderly relationship to subordinate such immediate purposes to our supreme and last end. If we faithfully observe this law, then it will follow that the particular purposes, both individual and social, that are sought in the economic field will fall in their proper place in the universal order of purposes.[14]

---

14. Pius XI, *Quadragesimo Anno*, nos. 42–43.

Pius's point is one also made by figures such as Karl Polanyi who argue that economic activity must always be understood as *embedded* within larger social structures with higher ends than merely increasing economic activity. Finn's moral ecology brings significant analytical clarity to the particular parameters of such an embedding, without indulging the temptation to nostalgia about an idealized past. When markets fail morally, it is not so much because they host self-interest, but because the background conditions fail to order economic activity toward genuinely productive ends. In highlighting this, Finn's moral ecological approach doesn't just aim to help us make better practical decisions within existing markets, but (perhaps even more importantly) foregrounds the ineliminably human and normatively laden nature of markets overall.

SOCIAL STRUCTURES AS MORAL ECOLOGIES: ANALYZING CAUSALITY AND CULPABILITY VIA CRITICAL REALISM

The moral ecology framework fundamentally moves the ball forward in terms of Niebuhr's first question, "What is going on?" In so doing, it shifts the debates about economic ethics to a higher and more integrated plane. But it doesn't (and doesn't purport to) give firm answers to the question "What shall I do?" Instead, the focus there was on developing tools for moving past "the lack of real dialogue between proponents with differing views" on economic justice. Indeed, using strong language, Finn argued that "it is a scandal" that even "well-educated" people have "stopped seeking each other out for criticism and now rarely read the writings of the 'other side' except to find fault."[15] A similar concern animated his well-known CTSA presidential address delivered in the same period, which focused on overcoming the tendencies to intellectual parochialism among those who share the same faith.[16]

But Finn's passion for fostering academic dialogue never came at the expense of his deep dedication to *effective social change* (a theme particularly noted in Regina Wentzel Wolfe's essay in this volume). For all his impressive devotion to articulating analytical frameworks, he has always been in the game of Christian ethics to make the world better—including by indicting us, awakening in readers a keener sense of our moral

15. Finn, *Moral Ecology*, 153.
16. Allen, "CTSA."

responsibility to make things better for those who suffer. Thus, even in *Moral Ecology*, his concluding chapter asks, "What do you do if you judge that the current system is not properly structured and yet does not call for an outright rebellion either?" His answer concludes with the following:

> Perhaps the key element here is the awareness that the economic defense of self-interest is conditional and that when the conditions are not fulfilled, those persons who benefit from a system while others are either harmed or excluded bear some degree of complicity in whatever injustice occurs. This is not the vivid culpability of an individual who has personally decided to take an unjust action that harms another. Nonetheless, it is a sense of a shared responsibility for a system from which we benefit.[17]

That shared responsibility, he quickly adds, should spur us to collective action "to improve the system."

We suggest that Finn's remarkable output over the past fifteen years can be understood as unpacking the insights articulated in this comment. Over this time, he developed an increasingly rich and nuanced account of "the system," which ultimately allowed him greater precision in naming our implication in and culpability for social structures, and identifying our capacities and thus responsibilities for improving them.

Driving Questions About Causation and Culpability

In many ways, Finn's move toward this theoretical sophistication was driven by his long-standing commitment to addressing two central themes within social ethics. One is the importance of gaining a better handle on causality in economic life. This was a key concern in Finn's analysis of trade in his first solo book, *Just Trading*. Written in the 1990s during the heated early days of NAFTA and other global free trade treaties, there Finn expresses suspicion about the aggregate abstraction and moral emptiness of those who dogmatically advocate in favor of free trade—but is even more direct in suggesting that free trade *critics* "are more frequently susceptible to making easy, unfalsifiable causal attributions."[18] Free trade critics are to be lauded for their concern for workers' struggles but are often mistaken when attributing these to international trade itself. Here, as in *Moral Ecology*, Finn's intervention was to direct our attention to the

17. Finn, *Moral Ecology*, 152.
18. Finn, *Just Trading*, 262.

complex trade-offs shaped by the "rules of the game"—and, moreover, to the prospects for improving these rules.[19]

Causality emerged again as critical in unpacking the legacy of Pope Benedict's encyclical *Caritas in Veritate*. Finn's practice was to conclude each True Wealth of Nations (TWN) conference by identifying a key question that has emerged from the in-person conversations and the ensuing volume, and then to use this as the framework for the following conference.[20] In the case of his second TWN volume, which resulted from a conference on Benedict's encyclical held in the wake of the 2008 financial crisis, the "most important single theme" generated was "the moral significance of causality in social and economic life. How should a moral analysis, like that provided in Benedict's encyclical, interact with the empirical analysis provided by the social sciences and policy analysis?"[21]

The other theme prominent throughout Finn's recent work is culpability and responsibility—or, put more theologically, sin. Here his reflections are regularly and noticeably driven by a sense of dissatisfaction with the terms available for conversation on sin in social life. As explained earlier, *Moral Ecology* pushed back on blanket indictments of self-interested behavior in markets as sinful, but by turning to the "conditions" question rather than by mounting a defense of economic self-interest. A similar instinct is visible in Finn's responses to early conversations on social sin and markets; as noted, he commended liberationists and other market critics for their attention to global inequalities, but without endorsing a view of either globalization or capitalism as intrinsically evil (indeed, Finn has tended to avoid using terms such as these, on the grounds that readers understand them differently).[22] However, neither did Finn align with those who effectively denied the structural dimensions of sin by centering their analyses on individual intentions. For Finn—quoting Benedict, in *Caritas in Veritate*—it is imperative to acknowledge "the presence of original sin in social conditions and in the structure of society."[23] But

19. Finn, *Just Trading*, 230.

20. Through USC's Institute for Advanced Catholic Studies, Finn led a series of seminar-style conferences resulting in a cumulative series of book publications. For more details on these, see especially the essay in this volume by Fr. James Heft, the director of the institute.

21. Finn, *Moral Dynamics*, 8.

22. E.g., Finn, "Promise of Interdisciplinary Engagement," 7.

23. Benedict XVI, *Caritas in Veritate*, no. 34, cited in Finn, "What Is a Sinful Social Structure?," 136.

what does this transpersonal aspect of sin mean, concretely? What moral responsibility does the average individual bear, for example, for the unjust outcomes generated by the imperfect systems in which they live? And in what sense can social structures be sinful?

It was this ongoing attention to both causality and culpability that led Finn to recognize the usefulness of critical realist sociology. As described in more detail in Douglas Porpora's chapter in this volume, Finn's discovery happens through a Vatican connection with British sociologist Margaret Archer. In Archer, Finn finds someone who is at least as determined to overcome intellectual dichotomies as he is and whose work offers an account of the interaction of individual choices and structural causality that neither prioritizes one over the other nor merely conflates them in a hazy both/and. Instead, Archer and others had developed a language that describes how social institutions can indeed "cause" phenomena within social life (as he insisted they can do, against libertarians and others espousing methodological individualism), but that avoids ascribing to them determinative powers (as he always insisted against materialists). Much of the rest of Finn's work can be understood as putting this language to work in various ways and using the conceptual traction it offers on complex social phenomena to advance reflection on a range of substantive and methodological questions within Christian social ethics.

How Structures Emerge from and in Turn Shape Our Action

Above all, a critical realist framework enabled Finn a greater level of granularity and precision in analyzing the complex and multidirectional relationship between structures and individual agency. As many of the chapters of this volume explain, critical realism assumes a stratified view of reality, in which social realities have characteristics and causal powers that are not reducible to a mere aggregation of their constituent members. Just as water "emerges" from hydrogen and oxygen and behaves very differently from either of those two elements, so too social structures emerge from and are sustained by individual actions but exist independently of those individuals and their intentions. As a result, social structures also exist at a "higher" level of reality; in this sense, critical realism presumes what can be called an emergent ontology.

For Finn, this vantage point provides a crucial opening in the debate over how to understand the individual's moral culpability in the distant harms caused by complex social structures, which is so often limited by traditional equations of responsibility with directly traceable causation. As he writes in the introduction to *Distant Markets, Distant Harms*,

> The discipline of ethics, whether in philosophy or theology, has traditionally identified individual causal efficacy as the primary reason for one's moral responsibility for harms caused in the lives of others. Putting it briefly, if I caused a problem, I am responsible for it. But my impact in global markets is vanishingly small. Thus our challenge is to articulate the moral responsibility that arises from our participation in markets even though none of us makes a perceptible difference in the harms caused.[24]

In Finn's view, even the most sophisticated extensions of the manualist category of cooperation with evil still fail to address this latter point: that we frequently act in ways that sustain unjust systems and yet have little to no impact on these when we refrain from acting. In *Consumer Ethics*, Finn surveys a number of attempts to name our responsibility for distant harms and finds that, in all of them, the problem is the derivation of "moral responsibility for harms caused to others from a form of individual causal efficacy."[25] This is demonstrably inadequate to represent the connection between an American purchasing a shirt and a seamstress working in a garment factory across the globe, the central illustration of *Consumer Ethics*. In contrast, critical realism enables the ethicist to articulate this connection in terms of "a long chain of social relations among preexisting positions that extends from the consumer to the seamstresses."[26] In this chain, each person is influenced by the constraints of the relations they find themselves in (consumer to store clerk, clerk to store manager, and so forth all the way to workshop manager and seamstress), just as each person in turn sustains and shapes those relations. Agency and structural positions never exist independently of each other, but neither are they conflated. Not only does noticing this allow the ethicist to look inside the "black box" of the market and begin to understand the moral context it provides for different parties, but it enables a more adequate understanding of the nature of the causal—and

---

24. Finn, *Distant Markets*, xi.
25. Finn, *Consumer Ethics*, 36.
26. Finn, *Consumer Ethics*, 101.

thus moral—relation between consumer and seamstress, mediated as it is by the social structure of the market.[27]

In turn, this approach also offers a rich explanatory scheme for describing how it is that social structures come to elicit the very behavior that gave rise to them in the first place. For this, critical realism uses the language of "enablements," "restrictions," and "incentives": each social position (such as that of an assistant professor, another example that Finn uses regularly) exists in relations to other positions (such as those of university student or dean) that present to the individual a set of preexisting opportunities, barriers to action, and incentives (which may be negative as well as positive). While these do not determine the agent's choices, they do influence them significantly. (While the professor is free to deliver boring lectures or prioritize teaching over publications, for example, the knowledge of how others in other positions will likely respond to these choices may shape her priorities.)

This framework enables ethicists to describe how it is that structures exercise such a "powerful causal impact" upon our lives with a new level of specificity, including by attending to the different "logics" of power they present—whether "constrictive" (that is, threat based), "enticive" (opportunity based), or "constitutive" (forming us as persons).[28] This approach also has the advantage of not requiring that ethicists ascribe actual agency to social structures themselves, which Finn has consistently avoided doing. Moreover, it does so in a way that directs attention to the implicit social norms governing relations between social positions, which often exert as much influence over our choices as do more explicit rules and laws. But perhaps most importantly, this approach provides tools for morally evaluating the influence that structures have in our lives, and thus structures themselves. Does a given structure encourage and incentivize right action, thus "helping" individual agents choose the good, or does it present barriers to this and instead encourage sinful forms of behavior, which also reproduce the distorting structure?

With this last question, Finn's work decisively moved from analyzing the moral ecology *of* structures to the way structures *themselves* also function as moral ecologies for their inhabitants. In *Moral Ecology*, the "subject" existing within an ecology is the market itself, and individual behavior is arguably held more or less constant. Indeed, the focus there

---

27. Finn, *Consumer Ethics*, 102.
28. Finn: *Moral Agency*, 50; *Consumer Ethics*, 77–92.

is on when a market's background ecology will generate just collective outcomes, assuming that individuals act in their own interest. Using critical realism, however, Finn has modeled how to ask how markets and other social structures also shape the way individuals behave in the first place—and as a result, how they come to shape us as moral agents.

Recent publications engaging Finn's scholarship—including by many of the contributors to this volume—have already begun illustrating the promise of this analytical approach for Christian ethics and exploring the new vistas this opens up for both moral theology and CST. How can this framework help us better understand the role of social context in the agent's pursuit of virtue, for example?[29] And what are the practical implications of Finn's use of causal chains of social relations to map consumer responsibility for distant harms—how does this concretely differ from more traditional analyses emphasizing complicity?

Finn's work also opens up generative questions about how to analyze structures themselves. While he has explicitly refrained from describing structures as having agency, others engaging his thought have raised the question of collective agency and the extent to which structures and collectives can be considered responsible moral agents; the essays by Albino Barrera and Daniel Daly in this volume both explore this theme.[30] And what about culture: how can a critical realist and moral ecological approach help ethicists in analyzing the power of culture in shaping behavior and individual responsibility for shared cultural values and institutions?[31]

How to Think About Structures Theologically

Some of these questions lead back to the theological underpinnings of Christian social ethics, including and especially fundamental claims about sin and the theological significance of our social contexts. Here, too, Finn's work has opened up new lines of inquiry, including by modeling how to let the tools of social sciences challenge and enrich theological reflection.

As he argued in an article in *Theological Studies*, while Catholic thought is replete with references to social and structural sin, "Catholic social thought has no coherent account of what a social structure

---

29. For example, this has been a primary question of Daly, *Structures of Virtue and Vice*.

30. See also Keenan, "Recognizing Collectives."

31. Shadle, "Culture," begins to ask questions in this regard.

is"—and, as a result, no reasoned criteria for what makes a structure sinful.[32] Speaking into this gap using a critical realist account of social structures, Finn has proposed that structures "can be described as sinful when the restrictions, enablements, and incentives those persons encounter encourage morally evil actions."[33] Reflecting on this theologically, Finn identifies key parallels between the operations of original sin and sinful social structures in our lives. Both influence our actions and inner dispositions by way of external environments, but precisely through our freely undertaken choices, rather than deterministically, and with each choice further shaping us. Moreover, while both facilitate sinful actions in which the agent feels that only a part of themselves is engaged—that is, that sinful structures and original sin are often experienced as external forces leading to actions that seem to contradict the person's deepest desires or true self—in reality, it is impossible to "draw a bright line between human choice and the influence of one's environment."[34]

With this helpfully precise anatomy of how it is that sin may reside "in social conditions and in the structure of society," Finn has offered tools for grounding the concrete analyses of Catholic social ethics more organically in the deeper theological vision of CST. As Finn has himself argued, however, this anatomy calls for the development of further diagnostic criteria for distinguishing "good from bad structures of a specific kind."[35] Given that all social structures enable and encourage *some* morally problematic actions, how should ethicists determine when to identify a given structure as "sinful" and discriminate between those that are more and less sinful? And what are the concrete implications of this theological labeling for the task of social analysis—what practical lines of action does it bring into view? Conor Kelly's essay in this collection, which identifies gerrymandering in the US as a sinful social structure, illustrates some of the analytical and practical promise of this framework.

At the same time, Finn's work on sinful structures also raises interesting questions about the grace-filled dimensions of our common life. Just as all structures facilitate sinful actions to some extent, so too do all structures enable and encourage morally praiseworthy actions and

---

32. Finn, "What Is a Sinful Social Structure?," 138.
33. Finn, "What Is a Sinful Social Structure?," 155.
34. Finn, "What Is a Sinful Social Structure?," 158.
35. Finn, "What Is a Sinful Social Structure?," 158. For an illustration of scholarship furthering this question, see Kelly, "Nature and Operation of Structural Sin"; and in response, Cloutier and Finn, "Complicity and Oppression."

dispositions. What are we to make of this aspect of social reality? If some social structures are sinful, can and should others be considered not just virtuous, but actually graced—that is, does grace also reside "in the structure of society," alongside sin? The concept of social or structural grace is comparatively underdeveloped within theology, and it stands to reason that Finn's use of critical realism may be of great use for ethicists aiming to understand its nature and operation in our lives. Moreover, Finn's bridging of doctrinal reflection on original sin with the categories of social ethics suggests parallel possibilities, when it comes to grace: how, his work invites us to ask, might nuanced attention to how social structures interact with our agency stand to advance theological reflection on sanctification, salvation, and the mediation of grace in history?

THE ONGOING CHALLENGE OF DOING TRULY INTEGRAL SOCIAL ANALYSIS

In his 2009 Society of Christian Ethics presidential address, Finn boldly named six propositions from economics that ethicists need to take seriously in their work, including the centrality of scarcity, the importance of self-interest, and the crucial role of prices. Like his CTSA presidential address of a few years earlier, he did not take the opportunity to preach to the choir, but to challenge the choir—in this case, to become more interdisciplinary, for the purposes of better combatting injustice. Commenting on his bold proposal that our doctoral programs include significant study of complementary disciplines outside of theology, he noted that this was not an end in itself, but aimed at

> our achieving the capacity to move among mutually enriching perspectives, especially among some that together create cognitive dissonance. The injustices of the world . . . so numerous in city and countryside around the globe, stand before us as witness to our inaction. We will not properly understand them without the capacity to grasp the contending accounts of their causes and we will be unable adequately to confront them without the capacity to evaluate the competing proposals for action. This understanding requires, then, both the grasp of multiple perspectives and a highly developed sense of wisdom in deciding when and how to move among them.[36]

---

36. Finn, "Promise of Interdisciplinary Engagement," 16.

This last claim, we propose, could arguably qualify as a third "big idea" animating Finn's scholarship: the recognition that understanding and changing complex social realities will require thinking with and critically about multiple disciplinary perspectives at once. One of the most central aims of Finn's work over the years has been cultivating the wisdom to do this, and then sharing this wisdom with others. His accomplishments in this regard, we think, are one of his greatest contributions to the field of Christian ethics.

As in his SCE presidential address, this has often led Finn to model how to use the perspectives and insights of economics to refine theological analyses of economic issues.[37] Indeed, a consistent concern of his has been to equip theological readers with the basic economic literacy required to make reasoned moral judgments about what goes on in markets. As Joseph Kaboski's contribution to this collection illustrates, however, Finn has also consistently critiqued the perspectives and methods of economics and argued that economics needs the insights of theology just as much as vice versa. Above all, his work engaging economic theory has taken aim at its alleged value neutrality; as noted, one of the central claims of *Moral Ecology* is that normative presuppositions are encoded within *all* arguments about economic matters—and, as a result, that debates over contested social questions would be more productive if participants developed the skills to be reflexive and transparent about their deeper moral and theoretical commitments (an argument critically revisited in Andrew Yuengert's essay in this volume, as well).

Indeed, for quite some time now Finn has been widely acknowledged—in both Catholic and Protestant scholarship alike—as a leading voice in economic ethics in no small part for his ability to think as a theologian and an economist at the same time, taking seriously the complexity of both disciplines, rather than merely cherry-picking favored thinkers or dismissing either. As one review essay praising his *Distant Markets, Distant Harms* notes, Finn's volume avoids the clunky nature of so many works aiming to be interdisciplinary in which "the theologians do a little talking, and then the economists do some talking."[38] Indeed, Finn's scholarship not only thoroughly integrates the theoretical perspectives of both fields but then also accessibly models this integration, inviting his readers to go and do likewise.

---

37. See also Finn, *Empirical Foundations*.
38. Ballor, "Affluence Agonistes," 282, citing Claar, "Joyful Economics," 132.

As so many of the contributions to this collection underscore, Finn's quest to understand causality and moral responsibility in social life ultimately led him to go beyond the dialogue with economics, despite its continued importance. As he remarks in the introduction to *Distant Markets, Distant Harms,*

> Mainstream economics has been notoriously individualist in its conception of economic life, and as a result, social structures of all kinds—whether firms, families, government, or markets—are undertheorized within economic science. Sociology is the discipline where there has been a consistent and careful analysis of social structures and their impact in people's lives. Thus Christian economic ethics has much to gain from a conversation with sociological colleagues.[39]

Alongside economics, then, Finn turned to sociology to help answer the question of what's going on with regard to social structures.

But *which* sociology? Douglas Porpora's essay makes clear that there, too, theories and methods that appear value free actually rest on contestable anthropological claims. Sorting through the normative underpinnings of different approaches to sociology, Finn—along with Porpora and a number of others contributing to this collection—advocates the use of critical realist sociological theory, on the grounds that its presuppositions are more descriptively realistic than other available options.

For the theological ethicist, attending to the theoretical foundations of other fields is not merely a matter of academic interest for the few scholars engaging in cross-disciplinary dialogue, but rather an integral part of the task of "seeing" social reality clearly. This is due to what critical realists describe as the "transfactual" nature of social structures and other social phenomena. Despite their objective existence, these are "not-sense-perceptible" in the way that physical phenomena are—that is, we cannot observe them the way we can icicles or geological strata.[40] As a result, those seeking to understand complex social dynamics and phenomena necessarily turn to the aid of the social sciences for insight. However, no social theory can be relied upon to provide complete and objective insight; instead, each offers a partial view of the subjects they bring into focus (and, moreover, some only offer distorted views). The theories, concepts, and metaphors we use to describe and analyze social realities significantly shapes our understanding of those realities.

39. Finn, *Distant Markets*, xi.
40. Finn, "What Is a Sinful Social Structure?," 149.

As a result, it is imperative that those seeking to make moral judgments about social life first critically reflect on the external disciplinary perspectives they rely upon, appreciating what they can offer while being mindful of their conceptual limitations. In his many publications engaging and employing critical realist sociology, Finn has done the field of Christian ethics a tremendous service in this regard. On one level, this is due to the theoretical advantages offered by critical realism itself, given that it so lucidly moves beyond simplistic binaries when it comes to representing the complex interactions between individual agency and social structures. Finn's explication and deployment of its grammar of social analysis in terms accessible for theologians renders any remaining ignorance of this complexity on our part vincible, moving forward!

On a more fundamental level, however, is the even greater gift of Finn's example of how to think about complex social questions using multiple disciplinary perspectives at once, whatever those disciplines may be. In modeling how to critically but appreciatively engage a range of social sciences with humility and rigor, Finn has given us a concrete illustration of how to answer Niebuhr's questions that sets a new standard for Christian social ethics more broadly.

CONCLUSION

It is impossible in an introductory essay like this to do justice to the full scope of the impact that Finn has had in his nearly fifty years of service to the church, academy, and wider society. In this essay, we haven't even mentioned his contributions to public discourse through his many columns and essays in popular journals like *Commonweal*, his leadership in the Association for Social Economics, or his years involved in interfaith community organizing working on issues such as affordable housing.[41] Nor have we said anything about his volume *Christian Economic Ethics*, which arguably provides the most comprehensive and yet accessible history of economic reflection in the Christian tradition.

But the deeper legacy of Finn's career is not restricted to the quantity or quality of his scholarly output, as if he was merely a scholar working ten hours a day in a dark library during the very long winters in central Minnesota. As we conclude, this is what we would like to underline most. Finn has been a kind and generous colleague, mentor, and friend to so

---

41. Many of these essays are now collected in Finn, *Faithful Economics*.

many people—not least the two of us. One of us (David) met him as a department colleague and immediately was shaped by his classroom visits with insightful advice for a young teacher, a memorable dinner for a CTSA newbie with senior colleagues in San Antonio, and friendly but sharp questions about whether my youthful sweeping criticisms of Walmart could be justified without learning more about economics. The other (Christina) is grateful for the years of conversations, feedback on written work, and the friendship between our families that have all followed from Finn's gracious choice to attend a paper by a graduate student at an SCE gathering in Toronto. In calling Dan a friend and mentor, our cup runneth over! And, as this Festschrift attests, there is no shortage of others whom he has likewise befriended, encouraged, challenged, and inspired over the years.

One final note: In the academic world, it can become easy to fall into repetitious ruts, where we rehearse the ideas and authors we learned early in our career. There's plenty of reasons for this—most of us got into this work because we read something and someone who changed our worldview, and that probably both shaped where and what we studied! But one privilege of the academic life should be that of constant growth—not the "growth" epitomized by consumption (e.g. our bookshelves or CVs!), but that of constantly *learning* more and more about the realities we are trying to understand. We see this kind of growth at every step throughout Dan's scholarly career. He has never stopped searching for better and better approaches with which to analyze the world, as a result of his commitment to helping us all to work hard to make it better.

But we are also invited to a life of continual growth because we are theologians. The ultimate object of our study—a God who is Goodness itself—always surpasses our understanding. And our calling to grow in understanding this divine mystery at the same time entails a calling to ever-greater communion with others. Finn's work serves not only the cause of justice but also this deeper communion, classically called "charity." All aspects of his life's work provide a model for seeking that communion, intellectually and personally, rather than settling back into our armed camps, ready for another theological battle. We know Dan is not averse to engagement and challenge. But it's not a battle. It's an opportunity. In modeling this, above all, Dan himself has been a gift to Christian ethics.

BIBLIOGRAPHY

Allen, John J. "CTSA: Group Should Stop Criticizing Vatican, Bishops, President Says." *National Catholic Reporter*, June 10, 2007. https://www.ncronline.org/news/ctsa-group-should-stop-criticizing-vatican-bishops-president-says.

Ballor, Jordan J. "Affluence Agonistes: A Review Essay." *Christian Scholar's Review* 45 (2016) 273–85.

Claar, Victor V. "Joyful Economics." *Econ Journal Watch* 11 (2014) 127–35.

Cloutier, David, and Daniel K. Finn. "Improving Theology's Understanding of Complicity and Oppression in Sinful Social Structures." *Horizons* 52 (2025) 26–49.

Daly, Daniel J. *The Structures of Virtue and Vice*. Washington, DC: Georgetown University Press, 2021.

De Vries, Jan. *The Price of Bread*. New York: Cambridge University Press, 2019.

Finn, Daniel K. *Christian Economic Ethics: History and Implications*. Minneapolis: Fortress, 2013.

———. *Consumer Ethics in a Global Economy: How Buying Here Causes Injustice There*. Washington, DC: Georgetown University Press, 2019.

———, ed. *Distant Markets, Distant Harms: Economic Complicity and Christian Ethics*. New York: Oxford University Press, 2014.

———, ed. *Empirical Foundations of the Common Good: What Theology Can Learn from Social Science*. New York: Oxford University Press, 2017.

———. *Faithful Economics: 25 Short Essays*. Minneapolis: Fortress, 2021.

———. "John Paul II and the Moral Ecology of Markets." *Theological Studies* 59 (1998) 662–79.

———. *Just Trading: On the Ethics and Economics of International Trade*. Nashville: Abingdon, 1996.

———, ed. *Moral Agency Within Social Structures and Culture: A Primer on Critical Realism for Christian Ethics*. Washington, DC: Georgetown University Press, 2020.

———, ed. *The Moral Dynamics of Economic Life: An Extension and Critique of Caritas in Veritate*. New York: Oxford University Press, 2012.

———. *The Moral Ecology of Markets: Assessing Claims About Markets and Justice*. New York: Cambridge University Press, 2006.

———. "The Moral Ecology of Markets: On the Failure of the Amoral Defense of Markets." *Review of Social Economy* 61 (2003) 135–62.

———. "Nine Libertarian Heresies Tempting Neoconservative Catholics to Stray from Catholic Social Thought." *Journal of Markets and Morality* 14 (2011) 487–503.

———. "The Promise of Interdisciplinary Engagement: Christian Ethics and Economics as a Test Case." *Journal of the Society of Christian Ethics* 30 (2010) 3–18.

———. "What Is a Sinful Social Structure?" *Theological Studies* 77 (2016) 136–64.

Keenan, James F. "Recognizing Collectives as Moral Agents." *Theological Studies* 85 (2024) 96–123.

Kelly, Conor M. "The Nature and Operation of Structural Sin: Additional Insights from Theology and Moral Psychology." *Theological Studies* 80 (2019) 293–327.

Niebuhr, H. Richard. *The Responsible Self*. New York: Harper & Row, 1963.

Pemberton, Prentiss L., and Daniel Rush Finn. *Toward a Christian Economic Ethic: Stewardship and Social Power*. Minneapolis: Winston, 1985.

Pius XI. *Quadragesimo Anno*. Vatican, May 15, 1931. https://www.vatican.va/content/pius-xi/en/encyclicals/documents/hf_p-xi_enc_19310515_quadragesimo-anno.html.

Shadle, Matthew. "Culture." In *Moral Agency Within Social Structures and Culture: A Primer on Critical Realism for Christian Ethics*, edited by Daniel K. Finn, 43–57. Washington, DC: Georgetown University Press, 2020.

Yuengert, Andrew M. *Catholic Social Teaching in Practice: Exploring Practical Wisdom and the Virtues Tradition*. New York: Cambridge University Press, 2023.

Reaching Out and Circling Back
Reconsidering Solidarity and Transformative Action in Daniel Finn's Catholic Social Ethics

CHRISTINE FIRER HINZE

DANIEL FINN'S FIRST BOOK, *Toward a Christian Economic Ethic: Stewardship and Social Power* (hereafter, *TCEE*), co-authored with distinguished Protestant ethicist Prentiss Pemberton, appeared in 1985.[1] In it, the authors present a biblically, historically, and interdisciplinarily grounded case for a contemporary Christian economic ethic. The book emphasizes Christians' vocational responsibility to inform themselves about economic matters and to work collectively to transform unjust social and economic structures. For executing these responsibilities Pemberton and Finn call for building networks of small, disciplined, justice-seeking groups; by carefully discerning and strategically embodied "structured, operative norms," these can generate and sustain effective, powerful action for change. *TCEE* sounded many themes that Finn's later work would continue to center, in particular, the importance of linking a full-bodied religious vision to an astute, social scientifically grounded understanding of social structures, power, and agency within economic and social relationships.

Intriguingly, in his many writings since 1985 Finn has never, to my knowledge, returned to this early discussion about "structured operative norms" empowering "small, disciplined communities" to effect justice-advancing societal change. Finn clearly values coordinated, collective action to ameliorate social injustice; he himself has participated in such

---

1. Pemberton and Finn, *Toward a Christian Economic Ethic*. On Prentiss Pemberton (1909–87), see Glock, "Prentiss L. Pemberton."

efforts over many years.² His later writings continue to affirm that such action is something that Christians and other concerned citizens ought to undertake or at least seriously consider.³ Yet within Finn's larger body of work, the 1985 volume, with its clarion call to Christians "to marshal a new kind of power ... to build counter-structures, and to effectively challenge the unjust social structures that are [at]the very root of the United States economy"—and its emphasis on small disciplined communities guided by sound, "structured operative norms" as key to living that call—remains an outlier.

This may be due to the 1985 book's co-authorship. Finn was the second author to Pemberton, a former teacher and senior colleague, and *TCEE*'s distinctive sensibility and focus may reflect Pemberton's concerns. Yet Finn's subsequent work retains many continuities with this first book. Most obviously, the concerns about power, social structures, and agency that *TCEE* evinced have continued in Finn's efforts to understand these foundational matters with greater precision, clarity, and nuance.

Over these same decades, the notion of solidarity received increasing attention among Catholic popes, scholars, and practitioners. By the early 2000s, solidarity had become enshrined in Vatican discourse as a fundamental principle of Catholic social teaching.⁴ Arguably, a full-orbed contemporary Catholic social ethics will connect critical analysis of social structures with an equally careful analysis of solidarity and its practical implications. Yet beyond presenting it as one of the tenets of Catholic social teaching, Finn's work has neither employed the language of solidarity nor analyzed its meaning and potential role in sparking and sustaining collective action for change.⁵

This brief essay suggests that Finn's robust contributions to Catholic social ethics may be further strengthened and burnished by "circling back" to retrieve themes from his 1985 volume and by "reaching out" to dialogue with Catholic and social science scholarship on solidarity.⁶ Undertaking this retrieval and outreach can, I propose, illumine, challenge, and enrich

2. See, e.g., Finn, "Power and Public Presence," 63–65.

3. Typical is Finn, *Christian Economic Ethics*, 385–86. Contrast Pemberton and Finn's treatments of "the Christian economic ethic and reformative structural power" and "the crucial issue of power in operative norms" (ch. 1); and "Empowerment Through Small Disciplined Communities" (ch. 9), in *TCEE*.

4. See Pontifical Council for Justice and Peace, *Compendium*, ch. 4, sec. 4.

5. See Finn, *Christian Economic Ethics*, 201, 308, 319–20, 340–41.

6. My terminology here is lightheartedly inspired by the ubiquity of these two phrases in current administrative jargon.

the contributions of our distinguished colleague in several directions. On one hand, Finn's recent critical-realist work on agency, power, and social structures presses Pemberton and Finn's treatment of social structures and structured action toward more theoretical precision and nuance. Including attention to solidarity would also enrich the 1985 book's argument. Conversely, Pemberton and Finn's compelling case for grassroots-based transformative action as key to Christian discipleship holds resources for translating Catholic discourse on solidarity and critical realism's explanatory insights into power-generating, solidary action capable of advancing, in concrete ways, a better social and economic order.

To illustrate these possibilities, I will first summarize significant contributions of Pemberton and Finn's 1985 volume. Next, contemporary Catholic teaching and scholarship on solidarity will be briefly surveyed, followed by a sketch of important ways that Finn's recent work employs critical realism to illuminate structures, power, and agency. Finally, I will consider contributions that *TCEE's* focus on gospel-inspired, collective transformative praxis, and CST's centering of solidarity, can make to the critical-realist Catholic social ethics that Finn and his colleagues are currently developing.

More broadly, bringing these three sites of social-ethical reflection into critical dialogue promises to enrich the theoretical and practical trajectories in Catholic social ethics to which Finn has so tirelessly contributed. And as I hope to show, far from replacing or adding extraneous elements, this exercise of circling back and reaching out can help re-center and integrate significant and long-standing concerns and themes that mark Finn's remarkable body of work.

DISCIPLESHIP AND STRUCTURED ACTION FOR JUSTICE IN *TOWARD A CHRISTIAN ECONOMIC ETHIC: STEWARDSHIP AND SOCIAL POWER* (1985)

This book's very first line throws down the gauntlet for its intended audience: "It is high time that all of us who claim to be Christians" take a second look at just "what Christian faith requires of us in regard to our economic values and commitments."[7] Given that "one of the clearest demands that Jesus articulated was for his followers to be on the side of the poor and downtrodden," Christians who assume that US economic

---

7. *TCEE* 1. Further references in text.

life is already structured as it ought to be need to look again, for: "It is not" (5). After surveying the current economic landscape and critiquing neoconservative and liberationist perspectives, the authors conclude that from a gospel perspective, the current US economy, which fails to adequately serve tens of millions of its citizens, requires "significant structural change." They then pose the critical question that the book aims to address: "How can committed Christians exert transformative structural power to alter our economic life in the U.S. in accord with more fully human values?" (12–13).

Against the backdrop of a substantive historical and ethical overview of Christian economic thought, Pemberton and Finn seek to answer that question by articulating a moral and practical framework whereby justice-seeking Christians and citizens can collaborate to generate power for positive social change. Central to this framework is participants' engagement in structured—that is, disciplined and collective—action, guided by relevant and strategic "operative structural norms." To explain what this entails, Pemberton and Finn cite a powerful historical case study: the US civil rights movement for racial justice, and the specific example of the 1955–56 Montgomery, Alabama, bus boycott, which after thirteen long months attained its goal of abolishing laws mandating segregated seating on city buses.

The authors emphasize the modern insight that because social structures are humanly constructed, unjust structures can be changed. But to do this requires collective action that translates ideals and principles into strategic action. Identifying what specific aim and action are best suited to advancing structural justice in particular circumstances is neither a quick or casual task. Thus, "any group of Christians who wants to live according to the demands of the gospel" by pursuing justice "will have to be attentive to the elements required for shaping sound moral structures" (207). Pemberton and Finn identify five such elements.

Justice-seeking groups must be motivated by (1) *conscientious intentions* and committed to (2) *just ultimate values*. To develop a sound and strategic plan of action, members must undertake a careful analysis of (3) *the factual situation* to be addressed, paying special attention to how *social norms* and other forms of *power* operate to uphold the unjust status quo.[8] Next, they must ask: "What prevailing norms are we challenging,

---

8. Christian social ethics "requires that we be clear and conscious about the norms that prevail in group life. We must move to take responsibility for them. We must address them with conscientious intentions and ensure that the expectations and

and what better norms do we want to empower in their place?" (213). Groups must then identify what (4) *structured norm* they will expect or require one another to adhere to (make *operative*) in taking collective action. Disciplined enactment of these norms is the key to generating nonviolent (5) *power to enact actions and policies capable* of advancing change. For participants in the Montgomery bus boycott, that norm was: "Responsible citizens should expect one another to refuse to ride buses until unjust seating arrangements are abolished." Adhering to that concrete, operative norm with discipline and perseverance for over a year, boycotters helped produce "a crescendo of power that mobilized new policies and actions" (209).[9]

Adumbrating a theme that would mark Finn's subsequent work, the authors underscore their third element—the importance of seeking an accurate and comprehensive understanding of "the factual situation." This requires the help of the social sciences ("psychology, economics, political science, and sociology") and of practical wisdom—"good old fashioned 'savvy' about how groups operate and about what is possible within this particular grouping at this time." They caution that "when a group [striving for social change] does not attend to the empirical situation, it often sets unrealistic goals and eventually dissolves in discouragement in the face of recurrent failure" (210). Indeed, "the shortcoming most prevalent" among social justice–disposed Christians is "naivete about the practical possibilities in a particular situation. Any norm the group proposes for its own life or for the life of a larger network of groups must be a feasible next step for those involved" (210). Implementing a worthy vision of structural transformation, on this view, also requires a practical incrementalism.

Pemberton and Finn thus urge justice seekers to focus upon "specific, easily interpreted, transformative policies" and "connect their simply-interpreted policies with transformative values" (22–23). Further, "vital operative norms need to be built upon the awareness that non-violent, deep-level social change in democracies can occur when large numbers of persons bring about small degrees of radical policy change" (22). The civil rights movement's multiple campaigns testify to the potential of

---

requirements in social life are in accord with just ultimate values" (*TCEE* 15).

9. Also: "Power is the capacity to bring about an intended result. P in social relations can be exerted by influence, by persuasion, by being able to provide rewards or impose deprivations, or by various kinds of coercion—e.g. physical or legal threat, or outright violence" (*TCEE* 23, citing Etzioni, *Active Society*, chs. 8, 12, 13–15).

wisely identified operative norms, hewed to by large numbers of committed persons and groups, to generate the power to make a difference in concrete policy outcomes.

TCEE's final chapter lifts up the crucial role of small, disciplined communities in grounding, seeding, and empowering collective work for structural transformation. A disciplined group is one whose members identify and bind themselves to behaviors by which they will, together, honor and seek to advance shared moral commitments: "Group members must agree to empower others in the group to expect certain behavior from them." Moreover, "in contrast to our often unreflective conformity to group norms," members of a disciplined, justice-seeking group "are critically conscious of the patterns of action they've agreed to expect of one another" (212). These commitments include informing themselves about the structures, policies, and institutions they wish to challenge or change.

These small disciplined communities of Christian disciples must be attuned to the facts and power relations in their situations; they must discern and be willing to take strategic, at times costly, group action to advance social justice. For moving ideals and general principles into operative norms that generate power for change, these local groups are often the first, indispensable vehicles. Groups that implement the above-mentioned five-point process for building sound moral structures will maximize their power and change-making potential.

The Montgomery bus boycott illustrates all of these points. As grassroots local leaders like Jo Ann Robinson would later recount, the boycott was initiated and sustained with remarkable alacrity, scope, and efficiency thanks to a large, established local network of African-American churches, civic associations, activists, and advocacy groups, most of whom had worked to advance racial justice over many years. These groups were "disciplined," in that members could rely on one another to show up, act consistently, and do their parts to accomplish what the cause required—whether it was leafleting, arranging alternate transportation for workers, or norm checking friends and neighbors to ensure people stayed off the buses.

For Pemberton and Finn, this historical case illuminates the concrete practicalities and embodied risk-taking that collective action for structural change entails.[10] This history also demonstrates that to enable effective public campaigns like the boycott and to sustain the capacity to work for change over the long haul, smaller, ground-level groups and

---

10. See American Archive of Public Broadcasting, "Interview with Jo Ann Robinson."

networks must continue to be built up, nurtured, and renewed over time. The work of civil rights leaders such as legendary community organizer Ella Baker, whose legacy lives on in the work of grassroots community coalitions across the US today, testifies to this crucial fact (211–32).[11]

Finally, as was also true for the civil rights movement, *TCEE* stresses that work for structural change does not end on the local level (171). Small local communities increase their efficacy by connecting to and cooperating within wider coalitions and networks striving to advance justice. Local networks, in turn, can fuel movements or multifaceted campaigns aimed explicitly at transforming larger social, political, and economic structures. From one perspective, the Montgomery bus boycott's victory—abolishing segregated seating on city buses—may appear rather narrow and modest in scope. But its power and impact multiplied as it inspired and lent momentum to a much larger movement intent on reshaping US social structures and institutions in the direction of racial justice (224–28).

SOLIDARITY IN RECENT CATHOLIC SOCIAL THOUGHT AND ETHICS

Though *TCEE* does not employ the term, "solidarity" aptly describes the dispositions and commitments to which the 1985 book called its readers. Solidarity has been a focus of Catholic teaching and thought since the Second Vatican Council (1962–65), and especially since the late 1980s.[12] Contemporary teaching describes solidarity as both a "fundamental social principle" and a "virtue"—a habituated disposition toward and a "firm and persevering determination to commit oneself to the common good."[13] As articulated by John Paul II, solidarity pertains to all human relationships; it entails acknowledging humans' de facto dignity and interdependence and taking moral responsibility for these in a "firm and persevering" commitment to the common good that motivates and sustains action. For Christians, solidarity also is also an explicitly religious virtue and duty, undertaken in response to the command to love God and neighbor.[14]

---

11. Cf. Payne, "Ella Baker"; and Stout, *Blessed Are the Organized*, 149–51, inter alia.

12. For one excellent survey and analysis, see Beyer, "Meaning of Solidarity."

13. See Pontifical Council for Justice and Peace, *Compendium*, no. 193, citing John Paul II, *Sollicitudo Rei Socialis*, no. 38; also no. 40.

14. Pontifical Council for Justice and Peace, *Compendium*, no. 196. Cf. Second

Official teachings stress several further points about solidarity. First, to build an inclusive common good, solidary people and communities must prioritize those who are currently deprived of rights and participation, making "a preferential option" for the poor, vulnerable, and marginalized.[15] Second, Vatican teaching describes solidarity as "above all" a principle and a moral virtue that determines the right ordering of institutions and is key to overcoming "structures of sin" that dominate and corrupt them. Solidary Christians and citizens are obliged to help transform structures of sin into "structures of solidarity" by creating or appropriately modifying "laws, market regulations, and judicial systems."[16] Third, to discern and respond to the demands of solidarity in particular times and circumstances are complicated and demanding tasks, to which the resources of the sciences and of human wisdom must necessarily contribute. Finally, solidarity is a pursuit expected of Christians, but also a responsibility of all persons of good will, with whom Christians are called to collaborate.

A number of US theological ethicists have analyzed and elaborated solidarity in recent Catholic teaching.[17] Gerald Beyer, for example, writes that solidarity awakens us to the reality and cries of the wounded and

---

Vatican Council, *Gaudium et Spes*, no. 30. *Gaudium et Spes*'s claim that human persons can fully discover themselves only "through a sincere gift of self" (no. 24) affirms an inextricable bond between personal flourishing and neighbor love; it is this bond that grounds solidarity as both fact and norm.

15. See, e.g., Francis, *Evangelii Gaudium*, no. 188: "The word 'solidarity' . . . refers to something more than a few sporadic acts of generosity. It presumes the creation of a new mindset which thinks in terms of community and the priority of the life of all over the appropriation of goods by a few." Also Francis, *Fratelli Tutti*, no. 116: "Solidarity . . . also means combatting the structural causes of poverty, inequality, the lack of work, land and housing, the denial of social and labor rights."

16. Pontifical Council for Justice and Peace, *Compendium*, no. 193. Further: "*Solidarity must be seen above all in its value as a moral virtue that determines the order of institutions.* On the basis of this principle the '*structures of sin*' [417] that dominate relationships between individuals and peoples must be overcome. They must be purified and transformed into structures of solidarity through the creation or appropriate modification of laws, market regulations, and juridical systems." Cf. Francis, *Evangelii Gaudium*, no. 189: "These convictions and habits of solidarity, when they are put into practice, open the way to other structural transformations and make them possible." Cf. Pontifical Council "Cor Unum," "World Hunger," no. 27.

17. US contributions include, e.g., Beyer, "Meaning of Solidarity"; Clark, "Anatomy of a Social Virtue"; Copeland, "Toward a Critical Christian Feminist Theology"; Firer Hinze, "Over, Under, Around, and Through"; O'Connell, "Dance of Open Minds"; Beyer, "Theoretical Appreciation"; Kelly, "Everyday Solidarity"; and Gichure and Pagnucco, "Solidarity."

impels us to find ways to respond not only affectively but intelligently and strategically. To do this we must attempt "to understand the causes of the suffering of the other." Echoing the "see-judge-act" formula commended by recent popes, he stresses that astute analysis and careful discernment are crucial to "understanding the cry of the wounded and formulating a plan of action in order to do good rather than harm."[18]

Beyer further argues that two marks of CST-inspired solidarity must be "*an emphasis on the participation of the marginalized*, and *continuity/perseverance*." Action—solidarity's culminating moment— "flows from the contemplation of the causes of suffering and calls for the participation of the sufferer/oppressed." Concretely, solidarity in action promotes the realization of human rights, particularly those of the oppressed, and seeks to ensure "solidarity as a principle of institutions and legislative policy."[19] Given this, "solidarity requires the sustained effort to go beyond short-term solutions and temporary aid toward long-term institutional change."[20]

Taken seriously, solidarity directs Christians to profoundly challenging conversions and paths of action. Persons and communities intending to undertake long-haul efforts to serve the common good by combating or transforming sinful social structures need also to dedicate themselves to their own, ongoing conversions of minds, hearts, and lives.[21] This conversion process, while deeply personal, requires the context and support of communities.[22]

Christian ethical investigations of solidarity also benefit from secular scholars' analyses of this descriptive and normative concept. Political philosopher Sally Scholz's thoughtful studies of solidarity, for instance, can help nuance and clarify both CST's treatment and Pemberton and Finn's analysis of "structured action." Scholz defines solidarity as a form of unity that binds members together into an identifiable group, mediates between individual and community, and, crucially, entails positive

18. Beyer, "Meaning of Solidarity," 16, citing John Paul II: *Sollicitudo Rei Socialis*, nos. 38–40; and *Novo Millennio Ineunte*, no. 43.

19. Beyer, "Meaning of Solidarity," 16–17, emphasis added. See also Hollenbach, *Common Good*, 159–65, 90–93; Beyer, *Recovering Solidarity*, 99–105.

20. Beyer, "Meaning of Solidarity," 17.

21. See, e.g., Pontifical Council for Justice and Peace, *Compendium*, nos. 42, 137, 328, 552, 579.

22. See also Francis, "Homily": "But [the gospel] also calls Christian communities to create 'circles of integrity,' networks of solidarity which can expand to embrace and transform society by their prophetic witness."

moral obligations for group members. While not denying the notion of universal human solidarity, Scholz argues that practices of solidarity are activated in one of three more specific forms: "social solidarity," "civic solidarity," and "political solidarity."[23]

Social solidarity prioritizes group membership and moral obligations springing from preexisting group bonds. These interdependencies may be natural or constructed, chosen or not, diffuse or tight, temporary or permanent. But insofar as they involve a unity that binds people together and entails positive moral obligations of some sort, social solidarity is present. *Civic solidarity* seeks to empower citizen participation and to redress or protect those vulnerabilities that would inhibit members from participating in the civic public. Here, positive moral claims are based both on rights of individuals and on the good of society. Scholz regards civic solidarity as a preeminent focus of Catholic social teaching.[24]

Political solidarity, finally, unites a group around a shared commitment to a cause. In contrast to civic and social solidarity, political solidarity involves "overtly political group action marked by multiple moral commitments," aimed at combating injustice or oppression and advancing, in particular ways, the communal good. Though not everyone in the group need be directly affected by the injustice being addressed, their political solidarity must be grounded in "a shared interpretation of the past and present, and [a shared] vision for the future."[25]

A distinctive feature of political solidarity—one that Scholz deems "rich with positive moral content"—is its "inherently oppositional nature." Political solidarity is not impartial or neutral. "Real people and real problems" are its moral starting point, and concrete human relations its content.[26] Political solidarity takes sides, and the solidary group's percep-

---

23. Scholz, *Political Solidarity*, 20–46. See also Scholz: "Duty of Solidarity"; "Political Solidarity and the More-Than-Human World"; "Solidarity, Social Risk"; "Persons Transformed"; "Trust in Solidarity."

24. In CST, "appeals to solidary duties are grounded in factual interdependencies of varied sorts, and there is an emphasis on the role of governments and policies in enforcing and protecting civic rights and duties" (Scholz, *Political Solidarity*, 33). A modern papal rhetoric of civic solidarity seeks "to hold the international community and powerful nations responsible for providing for and protecting the most vulnerable populations in the world" (Scholz, *Political Solidarity*, 32, citing John Paul II, *Centesimus Annus*, no. 58).

25. Scholz, *Political Solidarity*, 78.

26. Scholz, *Political Solidarity*, 35.

tions of injustice and vision for change are both shaped and limited by that group's cultural context and ideological framework.[27]

Scholz's description of political solidarity maps well onto Pemberton and Finn's discussion of structured action and the work of small disciplined groups. Her analysis also reveals an oft-noted ambiguity in CST's treatment of solidarity. Catholic teaching vigorously affirms de facto "human solidarity" and champions social solidarities that affirm members dignity and relationality. Scholz correctly observes, however, that in articulating solidarity's role in resisting and transforming sinful social structures, official teachings emphasize the less overtly conflictual form she calls civic solidarity. Resisting structural sin, making a preferential option for the poor, and joining in collective, change-seeking action will certainly bring persons and groups into opposition and conflict with the status quo. But with some exceptions—for instance, the Latin American bishops at Medellin and Puebla, and in some passages of Pope John Paul II's *Laborem Exercens*[28]—in official social teachings, the side-taking, political solidarity that this requires remains unmentioned or underdeveloped.[29] Scholz's and other philosophical and social-theoretical accounts of solidarity provide clarifying perspectives and language for addressing this and for strengthening Catholic reflection and solidary practice.

FINN'S RECENT WORK: A CRITICAL-REALIST PERSPECTIVE ON POWER, STRUCTURES, AND AGENCY

Finn's career-long quest to understand economic and social systems has led him more recently to sociology, where, with other Catholic social scientists and ethicists, he has found a philosophy of society known as "critical

---

27. Scholz and others who discuss political solidarity note that its side-taking need not conflict with broader human solidarity; rather it is a condition for ensuring human solidarity is realized and honored, especially for those currently deprived of their economic, social, and political rights.

28. See the Second General Conference of Latin American Bishops from Medellin (1968), *Church in Its Present-Day Transformation*, especially its chapter on peace, secs. 18–32.

29. On this tension in CST between the potentially conflictual demands of solidarity and modern social teachings' preference for "social harmony models," see, e.g. Donal Dorr's assessment of *Sollicitudo Rei Socialis* in *Option for the Poor*, 298–300; and Baum, "Class Struggle."

realism" a useful theory for understanding how social structures work.[30] As a metatheory that describes and relates individual agents and social structures in illuminating and non-reductionistic ways, critical realism offers Catholic social ethicists and practitioners language and frameworks for more precisely identifying the multiple relationships that comprise complex social structures; how such structures emerge, get reproduced; and how structures shape or influence agency. Better understanding equips persons and communities to better judge the moral responsibilities that those relationships entail and better decide how to respond to the opportunities and constraints they present. "Changing such structures will be less challenging if we understand how they work."[31]

Finn's recent works include critical-realism informed analyses of social structures, of power, of agency within social structures, and of what CST calls "sinful structures." For critical realists, a social structure is "a system of relations among pre-existing social positions into which persons enter." Structures exert "causal impact" on the people who inhabit them by "presenting them with restrictions—'conditional penalties' and opportunities—'conditional rewards.'"[32] By exerting "constitutive," "constrictive," or "enticive" power through rewards, norms, rules, or coercion, structures shape and can alter the decisions agents would otherwise make.[33] As agents repeatedly make choices in the directions that structures entice or constrain, they become habituated to those structures, which are, in turn, stabilized and reproduced.

Importantly, on this view, social structures do not abrogate agents' liberty; rather they have their impact through the ways we exercise our (constrained, but authentic) freedom within them. "Structures cause outcomes only in and through the decisions of people trying to accomplish their goals within them."[34] So, sinful social structures, Finn explains, do not incline people to evil by forcing individuals to be sinful. Instead, they make evildoing more likely by "generating restrictions and opportunities that encourage sinful decisions . . . by appealing to our disordered

---

30. Prominent sociologist Christian Smith holds that CR is not a sociological theory but a "philosophy of (social) science" ("Critical Theory"). A caveat: I am not an expert on critical realism. My discussion here relies primarily on Finn: *Consumer Ethics*; "What Can You Do?"; *Moral Agency*; and "What Is a Sinful Social Structure?"

31. Finn, *Moral Agency*, 32.

32. Finn, *Moral Agency*, 33–34.

33. Finn: *Moral Agency*, 33–34; *Consumer Ethics*, 69.

34. Finn, *Consumer Ethics*, 69.

beliefs and loves; by influencing and inclining members to choose sinfully and against their 'truer' selves; and by cultivating vice and inertia" as members' habituated sinful choices over time shape who they are, not just what they do.³⁵

Critical realists also depict individual agents as always enmeshed in preexisting social structures. Because we each are born into social matrices of language, beliefs and organizations, "agential power is always restricted to remaking... our social inheritance." Thus, "people... either reproduce or transform structure, rather than creating it." And because any structural status quo encourages inertia, "typically, people go along without much of a fuss, living within the restrictions and taking advantage of the opportunities they face."³⁶ All of this, Finn concludes, makes changing social structures "exceedingly difficult."³⁷

Difficult, but not impossible. Among human agents, "unpredictability" is always present. "Despite the costs, not everyone will go along" with the status quo; some people choose to resist. Often, those who are least privileged—"those who face the most restrictions and the fewest opportunities"—are the first to "choose to ignore restrictions, pay the price for that action, and if enough others do the same, can transform the structure."³⁸ And as modern struggles for racial, gender and worker justice attest, "significant structural change almost always arises not from the actions of formal leaders but from the conflict between persons enjoying many opportunities within a structure and others facing many restrictions."³⁹

Finn's recent work continues to affirm that "the Christian is obliged to improve sinful social structures," but with a clearer assessment of the structural and cultural forces that discourage this. Concluding his 2013 book, *Christian Economic Ethics: History and Implications*, he writes, "Most of us most of the time go along with the restrictions we face; we help to sustain the structures." Nonetheless, "personal moral responsibility requires not only virtuous decisions within structures (resisting

35. Finn: "What Can You Do?"; "What Is a Sinful Social Structure?" Also, Finn, *Moral Agency*, 32: "Since both we and the world around us are subject to sin, finitude, and ignorance, the structures within which we live all too frequently threaten personal morality and the common good, by placing restrictions on (thus penalizing) virtuous behavior and presenting opportunities for (thus promoting) vice."

36. Finn, *Moral Agency*, 34, citing Margaret Archer.

37. Finn, *Moral Agency*, 33.

38. Finn, *Moral Agency*, 33, 34. Cf. Finn, *Consumer Ethics*, 155–56.

39. Finn, *Consumer Ethics*, 73.

restrictions and opportunities that encourage morally evil decisions) but also effective efforts to alter social structures so that restrictions and opportunities make morally good decisions more likely and, in the long run, shape us to be morally better persons."[40]

But how does critical realism help to advance change? David Cloutier contends that this theory helps change-seekers tackle complex structural problems like climate change in two key ways: by offering "a *language* that allows us to name with some precision the actual structures facing agency"; and by providing a *structural analysis* that yields "a broader account of the possibilities for structural social change versus social stasis." Introducing this broader account, Cloutier limns more technical concepts such as stratified "emergent properties," interactions between reflexivity and material and cultural structures, and the level of "system," "where compatibilities and incompatibilities emerge that constitute the crucial leverage points for larger-scale change."[41] In the works of Margaret Archer, whether a social order is stable (reenacted by those within it) or vulnerable to change depends on the *relationship* between the structural system (what is actually going on) and the cultural system (the ideas about what is or should be going on).[42]

Put more prosaically, analyzing what Pemberton and Finn call "the factual situation" through a critical-realist lens can help change seekers grasp how present power relations operate, first, by illuminating how relationships among preexisting positions create and sustain opportunities and constraints that comprise "the way things are"; and second, by drawing attention to places where contradictions or disjunctions exist between current structures and what people think should be going on. These points of tension reveal sites where pressure can be exerted by agents seeking to effect structural change.[43] In 1955 Montgomery, Alabama, civil rights leaders correctly judged the tension between Jim Crow bus-seating laws and US values about equal rights, combined with heightened dissatisfaction with this contradiction among a united black community, to be one of those pressure points. "By providing a better understanding of the relation of structure and agency," then, a critical

---

40. Finn, *Christian Economic Ethics*, 350; cf. Finn, *Consumer Ethics*, 155–56.
41. Cloutier, "Critical Realism and Climate Change," 64, emphasis added.
42. Cloutier, "Critical Realism and Climate Change," 69.
43. Finn, *Moral Agency*, 33–34; Cloutier, "Critical Realism and Climate Change," 69.

realist analysis thus "illuminates the places where agents can or should act to transform structures."[44]

Cloutier concludes that "critical realism is not just a precision tool for analyzing issues. . . . It helps us realize how large-scale social changes can and do happen" and offers causal warrants for our moral responsibility to participate in action to improve them.[45] But, he adds, changed structures "are not merely the product of grassroots improvisations or intentional vanguard communities (even if both of these play vital roles)." They also require difficult, strategic, collective work to alter relationships between "the structural system and the cultural system," each with its manifold strata.[46] As for where to begin, Finn offers a concrete suggestion. "If you want to increase justice in any group," bring all stakeholders to the table and "start by identifying the differing restrictions and opportunities faced by different subgroups." This exercise "identifies privilege and disadvantage" and subjects taken-for-granted moral warrants for privilege to scrutiny. What happens next? Finn simply notes that while this process cannot in itself guarantee justice, "It's a good start."[47]

HOW DO WE MAKE THINGS BETTER? MUTUALLY ENRICHING CONTRIBUTIONS

Just as a high-resolution x-ray procedure assists doctors and patients, critical realist analysis discloses inner workings of agency within social structures, helping Christian ethicists and justice seekers "see" and differentiate the enabling and constraining relationships and norms that comprise and stabilize social and cultural institutions and practices. For the daunting work of understanding and shaping more just social structures, improved seeing sets the stage for sounder judging and more effective acting.

---

44. Cloutier, "How Critical Realism," 3. Cloutier adds that "a similar sort of analysis could be used to give a better, richer account of operationalizing 'the preferential option for the poor'" (6).

45. Cloutier, "Critical Realism and Climate Change," 68; Finn, *Consumer Ethics*, 157.

46. But a strong impediment to this work is the contemporary prevalence of what Margaret Archer calls "fractured reflexivity," which undermines agency even among the privileged. When reflexivity is fractured, "instead of agential action against violence [or complex structural problems like climate change], we get intensified affect." "If even academics deeply concerned with climate change get stuck at lament, imagine the problem of fractured reflexivity faced by so many others with so much less privilege than ourselves" (Cloutier, "Critical Realism and Climate Change," 68).

47. Finn: "What Can You Do?"; also *Consumer Ethics*, 155–57.

Arguably, recent critical-realism inflected work in Catholic ethics is developing and adding sophistication to Pemberton and Finn's earlier, more basic analysis of structured action and operative norms. Without explicitly discussing solidarity, this recent work also provides conceptual tools for better understanding the relationships, forms, and expressions solidarity may take. In particular, for confronting enormous, multidimensional, "wicked" structural problems such as climate change, economic inequality, or racism, critical realism offers important and needed contributions.

Critical realist analysis can also be useful in building on-the-ground practices of solidarity. In his examination of "everyday solidarity," for instance, ethicist Conor Kelly draws connections between Catholic teaching on solidarity and Finn's critical-realist approach to sinful structures. Kelly stresses that the virtue of "everyday solidarity entails a commitment to the transformation of social structures so that they can instead serve the common good." Advancing structural change requires "targeting the causal power of social groups" first, "by reforming the enablements and incentives that encourage personal agents to undermine the common good, and second, by challenging the restrictions that limit personal agents' abilities to promote the common good when they want to do so." Whether on the macro or everyday level, the goal of solidary practices is to contribute to "the emergence of 'structures of grace' to counterbalance existing structures of sin."[48]

Critical-realist ethics, then, can strengthen treatments of the social responsibilities of Christian disciples like Pemberton and Finn's and CST-inspired efforts to understand and enact solidarity. But the reverse is also true. *TCEE*'s prophetic call and concrete blueprint for pursuing structural transformation and CST's centering of solidarity both offer resources for enhancing critical-realist ethical analyses. They do so in several ways.

First, CST and Pemberton and Finn access the holistic, engaging, and motivating resources of Christianity's prophetic and narrative discourses.[49] Astute understanding is crucial but on its own cannot inspire or sustain the sturdy, power-bearing collective commitments and collective action that effective change requires. Recognizing this, *TCEE* proposes avenues for joining prophetic critique and vision to informed, discerning, and strategic planning and disciplined and courageous communal action for change.

---

48. Kelly, "Everyday Solidarity," 433, citing Ahern, *Structures of Grace*, 130–36.

49. Cloutier, "How Critical Realism," 1–2, discusses James Gustafson's fourfold taxonomy of moral discourse—prophetic, narrative, ethical, and policy, arguing that critical realism can assist and improve all four. See Gustafson, "Analysis of Church and Society."

Second, both make it clear that generating transformative agency requires agents who are personally converted to the common good but who are also committed participants in *groups and associations* that undertake *collective* action for justice. In an era of fraying civic bonds and waning associational engagement, stressing such embodied and committed participation is particularly urgent. Cloutier and Finn, in discussing critical-realist perspectives on agency and social transformation, often use examples that highlight personal choices and responsibility. Certainly, any Catholic social ethic must ensure that agency and structures do not become either conflated or untethered. But most scholars writing on solidarity, as well as Pemberton and Finn, also lift up the equally indispensable part that intentionally nurtured communal bonds and collective action play in advancing structural justice.[50]

Granted, as Cloutier states, large-scale social change is not effected solely by "grassroots groups or vanguard actions." But Pemberton and Finn, like movement leaders past and present, recognize that small, disciplined communities are necessary and potent players in such larger social change efforts. Pope Francis's multiple addresses to and enthusiastic encouragement of grassroots popular movements also reflect this insight.[51] Indeed, in the face of a powerful status quo, one might say that participating in communities or organizations dedicated to the common good becomes a condition for individuals' and groups' experiences of agency, and certainly for undertaking the structured action that addressing structural injustice requires.

Third, *TCEE* and CST highlight the distinctive capacities of faith communities to help ground, cultivate, and motivate collective action for structural change. As was true for the US civil rights movement, ethicist Melissa Snarr's 2011 study of contemporary grassroots living-wage campaigns observed that religious communities' understanding of solidarity as requiring ongoing "conversion" and renewal of commitments, and movement members' formation in practices and rituals of covenanting, forgiveness, and communal celebration, all made key contributions to the vitality and resilience—and thereby, the power—of justice-seeking coalitions.[52]

---

50. James F. Keenan, SJ, makes a related argument and surveys recent scholarship on collective agency and action in "Recognizing Collectives."

51. See Francis, "Address," as well as his addresses at subsequent meetings, most recently Sept. 20, 2024.

52. Snarr, *All You That Labor*.

In many different forms, times, and circumstances, such vital, resilient communities and organizations have addressed the complex relationships between opportunities and constraints, structures and power, social analysis and change strategies, personal agency and solidary action for change.[53] Susan Reynolds's 2022 ethnographic study of Our Lady of Angels Parish in Roxbury, Massachusetts, offers one local example.[54] Over several years of participant-observation in this culturally diverse and financially strapped community, Reynolds witnessed a process of ongoing conversion into solidarity whose linchpin has been members' long-term commitments to one another and to advancing gospel justice. As she recounts, the parish has endured periods of crisis and dramatic struggle. Yet more of its story consists in members' faithful accountability to less flashy practices: parish council meetings, liturgical planning and celebrations, tending to needy and hurting members of the church's economically challenged urban neighborhood.

Resonating with the community organizing philosophy of Ella Baker, Reynolds underscores the value of the formation in "slow solidarity" and "slow conversion" that these seemingly mundane but critically important associational settings can provide. Whether in local congregations, community organizations, or inter-group coalitions, when members hold each other accountable to doing the ongoing work of cultivating both inner-facing group bonds and the outward-facing virtue of solidarity, they also ready themselves to engage in civic and political solidarity in response to the "signs of the times." Thus prepared and grounded, such groups can detect and seize opportunities to engage in targeted collective action and exert nonviolent power to combat structural evils and advance structures that better support an inclusive common good.

CONCLUSION: CIRCLING BACK, REACHING OUT, AND MOVING FORWARD

As this volume in his honor testifies, Daniel Finn's labors in the field of Catholic economic and social ethics over the past forty years have born abundant fruit and planted many more seeds for the future. This essay has harkened back to the beginning of Finn's work and reached out to

---

53. Pemberton and Finn point to the US civil rights movement; Melissa Snarr to contemporary living-wage campaigns; Jeffrey Stout to grassroots community organizations. See Stout, *Blessed Are the Organized*.

54. See Reynolds: "Solidarity as Slow Conversion"; and *People Get Ready*.

a closely adjoining field where, over the same decades, Catholics have cultivated better understandings and more dedicated practices of solidarity. One can detect some cross-pollination between these adjoining fields, especially in Finn's early work, and in his own on-the-ground engagement in collective efforts for structural change. And over the past decade, the infusion of critical realist theory into Finn's work has yielded further good fruit.

Particularly for moving from theory to action, I have suggested that what Finn has produced so amply and well can be further fortified by first, retrieving and re-centering key themes in his early work with Prentiss Pemberton; and second, reaching out to connect with recent scholarship on solidarity and solidary practice.

So, for instance, an organization that undertakes Finn's critical-realism informed internal power analysis will benefit by also studying Pemberton and Finn's prescriptions for building sound moral structures. As they perform their power analysis and discern what to do with their findings, a *TCEE*-informed group will examine their intentions for proceeding and the justice of the values that motivate what they decide to do. Members will identify and evaluate the norms upholding current arrangements and determine what different norms they wish to advance. If the organization is bound by solidarity, members will prioritize for attention and redress structural relationships that negatively constrain or disadvantage people. Solidarity's commitment to the common good will expand their concern to encompass the organization's relationships and responsibilities to its external stakeholders and civic context. And in plotting specific courses of action, members will agree on factually informed strategic goals, identify sound operative norms to which they mutually commit themselves, and target their action at structural pressure points likely to yield to their nonviolent, collectively generated power.

Historically, as Finn notes, such dedicated action is more frequently initiated by a subgroup or groups that the status quo systemically disadvantages or oppresses. Pemberton and Finn helpfully expand this point by underscoring the importance of building small, disciplined solidary groups, who form networks with other like-minded groups whose members may include more advantaged allies. These networks provide the critical infrastructure for movements of political solidarity, helping fuel and sustain their efforts to alter unjust structures through nonviolent, collective actions and campaigns.

And engaging sources like Pemberton and Finn and CST on solidarity can enrich critical-realism informed ethical inquiry in one final, significant way: by wedding that inquiry to scriptural, narrative, and prophetic discourses capable of inspiring, motivating, and energizing action in ways that do not obviate but enhance and leaven the necessary and clarifying analysis it performs.[55]

For these reasons and more, we scholars, teachers, and practitioners who are indebted to Daniel Finn's inestimable contributions to Catholic economic and social ethics do well to circle back to his earliest work, reach out to recent teachings and scholarship on solidarity, and put these into creative, critical conversation. Doing so can deepen and strengthen our efforts to understand, critique, and join together to improve the structures in and through which we live and share our earthly lives.

BIBLIOGRAPHY

Ahern, Kevin. *Structures of Grace: Catholic Organizations Serving the Global Common Good*. Maryknoll, NY: Orbis, 2015.

American Archive of Public Broadcasting. "Interview with Jo Ann Robinson." *Eyes on the Prize; America, They Loved You Madly*, aired Aug. 27, 1979. Film and Media Archive, Washington University in St. Louis. https://americanarchive.org/catalog/cpb-aacip_151-wh2d796b02.

Baum, Gregory. "Class Struggle and the Magisterium: A New Note." *Theological Studies* 45 (1984) 690–701.

Beyer, Gerald. "The Meaning of Solidarity in Catholic Social Teaching." *Political Theology* 15 (2014) 7–25.

———. *Recovering Solidarity: Lessons from Poland's Unfinished Revolution*. Notre Dame, IN: University of Notre Dame Press, 2010.

———. "A Theoretical Appreciation of the Ethic of Solidarity in Poland Twenty-Five Years After." *Journal of Religious Ethics* 35 (2007) 207–32.

Clark, Meghan J. "Anatomy of a Social Virtue: Solidarity and Corresponding Vices." *Political Theology* 15 (2014) 26–39.

Cloutier, David. "Critical Realism and Climate Change." In *Moral Agency Within Social Structures and Culture: A Primer on Critical Realism for Christian Ethics*, edited by Daniel K. Finn, 59–72. Washington, DC: Georgetown University Press, 2020.

———. "How Critical Realism Can Help Christian Ethics." In *Moral Agency Within Social Structures and Culture: A Primer on Critical Realism for Christian Ethics*, edited by Daniel K. Finn, 1–8. Washington, DC: Georgetown University Press, 2020.

---

55. Cf. Gustafson, "Analysis of Church and Society," cited in Cloutier, "How Critical Realism," 1–2. My point here intends to highlight how prophetic and narrative discourse can enrich the theoretical and technical analysis that critical-realist ethics offers.

Copeland, M. Shawn. "Toward a Critical Christian Feminist Theology of Solidarity." In *Women and Theology*, edited by Mary Ann Hinsdale and Phyllis H. Kaminski, 3–38. Maryknoll, NY: Orbis, 1995.

Dorr, Donal. *Option for the Poor and for the Earth*. Maryknoll, NY: Orbis, 2012.

Etzioni, Amiati. *The Active Society: A Theory of Societal and Political Processes*. New York: Free Press, 1968.

Finn, Daniel K. *Christian Economic Ethics: History and Implications*. Minneapolis: Fortress, 2013.

———. *Consumer Ethics in a Global Economy*. Washington, DC: Georgetown University Press, 2019.

———, ed. *Moral Agency Within Social Structures and Culture: A Primer on Critical Realism for Christian Ethics*. Washington, DC: Georgetown University Press, 2020.

———. "Power and Public Presence in Catholic Social Thought, the Church, and the CTSA." *Proceedings of the Catholic Theological Society of America* 62 (2007) 62–77.

———. "What Can You Do? Understanding Sinful Social Structures." *Commonweal*, Sept. 20, 2018. https://www.commonwealmagazine.org/what-can-you-do.

———. "What Is a Sinful Social Structure?" *Theological Studies* 77 (2016) 136–64.

Firer Hinze, Christine. "Over, Under, Around, and Through: Ethics, Solidarity, and the Saints." *CTSA Proceedings* 66 (2011) 33–60.

Francis. "Address to Participants in the World Meeting of Popular Movements." Vatican, Oct. 28, 2014. https://www.vatican.va/content/francesco/en/speeches/2014/october/documents/papa-francesco_20141028_incontro-mondiale-movimenti-popolari.html.

———. *Evangelii Gaudium*. Vatican, Nov. 24, 2013. https://www.vatican.va/content/francesco/en/apost_exhortations/documents/papa-francesco_esortazione-ap_20131124_evangelii-gaudium.html.

———. *Fratelli Tutti*. Vatican, Oct. 3, 2020. https://www.vatican.va/content/francesco/en/encyclicals/documents/papa-francesco_20201003_enciclica-fratelli-tutti.html.

———. "Homily (Apostolic Visit to the Philippines)." Vatican, Jan. 16, 2015. https://www.vatican.va/content/francesco/en/homilies/2015/documents/papa-francesco_20150116_srilanka-filippine-omelia-cattedrale-manila.html.

Gichure, Peter Ignatius, and Ron Pagnucco. "Solidarity: A Catholic Perspective. Chapter 10 from *A Vision of Justice: Engaging Catholic Social Teaching on the College Campus*." *Journal of Social Encounters* 6 (2022) 87–100.

Glock, Charles Y. "Prentiss L. Pemberton." Hartford Institute for Religion Research, n.d. From *Encyclopedia of Religion and Society*, edited by William H. Swatos Jr. https://hirr.hartfordinternational.edu/articles/4495/.

Gustafson, James. "An Analysis of Church and Society Social Ethical Writings." *Ecumenical Review* 40 (1988) 267–78.

Hollenbach, David. *The Common Good and Christian Ethics*. New Studies in Christian Ethics 22. Cambridge: Cambridge University Press, 2002.

John Paul II. *Centesimus Annus*. Vatican, May 1, 1991. https://www.vatican.va/content/john-paul-ii/en/encyclicals/documents/hf_jp-ii_enc_01051991_centesimus-annus.html.

———. *Novo Millennio Ineunte*. Vatican, Jan. 6, 2001. https://www.vatican.va/content/john-paul-ii/en/apost_letters/2001/documents/hf_jp-ii_apl_20010106_novo-millennio-ineunte.html.

———. *Sollicitudo Rei Socialis.* Vatican, Dec. 30, 1987. https://www.vatican.va/content/john-paul-ii/en/encyclicals/documents/hf_jp-ii_enc_30121987_sollicitudo-rei-socialis.html.

Keenan, James F. "Recognizing Collectives as Moral Agents." *Theological Studies* 85 (2024) 96–123.

Kelly, Conor M. "Everyday Solidarity: A Framework for Integrating Theological Ethics and Ordinary Life." *Theological Studies* 81 (2020) 414–37.

O'Connell, Maureen H. "The Dance of Open Minds and Hearts: Aesthetic Solidarity as Antidote to an Anemic Solidarity." *Political Theology* 15 (2014) 74–87.

Payne, Charles. "Ella Baker and Models of Social Change." *Signs* 14 (1989) 885–99.

Pemberton, Prentiss, and Daniel Rush Finn. *Toward a Christian Economic Ethic: Stewardship and Social Power.* Minneapolis: Winston, 1985.

Pontifical Council "Cor Unum." "World Hunger, a Challenge for All: Development in Solidarity." Vatican, Oct. 4, 1996. https://www.vatican.va/roman_curia/pontifical_councils/corunum/documents/rc_pc_corunum_doc_04101996_world-hunger_en.html.

Pontifical Council for Justice and Peace. *Compendium of the Social Doctrine of the Church.* Washington, DC: United States Conference of Catholic Bishops, 2004.

Reynolds, Susan Bigelow. *People Get Ready: Ritual, Solidarity, and Lived Ecclesiology in Catholic Roxbury.* Catholic Practice in the Americas. New York: Fordham University Press, 2023.

———. "Solidarity as Slow Conversion." *Missiology: An International Review* 51 (2023) 31–45.

Scholz, Sally J. "The Duty of Solidarity: Feminism and Catholic Social Teaching." *Philosophy in the Contemporary World* 4 (Fall 1997) 24–33.

———. "Persons Transformed by Political Solidarity." *Appraisal* 8 (Oct. 2010) 19–27.

———. *Political Solidarity.* University Park: Penn State University Press, 2010.

———. "Political Solidarity and the More-Than-Human World." *Ethics and the Environment* 18 (Fall 2013) 81–99.

———. "Solidarity, Social Risk, and Community Engagement." *American Journal of Bioethics* 20 (2020) 75–7.

———. "Trust in Solidarity." *Rivista di estetica* 82 (2023) 16–29.

Second General Conference of Latin American Bishops. *The Church in the Present-Day Transformation of Latin America in the Light of the Council.* Washington, DC: US Catholic Conference, 1970.

Second Vatican Council. *Gaudium et Spes.* Vatican, Dec. 7, 1965. https://www.vatican.va/archive/hist_councils/ii_vatican_council/documents/vat-ii_const_19651207_gaudium-et-spes_en.html.

Smith, Christian. "Critical Theory." University of Notre Dame, Fall 2013. https://christiansmith.nd.edu/critical-realism/.

Snarr, C. Melissa. *All You That Labor: Religion and Ethics in the Living Wage Movement.* Religion and Social Transformation. New York: New York University Press, 2011.

Stout, Jeffrey. *Blessed Are the Organized: Grassroots Democracy in America.* Princeton, NJ: Princeton University Press, 2010.

The Unbearable Lightness of Work in an Affluent World

Mary Hirschfeld

The heaviest of burdens crushes us, we sink beneath it, it pins us to the ground. But in the love poetry of every age, the woman longs to be weighed down by the man's body. The heaviest of burdens is therefore simultaneously an image of life's most intense fulfillment. The heavier the burden, the closer our lives come to the earth, the more real and truthful they become.

Conversely, the absolute absence of a burden causes man to be lighter than air, to soar into the heights, take leave of the earth and his earthly being, and become only half real, his movements as free as they are insignificant.

What then shall we choose? Weight or lightness?

—Milan Kundera, *The Unbearable Lightness of Being*

When I was still an economist, I dipped my toe into theology by attending a Society for Christian Ethics conference. There, on introducing myself to various people and explaining why I was there, I was universally told that I should talk to Dan Finn. So I tracked him down, and sure enough, he graciously agreed to sit down for a chat. He was not just warmly encouraging. When I made the leap to go back to graduate school to study theology, Dan repeatedly created opportunities for me to develop my work. Indeed, it was the paper I wrote for the first volume of

Dan's True Wealth of Nations project that ended up being the foundation for my dissertation and subsequent book. In other words, I owe my entire career to Dan. It is a deep honor to have been invited to contribute to this Festschrift. Dan has been a leader in bringing Catholic social thought to bear on economic issues, and he has deployed Catholic social thought to address the ongoing concern about work and justice in a capitalist system.[1] In this essay (or better, meditation), I step back from the immediate concerns about justice to reflect on the meaning work can have in a world in which work is no longer essential for survival.

During the Covid-era lockdowns, a distinction was made between essential and nonessential workers. Even during what was perceived as a life-endangering public health crisis, between a third and a half of all workers needed to carry on, because a cessation of their work would issue in even worse consequences. Food needed to be provided, the utilities needed to be maintained, health care needed to be available, and so on. Perhaps not surprisingly, the essential or necessary workers were largely drawn from the bottom of the socioeconomic ladder. The demand that they keep working entailed shifting the burden of the risk from the pandemic onto the marginalized.[2] We thus repeated the pattern of elites shifting risk burdens onto the rest of the population that has been observed throughout human history.

What was different this time, however, was that those on whom the burden fell did not represent the overwhelming majority of the population. The widespread adoption of lockdowns around the world in the spring of 2020 was unprecedented, in no small part because in the history of the world no society could survive without a substantial majority of the population working in order to provision society with the essentials for maintaining life. To be in a world in which it was conceivable that economic life could be largely suspended for a considerable period of time is to be in an affluent world.[3]

While we can and should lament the burdens born by those who are "essential workers," this chapter takes up a question about the implications the distinction between essential and inessential work has for

1. Finn, "Human Work."
2. Tomer and Kane, "How to Protect Essential Workers."
3. Indeed, not all countries were in a position to weather Covid lockdowns well. There is considerable evidence that developing countries attempting to "lock down" inflicted severe harm in populations that were not affluent enough to do so without driving large numbers into deep poverty.

the majority of workers who were deemed to be *not* essential or necessary. Between half and two-thirds of American workers have jobs that in principle could be suspended without imposing an intolerable burden of suffering on society. On the one hand, an essential aspect of economic progress lies precisely in reducing the amount of labor that is needed to simply keep things going. There is a freedom to expand our work into other realms, building up the culture through education, the arts, communication, travel, and so on. But in a time in which there are increasing questions about the meaning of work, in which we hear about jobs that serve no purpose[4] and quiet-quitting or burnout,[5] we need to ask about the meaning of work that may be valuable in some sense, but which is not actually necessary.

I encountered this question when the governor of my state gave permission to colleges and universities to allow faculty back into their offices, sometime in the early summer of 2020. I went back to my office, since I do not work well at home. Nobody else did. Walking down the empty halls was an uncanny experience. The walls were plastered with posters advertising events that had not taken place, talks that had not been given, celebrations that had not been held. In early March of 2020 all those advertised events, talks, and celebrations had seemed to be important, signs of the raison d'être of academic life: the love of learning shared in community. All of that left behind in a blink because it was not essential. And although my university did open its doors in the fall, there were further signs that we didn't really think our work was all that important. Tenure clocks were stopped in deference to the decline in research productivity. Courses were taught mostly online, despite the manifest limitations of Zoom for genuine educational encounter. The gatherings and conversations that are the life-blood of intellectual life evaporated. Few were on campus, and those who were maintained social distance. I had thought my work was important. And suddenly it seemed it was not really all *that* important. Or at least it was not "essential" or "necessary." We might regret the loss, but we could survive without it.

In his encyclical *Laborem Exercens*, St. Pope John Paul II argues that work is an essential aspect of human nature, something which distinguishes us from all other creatures, and which is "the mark of a person operating within a community of persons" (Opening Blessing). He goes

---

4. Graeber, *Bullshit Jobs*.
5. Han, *Burnout Society*.

on to distinguish between the objective dimension of work, which refers to what we produce and how we produce it, and the subjective dimension, which refocuses on the person doing the work, who is "the image of God" (no. 6). The encyclical calls for us to recognize the importance of the subjective dimension. Yet as we might see in the image of Sisyphus pointlessly pushing a boulder up a mountain, the subjective dimension depends on the objective dimension. That is to say we must produce something that is valuable in order for our work to have meaning.

St. Pope John Paul II identifies the various purposes work might serve. Although work is first and foremost how we sustain ourselves, it is also how we build up society, both in terms of its science and technology and in terms of its cultural and moral dimensions (Opening Blessing). We might understand the Covid-era distinction between essential and inessential workers as an indication that while all work is valuable, in a situation in which survival is imperiled, only that work which itself is necessary for survival is essential.[6] One might think that in the return to ordinary times, the forms of work that involve building up the community in various dimensions would return precisely because they too are "necessary."

But my interest in pushing the question about the distinction between essential and inessential work rests in another artifact of the Covid period. In April 2020, I suddenly encountered multiple references to a short story by E. M. Forster I had never heard of, "The Machine Stops." The reason the story was suddenly circulating widely online was because it was a futuristic tale of a society in which "the machine" handled all the work that was essential, while humans lived a lock-down like existence, in which the only "work" being done by humans was remote, and . . . distinctly pointless. Forster plainly wonders whether the denizens of his futuristic world were fully human at all. There was a suggestion in that story that something goes missing when we relieve ourselves of the burden of the kind of work that is inescapably necessary. But before turning to those questions, we need to first think more about the kind of work that is "necessary."

---

6. I here represent a view that is possible. I myself believe the response to Covid was disproportionate to the threat the virus itself posed, but that is a debate for another day.

NECESSARY WORK

The distinction between the kind of work that sustains life and all other kinds of work was most notably taken up by Karl Marx. A simple version of the idea goes like this. If we consider the working day of a laborer, we can ask how many hours of that day are devoted to producing the means that would sustain the laborer. If, as is typically the case, the answer is less than the number of hours the worker works, the remaining hours generate "surplus value."[7]

James Suzman offers a useful framing of the point by grounding it in physics.[8] Energy represents the capacity to do something. And work involves transferring energy. As Suzman puts it, the distinctive feature of living organisms is that they actively harvest energy, which is used to maintain and grow the organism and to allow for its reproduction. But sometimes, organisms harvest more energy than they need for the purposes of simply sustaining life. Suzman introduces the case of the male masked weaver, a bird that builds elaborate nests and then puzzlingly proceeds to dismantle them. Suzman speculates that the behavior might represent a surplus of energy. Such an interpretation runs afoul of the idea of natural selection as the driver of evolution, a theory that requires that the essence of biological life be a competition to harvest enough energy to survive and reproduce. But whether or not examples of frittering away surplus energy occurs in nature, it certainly occurs in humans. Humans expend energy on all sorts of things that have nothing to do with harvesting enough energy to survive and reproduce.[9] Suzman goes on to celebrate the attitude toward work which he sees in hunter-gatherer societies. In such societies, people work for maybe ten to twenty hours a week, depending on their environment, to harvest enough energy to sustain life. They use the rest of their surplus energy to just enjoy life.

If we want to think about the meaning and purpose of work, we need to think in terms of this basic distinction between necessary work and work that involves the use of surplus energy. We will later discuss the meaning and purpose of necessary work, but no account of it can escape the fact that such work is the sine qua non of doing anything at all. But to understand human work, we cannot think of the division between necessary and surplus energy in terms of a single individual. We are social,

---

7. Hunt, *Property and Prophets*, 108–10.
8. Suzman, *Work*, 25–30.
9. Suzman, *Work*, 45–51.

and a key feature of our social nature is that we divide up work that is to be done. A group of humans can survive if enough of them do the necessary work and make the harvested energy available to those who do other things. So, it is typically the case that some workers do nothing but harvest energy, and whether through exchange or taxes or other modes of appropriation, they transfer the surplus energy to others.

The division of labor opens up two lines for reflection. First, we need to think about the implications for individuals. In particular, in most human societies, the group of people involved in necessary work are at the bottom of the socioeconomic ladder. The other forms of work are usually regarded as higher status, and presumably as being most important. The slaves, serfs, and peasants do the work essential for human survival, and their reward is often to be exploited and despised. And women, who are most heavily engaged in the labor of raising up the next generation, which is also a form of "work" necessary for survival, have likewise suffered low status. This is the line of thought that raises questions about exploitation and economic injustice that are the subject of most inquiries into the nature of work.

The second line of thought, which we can find in Hannah Arendt's book *The Human Condition*, is to reflect on where the weight in a culture falls between the types of activities that humans engage in. That weight is not just a matter of sheer numbers. Greek culture was centered in the ideal of political and cultural life (speech and actions), despite the fact that the elites who could partake of it were a small portion of the entire population. That said, Greek culture cannot be fully understood without attention to the presence of the laboring mass of slaves engaged in the necessary labor. Indeed, as William James Booth suggests, the Greek notion of freedom was largely centered on being free from the demands of necessary labor. Thinking about how the two forms of work are interconnected to shape the culture's experience of work is thus important. The two lines of thought are distinct, but interrelated. The fact that necessary work is virtually always at the bottom of the socioeconomic ladder leads some cultures to develop arguments about why such work *should* be disparaged.[10]

Since the Greeks offer a paradigmatic example of a culture that disparages necessary work, they provide a ready catalogue of "reasons" why such work should be disparaged. First, although John Paul II insists that

---

10. Booth, *Households*.

"only man is capable of work," Suzman's framing of work as "harvesting energy" makes it difficult to distinguish the peasant at his plow from the cat hunting a mouse. All living organisms have to find a way to "harvest energy." By contrast, other forms of work seem to be distinctively human. The male weaver bird may use its surplus energy to build and destroy elaborate nests, but we use our surplus energy to build civilizations. Greek culture distinguished humans from animals by emphasizing man's rational or political nature. The problem with the kind of work done by slaves is that it does not engage reason. Indeed, if we follow Aristotle, the reason some were slaves "by nature" is because they lacked sufficient reason to even govern themselves, and thus it was beneficial to them to be governed by their masters.[11] Not unlike a dog that can achieve some sort of perfection by becoming obedient to its master.

Second, the problem with necessary labor is precisely its necessity. In a world in which individuals produce very little surplus energy, necessity dictates the shape of life. If such a world were egalitarian, all humans would know nothing but the daily grind of harvesting enough energy to sustain themselves. And this, roughly speaking, was the predicament of humans engaged in early agriculture.[12] In a world without slaves, everyone would be a slave to the demands of the plow. Alongside the sheer necessity of such work is the toil it entails, toil that wears down the body. There could be no space in such a world to cultivate any of the distinctly human activities. We would be like ants, wearing ourselves out to sustain the colony, in an endless cycle.

Hannah Arendt shares in this devaluation of necessary work to some extent, and she adds the complaint that the work of *animal laborans* is "worldless," in the sense of not building a human world. The hunter-gatherers may have had an idyllic life, but they did not build up a world. And neither would have early agricultural humans, absent a state to marshal the energy of the masses through the enslavement or quasi-enslavement necessary to build up a city capable of sustaining cultural development.[13] For Arendt, necessary work, which she calls labor, is bound up with the life process which itself has no higher purpose and thus cannot absorb the human drive to make meaning through our work.

11. Aristotle, *Politics*, 14–17.
12. The question of why humans transitioned from the idyllic hunter-gatherer lifestyle that produced ample surplus energy to agriculture that produces very little has been raised not just by Suzman, *Work*, but also by Scott, *Against the Grain*, and Harari, *Sapiens*.
13. Scott, *Against the Grain*.

For animals, sustaining life is the very essence of their beings, but for humans the necessity of working to sustain life is a burden, because of our "innate 'repugnance to futility.'"[14]

If necessary labor really does hinder the full human development of the laborer, both by virtue of the nature of the work itself and by the fact that it has historically been exploited in order to sustain an "elite" that could engage in more fully human forms of work, then the advent of technological breakthroughs that have liberated an increasingly large percentage of the workforce from such labor must be celebrated. Aristotle himself imagined a world in which the shuttle might weave by itself.[15] Perhaps we should look forward to the day when not just 30 to 50 percent of the workforce engages in "necessary labor." With the advent of AI, can we not dream of a world in which all are liberated from the dread burden of necessity?

A WORLD WITHOUT NECESSARY LABOR

The question of what we might do in a world in which the economic problem has been solved dates back at least to John Maynard Keynes's essay "Economic Possibilities for Our Grandchildren," written in 1930. In that essay, Keynes argues that if we extrapolate the economic growth that had occurred over the preceding two centuries, we could expect that in a hundred years, everyone could enjoy a decent standard of living with little or no work required. He worries about whether we are prepared to use that free time well. We don't fully inhabit Keynes's future, largely because we have expanded our idea about what constitutes a decent standard of living.[16] But nonetheless, the question of whether everyone needs to work is increasingly being raised, especially as seen in the debate over universal basic income.

David Cloutier and Kate Ward recently engaged the debate over universal basic income, though they shared a common presumption, namely that work is good for human flourishing, and some sort of work should continue even if "necessary work" might disappear.[17] Their debate centers on whether that ongoing work should take place in the market

---

14. Arendt, *Human Condition*, 119, citing Thorstein Veblen.
15. Aristotle, *Politics*, 14.
16. Schor, *Overworked American*.
17. Cloutier, "Workers' Paradise"; and Ward, "Response to David Cloutier."

for a wage; or whether it might consist in unpaid work in the home or community that could be sustained with a universal basic income. I will return to that question below, but here I want to focus on what happens when a society is balanced around a norm that little if any work is actually necessary.

The specter of a world in which technology has displaced human labor has spawned dystopian fiction throughout the twentieth century. The most famous example is Aldous Huxley's *Brave New World*. In that world, work emphatically continues. But as Mustapha Mond, the technocratic overlord, reveals, the brave new world included full working days because experiments had shown that unrest and unhappiness ensued when working hours were greatly reduced.[18] But in his short story "The Machine Stops," published in 1909, E. M. Forster contemplates a different possibility. In his post-work world, the population does not engage in any sort of necessary labor. Instead, they occupy themselves with the higher calling of the life of the mind.

"The Machine Stops" describes a world in which technology, i.e., "the machine," meets all possible needs of the population at the push of a button. There is some division of labor in this world. There are a few people, entirely offstage in the story, who administer the society. A few of them seem to be tasked with maintaining the machine, though as the title suggests, it is not clear they are able to do so. We encounter one vestigial worker, a flight attendant, who is marked out as peculiar because she interacts with the physical world. But the vast majority of the population appears to live the sort of life we see in the main character in the story, Vashti. It is, therefore, their experience of work that dominates the culture.

So, what sort of work engages Vashti? It has nothing to do with meeting her physical needs. She lives in a single room, sitting in a chair. Everything she might need is delivered to her at the push of a button. It is an existence that might remind us of the movie *Wall-E*. Forster certainly suggests that the passive life of a consumer whose needs are met with no exertion on their part is dehumanizing. Vashti is physically atrophied. She can barely walk down a hallway on her own power. But she is not lazy.

In this world, although everyone lives in single cells and they only rarely see each other in person, there is a hive of activity online. Although it would be hard to say whether Vashti has a job—she "works." She attends online lectures, and she gives them. And when she is not doing

---

18. Huxley, *Brave New World*, 117.

these things, she participates in a constant conversation with her wide circle of "friends." The coin of this realm is "ideas," and activity centers on having ideas and sharing them. On the one hand, this online activity seems like work. Vashti perceives the demands on her time as pressing, and she resents interruptions. On the other hand, there is no sense that she works to make a living; no suggestion that if she failed to deliver her lectures, she would lose access to the perfect abundance offered her through the machine. Perhaps her motivation to constantly "work" is simply that this is how she participates in her community. And there is a suggestion that she derives pleasure from the applause she receives when she gives her talks.

This might seem to be the ideal. Freed from the demands of necessary labor, we can engage in activities such as intellectual pursuits that are intrinsically rewarding. But Vashti's dehumanization extends far beyond her physical atrophy. Forster pointedly never gives content to these "ideas." The one exception proves the rule. We are told of one lecturer who argued that people should stop seeking first-hand ideas (based on encounter with something), but rather should focus on second-hand or even tenth-hand ideas. This is a world in which nobody does necessary labor. It is also a world that is entirely divorced from the actual physical world.

The vapidity of Vashti's life prompted the title for this essay. She is a woman who, in grudgingly flying to visit her son in person, can draw the blinds on the Himalayas on the grounds that they can give her no "ideas." We are told that the last time humans tried to achieve anything substantive in relationship to the world, it entailed a failed quest to achieve speeds faster than the earth's rotation. In the wake of some unnamed catastrophe, humans moved underground and contact with the physical world essentially ceased. There can be no substantive ideas in a world that literally has no substance.

The move away from necessary labor seems to entail a move away from the body and from the world. And Forster suggests that true human flourishing requires bodies engaged with the world, forming a ground for the cultivation of genuinely human reason. First, as the title of the story advertises, the attempt to live human life virtually cannot succeed. In a culture that has forgotten that some work is necessary, a complacent expectation that all we need will always be ready to hand sets in. And when the machine starts breaking down, there is nobody left with the ability to fix it. Nor can anybody even save themselves. It is not just that they don't know how to survive as the machine starts to fail; the thought that they might try to do something in the face of a catastrophe never crosses their minds.

Second, even if such a life could be sustained, it cannot deliver anything like authentic human flourishing. Forster offers us a second character, Vashti's son, Kuno, to explore this theme. Kuno yearns for something beyond Vashti's vapid world. And a good chunk of the story entails Kuno's descriptions of his adventure to go back out into the world. What is significant is that because Kuno exercises agency, deviating from the path laid out by the machine, and especially because his agency is centered on physical engagement with the world, it is Kuno who can give voice to a string of ideas about human nature and the world in which we live that are the product of a living intellect:

> Cannot you see, cannot all you lecturers see, that it is we that are dying, and that down here the only thing that really lives is the Machine? We created the Machine, to do our will, but we cannot make it do our will now. It has robbed us of the sense of space and of the sense of touch, it has blurred every human relation and narrowed down love to a carnal act, it has paralyzed our bodies and our wills, and now it compels us to worship it. The Machine develops—but not on our lines. The Machine proceeds—but not to our goal. We only exist as the blood corpuscles that course through its arteries, and if it could work without us, it would let us die. Oh, I have no remedy—or, at least, only one—to tell men again and again that I have seen the hills of Wessex as Aelfrid saw them when he overthrew the Danes.[19]

Kuno describes a world in which humans need to struggle in order to live. But in that struggle, the potential glory of human nature might be found. Arendt's previously noted concerns about the futility of necessary work, which she calls labor, are largely centered on the fact that if we do nothing but labor, we cannot be lifted up to magnificent achievement. That said, she elsewhere suggests that necessary work provides the foundation for human happiness:

> There is no lasting happiness outside the prescribed cycle of painful exhaustion and pleasurable regeneration, and whatever throws this cycle out of balance—poverty and misery where exhaustion is followed by wretchedness instead of regeneration, or great riches and an entirely effortless life where boredom takes the place of exhaustion and where the mills of necessity,

---

19. Forster, "Machine Stops," 106–7.

of consumption and digestion, grind an impotent human body mercilessly and barrenly to death—ruins the elemental happiness that comes from being alive.[20]

Arendt's concern about the limited human fulfillment associated with labor might be less for the individual peasant laboring away in the fields. The peasant, at least, is sustaining a culture that might well be doing great things. And the peasant does have the kind of happiness Arendt describes. Her central concern rests with the road we are on—toward a consumeristic society in which people normatively have to work in order to claim a living; but one in which all of our efforts are to produce an abundance of disposable goods that do not lift us up. They live the grind and the futility but are too well off to experience the fundamental joy of work that immediately serves the end of life.

We can appeal to St. Thomas Aquinas to carry forward Arendt's point about a central joy of human labor in a theological key. Although Aquinas never takes up the theme of work as a subject for sustained reflection, he often addressed the question of his day about whether friars could escape the precept requiring manual labor. In Aquinas's day, manual labor would naturally refer to the work of peasants, who provision society with food. Manual work is a matter of precept because among other things that is how we sustain ourselves. But contra Arendt, Aquinas goes on to say that we *differ* from other creatures who are provided for by nature directly. We have only our reason and our hands, which we must then creatively use to engage with nature in diverse ways to meet our various needs.[21] I think of the distinction between the bird's nest which never varies and the diversity of means humans have found to shelter themselves. That creative engagement with the physical world to make a living is part of our position as creatures who can be provident for themselves.[22] Our creative engagement with the world through necessary labor is a way of manifesting our rational natures even in the "lowly" work of harvesting energy to sustain ourselves. The necessity to work is a reminder of our creatureliness. But our freedom to meet our necessity in diverse ways allows us to participate intimately in the natural order in a way that is fitting for rational creatures.

---

20. Arendt, *Human Condition*, 108.
21. Aquinas, *Quodlibet VII* 7.1.
22. Aquinas, *Summa Contra Gentiles*, III.112.

Aquinas goes on to argue that not every individual must engage in necessary labor. As a matter of divine providence, individuals contribute in diverse ways to the life of the community.[23] He compares this to the diverse roles of the organs within a body. We need the lungs to breathe, the stomach to digest, and so on. Thus, it is fitting that some should pray, some should teach, some should defend, and some should provide society with food and other necessities. A society that ceases to value those who pray might find itself losing the spiritual dimension of human life in its culture. And likewise, a society that no longer has need for necessary labor might lose an essential grounding in our creatureliness, along with the human capacity to creatively engage the natural world. "The Machine Stops" offers us a warning that without the anchor of physical necessity, we are at risk of weightlessly detaching from any real meaning or purpose altogether.

CONCLUDING THOUGHTS

It would be perverse to not welcome an escape from what Keynes called "the economic problem," the grind for survival that has characterized the lot of humanity at least since the rise of agriculture. Alongside the preference against necessary work revealed by the migration of multitudes from the farm into the cities, the fact that those doing necessary work have been subject to exploitation throughout history are sufficient reasons to not want to go back. And even if we did want to go back, we cannot. The occasional Wendell Berry can choose a life centered on farming. But once it is possible to use machines to do most of the necessary labor, the necessary labor we do engage in becomes voluntary. That sharp end of necessity (needed to ground ourselves) still goes missing. There is a paradox here. The sharp goad of necessity might be essential to human fulfillment; but it cannot be our business to actively put ourselves into its reach.

That said, we could first consider a realm of necessary labor that really cannot be replaced by machines: namely the business of caring for families and for our communities more generally. Arendt's point about the joy that lies in the point of connection between production and consumption can be most vividly seen in the work that takes place in the home. Economists sharply distinguish between production and

---

23. Aquinas, *Quodlibet VII* 7.1.

consumption. But when we look at the work that takes place in the household, we need to ask where to draw the line. Adam Smith famously remarked that if we want our dinner, we need to appeal to the self-interest of the butcher, baker, and brewer.[24] But if Smith only relied on the production in the marketplace for his dinner, he would go to bed hungry. For Smith to have had his dinner, someone had to go to the market to get the ingredients, and then come home and prepare the meal. All consumption requires work right up to and possibly through the point we would say consumption has happened. Buying toothpaste doesn't take care of my dental hygiene. I have to actually brush my teeth.

Modern economic progress can be narrated in terms of the steady transfer of such domestic work to the market. We have gone from grinding our own wheat into flour, to purchasing flour, to purchasing a cake mix, to purchasing a store-made cake, to having Uber deliver the store-made cake to our doorstep. It is possible that in the near future Elon Musk will deliver personal robots to us that can go to the doorstep to bring in the cake and put it on a plate and serve it to us in our chairs. Maybe the robot could even lift the fork for us. But if we take seriously the idea that necessary labor is actually good for us, perhaps we might step back from the encroachment of the market and technology into the household. Perhaps we could remember the joy of baking the cake for our daughter's birthday party. Or the joy of making the casserole to share at the community potluck. In the debate between Cloutier and Ward about universal basic income, Ward's point that important work remains for us in our personal lives is a good one.

Such domestic work might be immune from the pressures of technology if we note that a central characteristic of such work is that it is personal. The store-bought cake is not as wonderful as the one your mother baked for you. We could learn to re-see the lives we build in our homes and our communities as places in which the necessary labor involved is central to the flourishing that is to be had in such settings. And to the extent that such work involves direct personal care, such as tending infants and ministering to the sick, we can hope that it is still possible to see that one of Musk's robots cannot be a substitute for the human connection that is an essential component of such work.

A second resource for navigating the paradox posed by necessary labor is theological. It seems to me that a core element of Forster's vision

---

24. Smith, *Wealth of Nations*, 23.

of a world without necessary labor is that it detaches us from nature. The very possibility of escaping necessary work depends on the replacement of human effort with machines. And the technological developments of the last few decades should alert us to the fact that technology is pushing us more and more into a virtual world. But if, as we find in Catholic and Orthodox theology, the world is best understood as a sacramental reflection of God, then we have an imperative reason to engage seriously with the world, even if we no longer need to out of necessity.

The sacramental vision entails recognizing that in a world created by God ex nihilo everything we encounter manifests God's goodness in some particular way. In the words of Gerard Manley Hopkins, "The world is charged with the grandeur of God."[25] Every tree and every goose and every rock all manifest God's goodness. Josef Pieper invites us to remember the centrality of contemplation to human fulfillment.[26] If the form of all creatures lies in the divine ideas, opening ourselves to them is an act of communion with God that is possible in this life.[27] In *For the Life of the World*, Alexander Schmemann takes the idea a step further. We find communion with God not just in contemplating his creation, but also in the act of being nourished by creation. We find ourselves in a world that was created good; we are nourished by this world; and in celebrating the world and our sustenance, we become what we were created to be: creatures in communion with the God whom they rightly worship.

We may not wish to return to a mode of life consumed by necessary work. But the reminder of what might be lost should encourage us to think carefully about our connection with the world around us, and where our true meaning and purpose lie.

BIBLIOGRAPHY

Aquinas, Thomas. *Quodlibet VII*. Aquinas, n.d. https://aquinas.cc/la/en/~QVII.
———. *Summa Contra Gentiles*. Translated by James F. Anderson. Notre Dame, IN: University of Notre Dame Press, 1975.
Arendt, Hannah. *The Human Condition*. 2nd ed. Chicago: University of Chicago Press, 2018.
Aristotle. *Politics*. Translated by Ernest Barker. Revised by R. F. Stalley. Oxford World's Classics. Oxford: Oxford University Press, 1995.

25. Hopkins, "Grandeur of God."
26. Pieper, *Leisure*.
27. Warne, *Josef Pieper*.

Booth, William James. *Households: On the Moral Architecture of the Economy*. Ithaca, NY: Cornell University Press, 1993.
Cloutier, David. "The Workers' Paradise: Eternal Life, Economic Eschatology, and Good Work as the Keys to Social Ethics." *CTSA Proceedings* 75 (2021) 37–55.
Finn, Daniel. "Human Work in Catholic Social Thought." *American Journal of Economics and Sociology* 71 (2012) 874–85.
Forster, E. M. "The Machine Stops." *Oxford and Cambridge Review* 8 (1909) 83–122.
Graeber, David. *Bullshit Jobs: A Theory*. New York: Simon and Schuster, 2018.
Han, Byung-Chul. *The Burnout Society*. Translated by Erik Butler. Stanford Briefs. Palo Alto, CA: Stanford University Press, 2015.
Harari, Yuval Noah. *Sapiens: A Brief History of Humankind*. New York: Harper Perennial, 2015.
Hopkins, Gerard Manley. "The Grandeur of God." In *Gerard Manley Hopkins: The Complete Poems*, edited by Robert Bridges, 26. London: Milford, 1918.
Hunt, E. K. *Property and Prophets: The Evolution of Economic Institutions and Ideologies*. 7th ed. London: Routledge, 2003.
Huxley, Aldous. *Brave New World*. New York: HarperCollins, 2021. Ebook.
John Paul II. *Laborem Exercens*. Vatican, Sept. 14, 1981. https://www.vatican.va/content/john-paul-ii/en/encyclicals/documents/hf_jp-ii_enc_14091981_laborem-exercens.html.
Keynes, John Maynard. "Economic Possibilities for Our Grandchildren (1930)." In *Essays in Persuasion*. New York: Norton, 1963. Kindle.
Kundera, Milan. *The Unbearable Lightness of Being*. Translated by Michael Henry Heim. New York: Harper Perennial Classics, 1999.
Pieper, Josef. *"Leisure: The Basis for Culture," Including "The Philosophical Act."* Translated by Alexander Dru. San Francisco: Ignatius, 2009.
Schmemann, Alexander. *For the Life of the World: Sacraments and Orthodoxy*. Yonkers: Saint Vladimir's Seminary Press, 2018.
Schor, Juliet. *The Overworked American: The Unexpected Decline of Leisure*. New York: Basic Books, 1992.
Scott, James C. *Against the Grain: A Deep History of the Earliest States*. New Haven, CT: Yale University Press, 2018.
Smith, Adam. *The Wealth of Nations*. Edited by Edwin Cannan. New York: Bantam Dell, 2003.
Suzman, James. *Work: A Deep History, from the Stone Age to the Age of Robots*. New York: Penguin, 2021.
Tomer, Adie, and Joseph W. Kane. "How to Protect Essential Workers During COVID-19." Brookings Institute, May 31, 2020. https://www.brookings.edu/articles/how-to-protect-essential-workers-during-covid-19/.
Ward, Kate. "A Response to David Cloutier's 'The Workers' Paradise: Eternal Life, Economic Eschatology, and Good Work as the Keys to Social Ethics': Shifting the Balance: The Work Before Us." *CTSA Proceedings* 75 (2021) 56–61.
Warne, Nathaniel A. *Josef Pieper on the Spiritual Life: Creation, Contemplation, and Human Flourishing*. Notre Dame, IN: University of Notre Dame Press, 2023.

Economic Analogies for the Sacraments in the Middle Ages

Matthew Shadle

Pope Francis has called on theologians to undertake a "paradigm shift," and one of the characteristics of this fresh way of doing theology is what Francis calls "transdisciplinarity."[1] Theology and other disciplines must enter into dialogue with one another and ultimately be transformed by one another. One of the most fruitful examples of transdisciplinarity today is the dialogue between theology and economics, and few have illustrated the promise of this dialogue more than Daniel Finn. During his long career, Finn has insisted that Christian theology has something to say to economists, particularly on questions of ethics. For example, he has traced how the Christian theological tradition has contributed to how we think ethically about economic life[2] and how the integral, theological vision of Catholic social teaching can inform our understanding of economic development.[3] But Finn has also explored what economics might teach theologians, including how to think about self-interest[4] and the social structures that condition the global economy.[5]

This dialogue between theology and economic thinking is not new, however. Christian theologians have long turned to metaphors

---

1. Francis, *Ad Theologiam Promovendam*, nos. 4, 5.
2. Finn, *Christian Economic Ethics*.
3. Finn, *True Wealth of Nations*.
4. Finn, *Moral Ecology*, 34–75.
5. Finn: *Distant Markets*; and *Moral Agency*.

and concepts from economic life to help explain theological ideas. One noteworthy example is the debate among medieval scholastic theologians over how the sacraments cause grace in their recipients. Some argued that the sacraments are like tools in the hands of a worker, for example, the hammer or saw used by a carpenter. Only God can cause grace in the human heart, but the sacraments have the capacity to be used by God as instruments for that purpose. Others argued that the sacraments work like coins whose exchange value comes not from the inherent value of the metal from which the coin is made, but from the decree of the king who had them minted. In a similar way, the sacraments' ability to confer grace does not arise from anything inherent to the rituals, but rather from the covenant instituted by God with the church. This essay will explain these competing metaphors and the theories of sacramental efficacy behind them and how the economic context of the thirteenth century can enrich our understanding of medieval sacramental theology. Finally, it concludes by briefly arguing that these medieval debates about causality serve as an invitation for us to think more deeply about causality in both theology and social theory.

SACRAMENTS AS INSTRUMENTAL CAUSES

The great theologians of the thirteenth and fourteenth centuries inherited from their eleventh- and twelfth-century predecessors both a shared understanding of the sacraments and unresolved problems.[6] By the time Peter Lombard wrote his *Book of Sentences* in the twelfth century, theologians had settled on seven sacraments and a bare definition of what a sacrament is. The sacraments are *signs* of God's grace, that is, visible or auditory rituals that signify the transformation of the recipient by God. But the sacraments don't simply *represent* God's grace; in some sense, they *cause* it and therefore can be considered *efficacious* signs of grace. Here the scholastics appealed to St. Augustine, who in his fifth-century controversy with the Donatists established that this efficacious power of the sacraments ultimately comes from God and inheres in the sacraments themselves (*ex opere operato*) rather than arising from a personal quality of the one performing the sacraments (*ex opere operantis*). It was left to the medieval theologians of the thirteenth and fourteenth centuries,

---

6. For a summary of the state of sacramental theology as the thirteenth century began, see Wawrykow, "Sacraments in Thirteenth-Century Theology."

though, to further think through what it means to say that this power of the sacraments to cause grace inheres in the rituals.

One of the most challenging problems faced by the medieval scholastics arose from the tension between the sacraments necessarily being *material* rituals and their being the cause of the *spiritual* effect of grace.[7] For example, St. Thomas Aquinas has one of his objectors pose this challenge: "Nothing corporeal can act on a spiritual thing.... But the subject of grace is the human mind, which is something spiritual. Therefore the sacraments cannot cause grace."[8] This is an interesting problem in its own right, but it had added salience because the Cathars or Albigensians, a heterodox religious movement that emerged in southern France in the twelfth century that rejected the material world as evil, had denied the validity of the church's sacraments precisely because they were material rituals.[9] It behooved Catholic theologians, then, to develop an explanation of how God makes use of the material realities of the sacraments in causing the spiritual reality of grace.

One of the most important responses to this question argued that the sacraments are efficacious not through their own power, but because God uses them as instruments to cause grace. Advocates for this position drew analogies from the world of work, typically a carpenter hammering a nail or sawing a piece of wood. In one sense, one can rightly say that the hammer causes the nail to enter the wood, but in another sense, tools are efficacious because the carpenter acts as the primary cause of the action. This argument was developed early in the thirteenth century by a number of theologians.[10] The most famous exposition of the argument comes from Aquinas in his *Commentary on the Sentences*, where he draws on the Aristotelian concept of instrumental causality.[11] Aquinas compares the sacraments to an axe used by a craftsman to make a piece of furniture.[12] The axe cuts the wood in virtue of its own powers, but it is the carpenter who makes the furniture, using the axe as an instrument.

---

7. Adams, *Theories of the Eucharist*, 51–54.

8. Aquinas, *Summa* III, q. 62, a. 1, obj. 2.

9. On the role of the Cathars as an impetus to the scholastic debate on the efficacy of the sacraments, see Courtenay, "King," 188–89.

10. Courtenay, "King," 189–91.

11. Lynch, *Cleansing*, 67–87.

12. Aquinas, *Sent* IV, d. 1, q. 1, a. 4, qc .2.

In the same way, the sacraments dispose their recipients for grace, but it is God who causes grace in the recipients.[13]

In economic terms, Aquinas's analogy of the carpenter demonstrates the inklings of a humanistic conception of work. Although work involves physical tools like an axe and physical actions like cutting wood, work cannot be reduced to physical labor. As Marilyn McCord Adams explains, for Aquinas, "an instrumental cause qua instrument is moved by and so participates in the power of the principal agent and thereby receives a further intentionality or direction, toward the end at which the principal agent aims."[14] The nature of work is defined by the aims and intentions of the laborer and is a truly human act. Here Aquinas foreshadows Pope John Paul II's modern teaching that the subjective or personal dimension of work is primary relative to its objective dimension,[15] although Aquinas does not yet derive from this John Paul's conclusion that work has inherent dignity.

That being said, as an argument for how the sacraments cause grace, Aquinas's metaphor of the carpenter raises some problems that were identified almost immediately by his critics.[16] For one, as the Franciscan John Duns Scotus noted, this theory does not adequately explain how a sacramental act can cause a spiritual effect; even if God is the immediate cause of grace, the disposition for grace is likewise a spiritual reality, and Aquinas does not sufficiently explain how the sacramental acts cause that reality.[17] Similarly, the metaphor of the carpenter appeals to the natural power of the axe to cut, contributing to the ability of the carpenter to make furniture. But it is unclear what analogous natural powers the sacraments have to dispose their recipients for receiving grace.[18] Finding Aquinas's theory unconvincing, his contemporaries embraced alternative theories to explain the efficacy of the sacraments.

---

13. Aquinas, *Sent* IV, d. 1, q. 1, a. 4, qc .2.
14. Adams, *Theories of the Eucharist*, 57.
15. John Paul II, *Laborem Exercens*, 6.
16. Adams, *Theories of the Eucharist*, 61.
17. Duns Scotus, *Ordinatio* IV, d. 1, pt. 3, qq. 1–2, nn. 285–86.
18. In his later work the *Summa Theologiae*, Aquinas avoids this problem by abandoning the claim that, as instruments, the sacraments *dispose* their recipients for grace, instead arguing that the sacraments are instrumental causes of grace because they *participate* in the work of the primary agent, God (*Summa* III, q. 62, a. 1). See Blankenhorn, "Instrumental Causality"; Lynch, *Cleansing*, 111–28.

SACRAMENTS AS TOKENS OF DIVINE POWER

A second, quite different, theory emerged around the same time as the first. According to this theory, the power of the sacraments to cause grace does not come from anything inherent to the sacraments, but rather from a decree or covenant established by God. God decrees that whenever a sacrament is performed, the appropriate grace will assuredly be conferred. Although a version of this theory is sometimes attributed to St. Bernard of Clairvaux as early as the twelfth century, the notion that the sacraments are tokens of divine power is first fully developed in the middle of the thirteenth century by the English Dominicans Richard Fishacre and Robert Kilwardby, both of whom taught at the University of Oxford and the latter of whom was appointed archbishop of Canterbury in 1272. The theory was then adopted by the Franciscan St. Bonaventure in his *Commentary on the Sentences* written in the early 1250s and the *Breviloquium* written in 1257.

The most provocative analogy proposed in support of this theory is that of a coin whose exchange value is determined by a decree of the king rather than by the value of the material out of which it is made. In fact, we are presented with two different analogies of coins, although both making a similar point. In the first, Fishacre asks us to imagine that a minister of the king distributes to the poor tokens (*signi*) made from an alloy of silver and lead, and, by the authority of the king, this token admits its holder to a meal with the king.[19] In this case, the coin's value, its ability to be exchanged in return for admission to the meal, far exceeds the value of the material from which it is made; rather, its value is conferred on it by the king. In the same way, the efficacy of the sacraments does not come from the sacramental act, but rather from a covenantal decree of God.

Bonaventure presents a somewhat simpler analogy. He proposes that the king could ordain that a certain coin or token (*signum*) has an exchange value of a hundred marks of silver. Again, just as the value of the coin is not intrinsic but rather a consequence of the king's decree, the sacramental rituals have no efficacy in themselves but rather because they are ordained by God. Aquinas presents a slightly different variation of this analogy, attributed to an unnamed opponent. In this case, the coin is a lead denarius (the most common coin of the thirteenth century,

---

19. Fishacre, *Sent* IV, d. 1.

although typically made of silver) which, according to the will of the king, can be exchanged for a hundred pounds of silver.[20]

Both of these analogies using a coin draw on the economic practices of their time, but for contemporary readers their context is obscure. In regard to Fishacre's analogy, William J. Courtenay has explored the various uses of tokens made of metal, or other materials like leather, during the Middle Ages and concludes that Fishacre is making an early reference to charity tokens, lead coins distributed by ecclesiastical institutions that could be exchanged for food or clothing.[21] I would argue that the more likely source for Fishacre's analogy is the feeding of paupers by King Henry III of England, who reigned from 1216 to 1272.[22] On various occasions, Henry would invite the poor to be fed in the halls of Westminster Palace and other palaces throughout the realm. These meals could be quite extravagant; in 1242, for example, fifty thousand poor people were fed on one occasion, and on a handful of others ten thousand or more were fed.[23] In addition to these more elaborate affairs, the king also ensured that at least five hundred poor were fed by his household each day wherever he was present, even when abroad.[24] Although there is no extant evidence that tokens were used to regulate attendance at these events, there are good reasons to think they may have been on at least some occasions; the royal almoners who organized them were responsible for determining who would be eligible to attend,[25] and tokens were being used to mark eligibility for alms in other contexts, for example, by the papal almoners in Rome.[26] Fishacre surely would have been aware of these meals, and not just by reputation; the Dominicans and Franciscans

---

20. Aquinas, *Summa* III, q. 62, a. 1.

21. Courtenay: "King," 193–200; "Token Coinage." See also Mitchiner and Skinner, "English Tokens." Other uses for tokens included as a badge for having gone on a particular pilgrimage; as a sign of royal authority to engage in a particular trade; as a sign that the bearer was exempt from paying a toll; and as a means of tracking accounts within the royal household or an ecclesiastical institution. As Courtenay admits, the weaknesses of his theory are that, first, Fishacre's *Commentary on the Sentences*, written in the 1240s, predates the first known evidence of the use of charity tokens by a few decades, and second, charity tokens were primarily used by ecclesiastical institutions rather than by royal households.

22. Dixon-Smith, "Feeding the Poor"; Phillips, "Devotion by Donation."

23. Phillips, "Devotion by Donation," 83.

24. Dixon-Smith, "Feeding the Poor," 84–87.

25. Cole, "Ritual Charity," 234–35.

26. Dixon-Smith, "Feeding the Poor," 167–68.

were included among the poor fed at these meals,[27] and Henry had even visited and fed the Oxford Dominicans in 1233.[28]

Although these meals were certainly political spectacles, Henry also had deeply spiritual motivations; as Katie Phillips notes, Henry saw these events as "nourishing the mystical body of Christ" and inspired, in part, by the spirit of the mendicant orders.[29] If they inspired Fishacre's metaphor for the sacraments, we then have a fascinating example of religious belief being expressed in a concrete economic practice, and then this practice in turn being used to inform theological reflection. This attempt to create a foretaste of the kingdom of God on earth, then, provided a fertile source for Fishacre's thinking on the sacraments, and knowing this background enriches our understanding of his argument.

Bonaventure's analogy and that of Aquinas's unnamed opponent are more commercial in nature and seem to reflect the changing nature of money in Western Europe in the twelfth and thirteenth centuries. After a long period in which the use of money was relatively rare and disorganized, the Carolingian monarchs of the eighth century imposed a new system of units of account, modeled on the old Roman system, that influenced European currencies for centuries. The most basic unit of account was the pound (or livre), which, at least at first, was the equivalent in value of one pound weight of silver; a pound could be divided into twenty sous (also known as a shilling). The pound and the sou were not coins but simply units of account used by merchants to measure the value of goods and services. A sou, however, could be divided into twelve denarii (which came to be called deniers or pennies), which were both units of account and silver coins used to conduct business.[30] These denarii were made from a weight of silver proportionate to their value relative to the pound, and although monarchs tinkered with the exact value of the pound and the denarius in terms of silver weight, the value of the denarius as a currency remained based on the intrinsic value of the metal from which it was made.[31]

---

27. Dixon-Smith, "Feeding the Poor," 164–65.
28. Dixon-Smith, "Feeding the Poor," 158–59.
29. Phillips, "Devotion by Donation," 82–83.
30. Depeyrot, "Monetary System," 131–33; Spufford, *Money and Its Use*, 33–34. Gold was relatively scarce in Western Europe at the time, in contrast to the Byzantine Empire and Arab lands, and as a result gold coins were rare until the end of the thirteenth century.
31. Spufford, *Money and Its Use*, 43.

By the eleventh century, however, this system had broken down. Feudal lords throughout Charlemagne's former empire, including ecclesiastics like bishops and abbots, began operating their own mints and issuing their own denarii; they also began to debase their currencies, minting coins with an increasing quantity of lead mixed with the silver. To conduct business, merchants needed to know the value of their coins, which meant they had to keep track of the sources of the currencies they were using and the amount of silver they contained.[32] This situation was not sustainable, and an alternative way of managing currency was needed.

In England, the Anglo-Saxon monarchs of the tenth and eleventh centuries had never lost control over the minting of coins. Rather than seeking to maintain the intrinsic value of the currency, however, the English kings instead regularly reissued the currency, minting new pennies every few years that varied in weight and fineness (i.e., the proportion of silver and lead). These regular remintings, which continued after the Norman Conquest of 1066 until the middle of the twelfth century, served as a kind of tax—currency holders might exchange ten old coins and get eight of the newly minted ones in return, for example—but they also had the effect of disconnecting the value of the coin from the intrinsic value of the metal. According to Peter Spufford, these English coins "fluctuated quite considerably in weight and fineness from one issue to the next and yet their value remained constant, since it derived not from their intrinsic worth, but from the word of the king."[33]

The French kings of the era were never able to control the mints to the same extent as the English monarchs, but in the early decades of the thirteenth century, Philip II Augustus and Louis VIII were able to either eliminate or coopt the feudal coinages in the areas of France that had come under royal control.[34] The monarchs allowed royal deniers to be debased, however, and they came to be referred to as "black money" (*monnaie noire*) due to their low silver content. The value of the deniers in relation to the standard units of account (livre and sou) was now dependent on their weight and fineness as decreed by the king. In 1266, King Louis IX began minting a new, larger silver coin called the gros, whose weight and fineness, unlike those of the denier, were maintained; the value of the denier was set by royal decree at twelve per gros, regardless

---

32. Depeyrot, "Monetary System," 133–36; Spufford, *Money and Its Use*, 101.
33. Spufford, *Money and Its Use*, 94.
34. Spufford, *Money and Its Use*, 197–200.

of the former's weight and fineness, reinforcing the fact that it had merely token value rather than intrinsic value.[35]

Bonaventure wrote his *Commentary on the Sentences*, where he draws on the analogy of the coin, in the decade before King Louis issued the gros, whereas the new coin was issued as Aquinas was completing his *Summa Theologiae* a few years later. Both theologians, though, certainly would have been familiar with the denier's function as a token currency due to the variations in its weight and fineness. This helps us better understand the analogy of the coin used by Bonaventure and Aquinas's unnamed opponent. For one, Bonaventure refers to the coin as a token (*signum*), suggesting it is something without intrinsic value, and Aquinas's opponent more explicitly refers to it as a lead denarius (*denarius plumbeus*), which is likely a reference to the debased deniers of the day. Aquinas (or at least his opponent) may even be exaggerating for effect here by suggesting that the coin is *entirely* made of lead, having no silver content and therefore lacking *any* intrinsic value. Second, Bonaventure says that, due to a decree of the king, those who have this coin "have a hundred marks" (*habeant centum marcas*). Aquinas phrases it somewhat differently, suggesting that someone who produces the lead denarius can, based on the king's decree, receive a hundred pounds (*accipit centum libras*). Contrary to modern usage, in the Middle Ages "mark" and "pound" were units of weight and units of account, but not currencies (a mark was two-thirds of a pound). The coins described by Bonaventure and Aquinas, then, have value in relation to a specific weight of silver, but this value is ordained by the king rather than based on the silver content of the coins.

Third, in both cases the ascribed value of the coins is comically absurd, probably intentionally so. Typically, there were 240 denarii in a pound, and so Aquinas's coin, worth a hundred pounds, is overvalued by a factor of 24,000! Bonaventure is only somewhat less generous. It seems possible, then, that contemporaneous readers would have understood that this exaggeration was meant to illustrate the immense value of the grace effected through the sacraments, particularly in relation to the value of the sacramental acts considered in themselves. Finally, it is interesting that Aquinas's opponent describes the hundred pounds of silver as something received in exchange for the coin, whereas Bonaventure describes the owner of the coin as already, in a sense, *having* the hundred marks.

35. Spufford, *Money and Its Use*, 229, 237.

The former puts the emphasis on the coin as a means of exchange, while the latter emphasizes the coin as a holder of value. This difference may just be a coincidence, but it may be that Aquinas's opponent intended to put even greater emphasis on the point that the value of the coin is not inherent.

Aquinas, among other theologians, was not convinced by this argument that the sacraments are tokens of divine power. His primary argument was that, while this theory certainly accounts for the nature of the sacraments as signs, it does not explain how they *cause* grace. Aquinas's point seems to be this. When the holder of the lead coin presents it to another person, it communicates the king's wish that the original holder be given one hundred pounds of silver, but the coin doesn't *cause* the recipient to hand over the silver. If this were the way the sacraments worked, Aquinas argues, this would mean that the sacraments are signs upon the performance of which God bestows grace, but the sacraments themselves would not be the cause of grace, a conclusion which all involved in the debate agreed was unacceptable.

Aquinas goes even further, alleging that, in this analogy, the coin is merely an *accidental* cause.[36] Here he is appealing to Aristotle's distinction between efficient causes *per se* and *per accidens*, or accidental causes. For example, Aquinas states that the builder is the efficient cause *per se* of a house, but the fact that the builder happens to be pale is only accidentally the cause of the house, or we might say his paleness is accidental to the relationship of causation; it does not bring about the completion of the house.[37] Similarly, Aquinas believes that the coin plays a merely accidental role in its possessor obtaining a hundred pounds of silver because, in his view, it is not the coin that effects the transfer of silver, but rather the will of the king. But the sacraments must effect what they signify, and so the metaphor of the coins cannot be an adequate explanation of sacramental efficacy, in Aquinas's view.

But surely, contra Aquinas, the coin plays some kind of causal role that the builder's paleness does not. Causality provides us with an explanation of *why* things happen, and Aquinas is surely right that the builder's paleness is extraneous to an adequate explanation of why the house is built. But the lead coin *does* play an important role in explaining why a

---

36. Adams, *Theories of the Eucharist*, 56.

37. Aquinas, *Sent* IV, d. 1, q. 1, a. 4, qc. 1. For a brief, helpful explanation of the distinction between causes *per se* and causes *per accidens*, see Toth, "Sine Qua Non Causes," 141–42.

hundred pounds of silver are exchanged; the coin is not extraneous to understanding the causal sequence and therefore is not merely an accidental cause in the sense intended by Aquinas. The coin does act as a cause, according to Fishacre and Bonaventure, even if by extrinsic rather than natural powers. By analogy, the sacraments are causes of grace, even if that causal power is not intrinsic to the sacramental acts.[38] Still, Aquinas correctly identifies that his opponents lack an adequate explanation of the causality of the coin, and by extension the sacraments.

FOURTEENTH-CENTURY LEGACIES

At the beginning of the fourteenth century, Scotus took up the argument of Fishacre and Bonaventure regarding the efficacy of the sacraments but incorporated a key element of Aquinas's theory. Like his Franciscan confrere Bonaventure, Scotus argues that the sacraments are efficacious because they are ordained by God as the means of grace. Scotus, for unclear reasons, abandons the analogy of the coin, however. Like Aquinas, Scotus also insists that the sacraments are a kind of instrumental cause, not, however, because of any inherent powers they possess, as Aquinas had believed, but because of a power arising precisely from the covenantal relationship between God and the church that performs the sacraments.[39]

Scotus here draws on an innovative way of thinking about causal relationships that goes beyond Aristotle's four types of causes (efficient, formal, final, and material). According to Scotus, causation is only one type of what he calls an essentially ordered relationship or essential dependence.[40] For instance, Scotus argues that when two things co-cause the same effect, but each contributes to the effect in a different manner, there is an essentially ordered, but noncausal, relationship between the two co-causes; the relationship between a male and a female in the act of reproducing offspring, for example, would be an example of this type of essentially ordered relationship.[41] Similarly, one thing could necessarily

---

38. Aquinas himself seems to move closer to this view in the *Summa Theologiae*, where he argues that the sacraments cause grace by participating in God's principal agency. See n18 above. By the same token, why couldn't one say the coin is efficacious by participating in the authority of the king?

39. Duns Scotus, *Ordinatio* IV, d. 1, pt. 3, qq. 1–2, n. 311.

40. Adams, *Theories of the Eucharist*, 67–74.

41. Scotus distinguishes this type of relationship from one in which the two things cause the effect in the same way, such as two men pulling a boat into a dock. In the

cause two effects, one preceding the other; to use a contemporary example, if I drink a soda, I will immediately experience the gas in my digestive system, and then later I will feel more alert and awake as a result of the caffeine in the soda. According to Scotus, there is an essentially ordered relationship between my experiencing gas and my feeling alert since one necessarily follows the other, even though neither causes the other.

Finally, an essentially ordered relationship exists when one causal relationship (i.e., the relationship between a cause and an effect) is a condition for the possibility of a separate causal relationship. For example, if a faulty pipe causes gas to leak into a home, and a person lights a match, the lighted match will cause an explosion; the gas leak was a necessary condition for the explosion but was not the efficient cause of the explosion. Scotus believes that the efficacy of the sacraments depends on this latter type of essentially ordered relationship. God has ordained that when Christians properly perform a sacrament, this unfailingly creates the occasion for God, acting in and through the sacrament to cause grace in the sacrament's recipients. In this limited sense, the sacraments can be called instrumental causes of grace because they have an efficacy of their own in bringing about grace, albeit one derived not from natural powers but from the essentially ordered relationship established by God's covenant.[42]

It's a shame that Scotus did not use the analogy of the coin to illustrate his argument (and that we don't know why he doesn't use it) because it could serve as a starting point for applying his rich description of the variety of essentially ordered relationships to economic phenomena. For example, the complex relationship of behaviors of producers and consumers creates the conditions in which sellers decide on prices. Institutions like currency, corporations, and banks operate in particular ways not because of anything inherent in the nature of things, but as creations of society. Scotus's account of the different types of essentially ordered relationships, had it become more widely accepted, could have provided a fruitful theoretical foundation for explaining these and other economic phenomena.

In contrast, Courtenay insightfully argues that Aquinas's strict adherence to Aristotelian notions of causality in the debate over sacramental

---

latter, a single, stronger man could conceivably pull the boat (*Quaestiones Quodlibetales* 15.33, in Duns Scotus, *God and Creatures*, 353).

42. The type of essentially ordered relationship that Scotus believes helps explains the sacraments is similar to what earlier theologians had called sine qua non causality, but Scotus rejects this term, primarily because he doesn't think he is describing a type of causality. See Toth, "Sine Qua Non Causes," 146–49.

efficacy is closely linked to his positions on economic questions like the just price and usury.[43] These latter stances were based on his insistence that money must have an intrinsic value as a commodity, a premise central to his rejection of the analogy of the coin.[44] Whereas in important ways Aquinas was a theological innovator, here we potentially see him from another angle as conservative, disdainful of and unable to learn from the transformations taking place in the increasingly urban and commercial world of the thirteenth century. On the other hand, his own analogy of the worker and his tools may hint at a valiant defense of the inherent value of work in resistance to the increasing commodification of labor.

The argument that the sacraments are tokens of divine power was taken up later in the fourteenth century by representatives of the *via moderna* like the Franciscan William of Ockham, the Dominican Robert Holcot, and the secular priest Pierre d'Ailly, the former two of whom likewise revived the analogy of the coin.[45] These theologians situated this argument about the sacraments in the broader context of a theology of covenant (*pactum*), emphasizing the contingency of the economy of salvation ordained by God in light of God's absolute power.[46] That being said, they put the emphasis on divine power, rather than the essentially ordered relationship between God's gift of grace and the performance of the sacraments, as the source of sacramental efficacy (whereas Scotus had emphasized both); indeed, Ockham denied the reality of essentially ordered relationships, arguing that they could be explained entirely in terms of efficient causation.[47] Here again, as with Aquinas although from a quite different direction, we see a narrowing of options when it comes to describing causal relationships. Although Scotus continued to exert some influence on the Catholic intellectual tradition, the impact of the *via moderna* on subsequent thought and the revival of Thomism in the fifteenth

---

43. Courtenay, "King," 202–9.

44. As his treatment of the analogy of the coin makes clear, Aquinas did not believe that it was *impossible* for a coin to be ascribed token value; rather, he believed such a coin was debased and that its use was dishonest (Courtenay, "King," 206).

45. William of Ockham, *Sent* IV, d. 17, q. 1; Holcot, *Super Libros Sapientiae*, bk. 3, n. 35.

46. This theology of covenant took embryonic form in the work of Scotus but was fully developed by the theologians of the *via moderna*. It draws on the distinction between God's "ordained power" and "absolute power." See Adams, *William Ockham*, 1186–207; Slotemaker and Witt, *Robert Holcot*, 17–39; Courtenay, "Covenant and Causality."

47. Adams, *William Ockham*, 772–84.

and especially the sixteenth centuries left Catholics, at the dawn of the modern age, with a limited set of tools for understanding causality, not just in the sacramental realm but also in the social and economic fields.

"Transdisciplinary" theology is not a modern innovation; the medieval scholastics drew on their knowledge of their economic context to help explain theological concepts. For example, these medieval theologians appealed to metaphors of an artisan exercising his craft and a coin whose value depended on the decree of the king to explain competing theories of how the sacraments cause grace in their recipients. For us today, understanding this medieval debate requires transdisciplinarity on our part, as well. Although the significance of these economic metaphors may have been obvious to their originators, we require research into the economic realities of the medieval era to deepen our understanding of the theological arguments made by the scholastics. At the same time, further exploration of the theories of causality developed by these theologians in this debate over the sacraments can prove useful to us, as well, especially as scholars seek out more adequate accounts of causality in the economy and other aspects of social life.[48]

BIBLIOGRAPHY

Adams, Marilyn McCord. *Some Later Medieval Theories of the Eucharist: Thomas Aquinas, Giles of Rome, Duns Scotus, and William Ockham.* New York: Oxford University Press, 2010.

———. *William Ockham.* Vol. 2. Notre Dame, IN: University of Notre Dame Press, 1987.

Aquinas, Thomas. *Scriptum Super Libros Sententiarum.* Edited by P. Mandonnet and M. F. Moos. 4 vols. Paris: Lethielleux, 1929–47.

———. *Summa Theologiae.* Edited by Petrus Caramello. 3 vols. Turin and Rome: Marietti, 1952–56.

Blankenhorn, Bernhard. "The Instrumental Causality of the Sacraments: Thomas Aquinas and Louis-Marie Chauvet." *Nova et Vetera* 4 (2006) 255–94.

Cole, Virginia A. "Ritual Charity and Royal Children in Thirteenth-Century England." In *Medieval and Early Modern Ritual: Formalized Behavior in Europe, China and Japan,* edited by Joelle Rollo-Koster, 221–44. Cultures, Beliefs and Traditions: Medieval and Early Modern Peoples 13. Leiden: Brill, 2002.

Courtenay, William J. "Covenant and Causality in Pierre d'Ailly." *Speculum* 46 (1971) 94–119.

---

48. For example, Scotus arguably anticipated certain aspects of the contemporary social theory known as critical realism. See my explanation of critical realism's understanding of the economy in Shadle, "Critical Realism and the Economy."

———. "The King and the Leaden Coin: The Economic Background of 'Sine Qua Non' Causality." *Traditio* 28 (1972) 185–209.

———. "Token Coinage and the Administration of Poor Relief in the Late Middle Ages." *Journal of Interdisciplinary History* 3 (1972) 275–95.

Depeyrot, Georges. "Monetary System of the 'Ancient Régime' (Third to Eighteenth Centuries)." In *Handbook of the History of Money and Currency*, edited by Stefano Battilossi et al., 107–58. Springer Reference. Singapore: Springer, 2020.

Dixon-Smith, Sally Angharad. "Feeding the Poor to Commemorate the Dead: The *Pro Anima* Almsgiving of Henry III of England, 1227–72." PhD diss., University College London, 2016.

Duns Scotus, John. *God and Creatures: The Quodlibetal Questions*. Translated by Felix Alluntis and Allan B. Wolter. Princeton, NJ: Princeton University Press, 1975.

———. *Ordinatio Liber Quartus, Distinctiones 1–7*. Edited by P. Barnaba Hechich. Opera Omnia 11. Vatican City: Vatican, 2008.

Finn, Daniel K. *Christian Economic Ethics: History and Implications*. Minneapolis: Fortress, 2013.

———, ed. *Distant Markets, Distant Harms: Market Complicity and Christian Ethics*. New York: Oxford University Press, 2014.

———, ed. *Moral Agency Within Social Structures and Culture: A Primer on Critical Realism for Christian Ethics*. Washington, DC: Georgetown University Press, 2020.

———. *The Moral Ecology of Markets: Assessing Claims About Markets and Justice*. New York: Cambridge University Press, 2006.

———, ed. *The True Wealth of Nations: Catholic Social Thought and Economic Life*. New York: Oxford University Press, 2010.

Fishacre, Richard. *In IV Libros Sententiarum Petri Lombardi* [excerpts]. In *De Sacramentorum Efficientia apud Theologos Ord. Praed., Fasc. 1, 1229–1276*, edited by Henri-Dominique Simonin and Gilles Gérard Meersseman, 17–20. Rome: Pont. Institutum Internationale Angelicum, 1936.

Francis. *Ad Theologiam Promovendam*. Vatican, Nov. 1, 2023. https://www.vatican.va/content/francesco/la/motu_proprio/documents/20231101-motu-proprio-ad-theologiam-promovendam.html.

Holcot, Robert. *Super Libros Sapientiae*. Hagenau, 1494. Repr., Frankfurt: Minerva, 1974.

John Paul II. *Laborem Exercens*. Vatican, Sept. 14, 1981. https://www.vatican.va/content/john-paul-ii/en/encyclicals/documents/hf_jp-ii_enc_14091981_laborem-exercens.html.

Lynch, Reginald M. *The Cleansing of the Heart: The Sacraments as Instrumental Causes in the Thomistic Tradition*. Washington, DC: Catholic University of America Press, 2017.

Mitchiner, Michael, and Anne Skinner. "English Tokens, c. 1200 to 1425." *British Numismatic Journal* 53 (1983) 29–77.

Phillips, Katie. "Devotion by Donation: The Alms-Giving and Religious Foundations of Henry III." *Reading Medieval Studies* 43 (2017) 79–98.

Shadle, Matthew A. "Critical Realism and the Economy." In *Moral Agency Within Social Structures and Culture: A Primer on Critical Realism for Christian Ethics*, edited by Daniel K. Finn, 73–88. Washington, DC: Georgetown University Press, 2020.

Slotemaker, John T., and Jeffrey C. Witt. *Robert Holcot*. New York: Oxford University Press, 2016.

Spufford, Peter. *Money and Its Use in Medieval Europe*. New York: Cambridge University Press, 1988.
Toth, Zita V. "Sine Qua Non Causes and Their Discontents." *Res Philosophica* 99 (2022) 139–67.
Wawrykow, Joseph P. "The Sacraments in Thirteenth-Century Theology." In *The Oxford Handbook of Sacramental Theology*, edited by Hans Boersma and Matthew Levering, 218–34. Oxford Handbooks. New York: Oxford University Press, 2015.
William of Ockham. *Quaestiones in Librum Quartum Sententiarum*. Edited by Gideon Gal et al. Opera Theologica 7. St. Bonaventure, NY: Franciscan Institute, 1984.

The Advancement and Economic Empowerment of Women
How Far Have We Come?

Regina Wentzel Wolfe

THE WORKPLACE AND WOMEN'S status in it has been a long-standing interest and focus of mine, particularly the inequities of the gender wage gap and barriers which preclude women from full participation in meaningful work. Many things assist the advancement and economic empowerment of women. Some require modification of systems and structures, policies and procedures. Others are more personal and relational. Among the latter are mentors, leaders, and colleagues who acknowledge and respect women's human dignity, value their talents and contributions, listen to and engage their perspectives, treat them equitably, and work with them collaboratively. In a Festschrift honoring Daniel K. Finn, it seems appropriate to consider the current state of women in the workplace not simply because of his scholarly interests in systems and structures but because these are attributes, attitudes, and actions he has long embodied. I am among many women, and others too, who have benefited from his example and encouragement.

My first encounter with Dan was in 1983 at the American Academy of Religion Midwest Regional Meeting. Still in the throes of doctoral course work, I had just presented my first academic paper when he introduced himself. We had a good discussion; I was pleased to find someone was genuinely interested in my ideas. He mentioned the Ecumenical Institute, as the Collegeville Institute was then called, and suggested I consider applying for residency when I got to the dissertation stage. He followed up a few weeks later with an encouraging note and information on the institute. Little did I know that a decade later I not only would be his colleague but also would be the junior faculty member on the Faculty Handbook Committee which he chaired. Working with him as the handbook underwent a major revision and watching his leadership skills and the way he engaged others and listened to a multitude of voices in a collegial and collaborative manner—even when there were disagreements—taught me a great deal; it was among many things I learned from him.

It should also be noted Dan is a man of action when necessary. When Jane Kathman, the first woman to join the Department of Economics faculty, arrived, she was given a desk in the mimeograph room. In Dan's view this was undignified and unacceptable. He set to work rectifying the situation. Purchasing appropriate materials, he enlisted the help of two colleagues. Together the three of them went in one Saturday and put up partitions and a door at the end of the room. Voila! She had an office, with a window no less! As I did, she, too, observed Dan's sincere and respectful manner as he engaged with others, particularly women, as mentor, colleague, and leader supporting them and bringing out the best in them as they advanced in their careers.

HISTORY OF THE ADVANCEMENT AND ECONOMIC EMPOWERMENT OF WOMEN

The focus of this chapter considers the advancement and economic empowerment of women with a particular focus on wage inequities and participation in the workforce. These are only two aspects of what is, necessarily, a larger project to address the many systems and structures which limit women's human rights, particularly the right to work and the right to a just wage. These systems and structures also impede women from meeting their responsibility to participate in society and promote the common good. Though he does not deal specifically with women's economic empowerment, doing so here resonates with various aspects of Finn's work including his writings on just wages and the meaning of work found in Catholic social thought.[1] Of particular import is his work on social structures and the Catholic understanding of sinful social structures.[2]

---

1. See, for example, Finn: *Faithful Economics*, particularly ch. 7; *Christian Economic Ethics*, particularly ch. 14 and conclusion; and "Human Work."

2. See, for example, Finn: "Social Structures"; and "What Is a Sinful Social Structure?"

Early Calls for Equal Wages

In *A Living Wage: Its Ethical and Economic Aspects*, published in 1906, Monsignor John A. Ryan called for women to be paid a living wage and, in addition, as a matter of distributive justice insisted men and women doing the same work should receive the same pay. As I have argued elsewhere, this position was ahead of its time.[3] In the early 1900s, even the International Ladies' Garment Workers Union accepted contracts setting women's wages below men's and restricting women to less skilled jobs.[4]

It took until 1963 for the Equal Pay Act targeting the disparity in wages to be enacted in the United States. It was seen as a first step in addressing equal economic opportunity for women. At that time, compared to men, women were earning fifty-nine cents on the dollar—a wage gap of forty-one cents. President John F. Kennedy established the Commission on the Status of Women to develop programs addressing the needs of working women, including expanding child care and increasing the tax deductions working mothers could take for child care costs.[5]

The work of Esther Peterson, director of the Department of Labor Women's Bureau and executive vice-chairman of the President's Commission on the Status of Women, was crucial to passing the legislation. She expanded the focus of the Women's Bureau to include women who worked in low wage jobs and recognized the need to build support and coalitions. Peterson looked to the National Equal Pay Committee and women's groups whose representatives made up that committee.[6] This included the National Council of Catholic Women, represented by Irma Piepho, who served on the staff of the National Council of Catholic Women and was involved with the National Committee on the Status of Women.[7]

Catholic Social Teaching Mid-Century and Beyond

In 1891, a decade or so before John Ryan's book, Pope Leo XIII promulgated *Rerum Novarum*, heralding in what is known as Catholic social

---

3. Wolfe, "John Ryan and Women's Wages."
4. Hymowitz and Weissman, *History of Women*, 253.
5. Kennedy, "Remarks on Signing Equal Pay Act."
6. Peterson, "Oral History Interview."
7. *Catholic Transcript*, "Untitled Photo."

teaching (CST).[8] Not to be confused with the social implications of faith, CST is understood as an "effort to provide systematic, normative theory relating the social vision of faith to the concrete conditions" in which contemporary women and men find themselves.[9] As did Pope Leo XIII, his successors continued to respond to challenges and concerns of their own time, thereby contributing to the development of CST. In *Christian Economic Ethics*, Finn investigates "the history of Christian life so the reader can better decide how to apply the insights of that tradition to economic life in the twenty-first century."[10] As will be seen, his work sheds light on the economic empowerment of women, particularly responses to the gender wage gap and barriers to participation in the workforce.

Despite addressing contemporary circumstances, it is important to acknowledge the commonalities in the underlying assumptions across the decades. The most obvious is the insistence that human persons possess an inherent dignity and are inherently social beings. Claims about human rights are founded on the dignity of the human person. Furthermore, as David Hollenbach has observed, the church's approach to human rights is dynamic. Citing the *Declaration on Religious Freedom* and *Gaudium et Spes*, no. 41, he notes "the Council linked the full gambit of human rights with the very core of Christian faith. Since the Council, the church has become an important institutional activist for human rights."[11]

A second commonality concerns the understanding of the role and function of the state. While there has been a shift in the paradigmatic understanding of the relationship of the church to the state and the broader society, there is a general acceptance that the basic purposes of the state include promoting the common good and ensuring the welfare of citizens entrusted to it.[12] The details of what this role entails have become more specific with each subsequent teaching.

Also found throughout CST is concern for economic life. Here too, "the central importance of human dignity in the Christian vision of the

---

8. Some, including Schuck, *Social Catholicism*, have argued pre-Leonine encyclicals dating back to those of Pope Benedict XIV (1740–58) belong in the corpus of papal social teachings.

9. Hehir, "John Paul II," 125.

10. Finn, *Christian Economic Ethics*, 383. See also B. Brady, "From Catholic Social Thought"; and Dorr, "Themes and Theologies."

11. Hollenbach, "Human Rights," 260.

12. For a discussion on the way in which the relationship between church and state was reconceived by the bishops at Vatican II, see the commentary on *Gaudium et Spes*, pt. 2, ch. 4, by Nell-Breuning, "Life of the Political Community," particularly 5:323–27.

person also led to a strong emphasis on the importance of social and economic rights in the developing Catholic tradition."[13] In *Gaudium et Spes*, specific areas were singled out and addressed in a concrete manner in an attempt to avoid a merely intellectual or emotional acceptance of the view of the human person which Vatican Council II had presented. Insisting all people are worthy of respect, are essentially equal, and must develop a sense of responsibility is important; it provides common ground from which dialogue, relationships, and social commitment arise. In addition, true respect for all human beings implies fostering the common good by working to ensure the right to those conditions of political, economic, and social life which foster and promote their own and others' fulfillment and flourishing (nos. 12, 15, 16, 18, 22, 29, 30). As noted above, there was not much specificity about those conditions, particularly those affecting economic life, the way it is organized, and its obligation to pay just wages.

Pope John Paul II expanded this area of CST adding specificity to the understanding of the place and meaning of work in human life in *Laborem Exercens* (1981) and giving consideration to the organization of work in *Centesimus Annus* (1991). The focus is on fostering environments which will ensure the rights of all who work are realized. These rights have their basis in the basic human rights which are fundamental to human persons.[14] Among them are the right to work, the right to just wages, the right to organize, and the right to social benefits, including pensions, health care, and education.

Pope Benedict XVI took up many of these themes in *Caritas in Veritate*. His comments on wages, particularly in terms of the persistent gender wage gap, are important. He notes work "expresses the essential dignity of every man and woman in the context of their particular society" and goes on to specify the content of such work, which is

> work that is freely chosen, effectively associating workers, both men and women, with the development of their community; work that enables the worker to be respected and free from any form of discrimination; work that makes it possible for families to meet their needs and provide schooling for their children,

---

13. Hollenbach, "Human Rights," 261.

14. For a discussion of how Catholic rights theory differs from other rights theories in that it is grounded in the Catholic understanding of human dignity and social solidarity, see Coleman, "Neither Liberal nor Socialist," 35; and Hollenbach, *Justice, Peace, and Human Rights*, 93–98.

without the children themselves being forced into labour; work that permits the workers to organize themselves freely, and to make their voices heard; work that leaves enough room for rediscovering one's roots at a personal, familial and spiritual level; work that guarantees those who have retired a decent standard of living.[15]

Of course, as Finn reminds us, determining what constitutes an adequate wage is not easy.[16] This is particularly true of CST, which argues it must be a living wage. University of Notre Dame's Center for Social Concern's Just Wage Initiative is taking up the challenge by considering the question "What makes any given wage just or unjust?"[17] With roots in the Just Wage Working Group convened in 2017, it considers that question. "The group was interdisciplinary—made up of scholars and students—and their work was rooted in the Catholic social tradition's (CST) commitment to the dignity of work and those who perform it. In their first year they identified seven core criteria that together provide a framework for determining the justness of any given wage scenario. Those criteria are visually represented as a honeycomb of hexagons to show their interconnectedness, as well as their embedding within larger political, economic, and cultural contexts."[18] The seven criteria are:

1. A just wage enables a decent life for a worker and their household.
2. Wage enables asset building.
3. Wage provides basic social security for worker and household.

---

15. Benedict XVI, *Caritas in Veritate*, no. 63.

16. Finn, *Faithful Economics*, particularly ch. 7.

17. This initiative is one of a number of interdisciplinary approaches at Catholic colleges and universities. Examples include Georgetown University's Institute for Women, Peace and Security, which insists on recognizing the role women have in achieving peace and calls for women's empowerment, including economic empowerment, in efforts to achieve peace; see https://giwps.georgetown.edu for more information on their work, including both the US and global indices which, among other areas, measure women's achievements in employment and access to financial services. The John A. Ryan Institute for Catholic Social Thought at the University of St. Thomas brings Ryan's legacy into the twenty-first century through its research and partnerships with business and focus on the integration of work and life; for more information see https://cas.stthomas.edu/departments/areas-of-study/catholic-studies/john-a-ryan-institute/. A final example is the Kalmanovitz Initiative for Labor and the Working Poor at Georgetown University; grounded in Catholic and Jesuit traditions, the initiative focuses on empowering workers through research, education, and advocacy all in service to the common good; see https://lwp.georgetown.edu.

18. Just Wage Tool.

4. Wage structure is non-discriminatory.
5. Wage is not excessive.
6. Wage reflects participation by workers.
7. Wage considers performance, qualification, and type of work.[19]

Each is described in detail, beginning with a paragraph defining the criterion. A discussion follows on how each criterion relates to CST. There is also discussion of research findings and legislative requirements as well as exemplars from across sectors. In addition, a Just Wage Tool was created fostering greater understanding of just wages and used to encourage dialogue among and across stakeholders.[20]

The Equal Pay Act at Thirty and Beyond

By 1993, the thirtieth anniversary of the Equal Pay Act, women were earning seventy cents on the dollar compared to men. While the gender pay gap had decreased by eleven cents, a portion of the decrease was the result of men's wages decreasing. As Rosemary Yardley reported, "In 1992 a woman's median hourly wage was $8.42, or 31 cents more than in 1979. A man's median hourly wage was $11.03, a $1.84 decrease during the same period."[21] At the turn of the millennium women were earning seventy-six cents on the dollar; the gap had now closed by seventeen cents compared to 1963.[22]

For some, this progress meant disparities were resolved. Market forces, educational and skill levels, and/or personal choices explained remaining differences. Often, this perspective reflects more traditional understandings of women's social roles arguing women prefer to remain at home. Those who choose work do so in occupations more suited to women. That those occupations pay lower wages is simply coincidence. Today, many hold this position.[23]

19. Just Wage Tool.
20. For more details and discussion of the seven criteria, see Just Wage Tool.
21. Yardley, "U.S. Women Still Undervalued."
22. U.S. Bureau of Labor Statistics, "Women's Earnings."
23. A 2019 ILO report found only 45.3 percent of women worked and discredited the view that "women do not want to work outside their home. Based on a representative global sample, about 70 per cent of the women interviewed said that they would prefer to be in paid work, and 66.5 per cent of men agreed that they should be." For more details, see International Labour Organization, *Quantum Leap*, 12.

Critics argue this view ignores the manifold barriers to gender equity and their impact on efforts to attain wage parity between women and men. The complexity and the systematic nature of the inequities and barriers can be seen in efforts to address gender equity at the Fourth World Conference on Women held in Beijing, China, in 1995 and the resulting Beijing Declaration and Platform for Action (BPfA). The declaration identified twelve areas of critical concern:

- The persistent and increasing burden of poverty on women
- Inequalities and inadequacies in and unequal access to education and training
- Inequalities and inadequacies in and unequal access to health care and related services
- Violence against women
- The effects of armed or other kinds of conflict on women, including those living under foreign occupation
- Inequality in economic structures and policies, in all forms of productive activities and in access to resources
- Inequality between men and women in the sharing of power and decision-making at all levels
- Insufficient mechanisms at all levels to promote the advancement of women
- Lack of respect for and inadequate promotion and protection of the human rights of women
- Stereotyping of women and inequality in women's access to and participation in all communication systems, especially in the media
- Gender inequalities in the management of natural resources and in the safeguarding of the environment
- Persistent discrimination against and violation of the rights of the girl child[24]

Not all of these directly address barriers to the advancement and economic empowerment of women in the workplace. However, recognizing the complexity, interdisciplinary, and systemic nature of barriers which limit progress toward gender equity, Beijing Conference participants and

---

24. United Nations, "Beijing Declaration."

drafters of BPfA adopted an integrative approach echoing CST with its insistence on the dignity of all persons and emphasis on the common good leading to a society in which all humans will flourish.

The BPfA was taken up by a range of institutions intent on developing strategies to address the lack of gender equity. The United Nations, the largest of these, does so through UN Women, its entity for gender equality.[25] It is joined in this work by other intergovernmental bodies including the World Bank, the International Monetary Fund, the International Labour Organization, and the Asian Development Bank. Many NGOs and foundations also address issues of gender equity including the Gates Foundation Gender Equality Division with its programs that address the complexity of women's lives.[26] The resulting responses include increased access to financial services, assistance in finding employment in higher paying sectors, creative approaches to meeting child care needs, and strategies for systemic change in institutional cultures and structures of organizations. Businesses of all sizes were also challenged by BPfA to be proactive in the advancement and economic empowerment of women.

Most of the challenges, whether to individual governments, intergovernmental bodies, NGOs, or businesses, were spearheaded by the United Nations, primarily through the Millennium Development Goals (MDGs) which addressed many of the concerns identified in BPfA. In 2000, Kofi Annan established the United Nations Global Compact (UNGC), a voluntary initiative targeted at the business community.[27] First broached in 1999, "Annan argued that shared values provide a stable environment for a world market and that without these explicit values business could expect backlashes from protectionism, populism, fanaticism and terrorism."[28] In line with the UN Convention Against Corruption, a principle on corruption was added to the original nine UNGC principles focusing on human rights, labor, and the environment.[29]

25. For more information on UN Women, see https://www.unwomen.org/en.

26. For more information on these two programs, see Gates Foundation: "Women in Leadership"; and "Women's Economic Empowerment."

27. For a discussion of the Global Compact, see Williams, "United Nations Global Compact."

28. Williams, "UN Global Compact," 755.

29. The Universal Declaration of Human Rights (1948), the Rio Declaration on Environment and Development (1992), and the International Labour Organization's Fundamental Principles and Rights at Work (1998) are the other multilateral UN treaties undergirding the principles.

Another significant initiative came from Calvert Investments, a US mutual fund manager known for socially responsible investing.[30] Unable to find adequate metrics or tools to assess investments and screen companies for issues related to gender equity, Calvert developed its own—the Calvert Women's Principles (CWP).[31] Introduced in 2004, they were "the first global code of conduct for corporations focused exclusively on empowering, advancing and investing in women worldwide."[32] Calvert sought input from a wide range of researchers, NGOs, and practitioners, including UNIFEM.[33] The CWP were aligned with gender equity related aspects of the MDGs; using BPfA as a model, specific actions were linked to each principle and set out as follows:

1. Disclosure, Implementation and Monitoring

   Corporations will promote and strive to attain gender equality in their operations and in their business and stakeholder relationships by adopting and implementing proactive policies that are publicly disclosed, monitored and enforced.

2. Employment and Income

   Corporations will promote and strive to attain gender equality by adopting and implementing wage, income, hiring, promotion and other employment policies that eliminate gender discrimination in all its forms.

---

30. In December 2016, Eaton Vance Corporation acquired Calvert Investments, which was renamed Calvert Research and Management, a subsidiary of Eaton Vance. In 2021, Morgan Stanley acquired Calvert Research and Management, which is now part of Morgan Stanley Investment Management, the asset management division of Morgan Stanley.

31. For a more extensive discussion of the CWPs, see Wolfe, "Calvert Women's Principles."

32. D. Brady and Sager, "Is Your Company up to Code?"

33. UNIFEM is now called UN Women.

3. Health, Safety and Violence

Corporations will promote and strive to attain gender equality by adopting and implementing policies to secure the health, safety and well-being of women workers.

4. Civic and Community Engagement

Corporations will promote and strive to attain gender equality by adopting and implementing policies to help secure and protect the right of women to fully participate in civic life and to be free from all forms of discrimination and exploitation.

5. Management and Governance

Corporations will promote and strive to attain gender equality by adopting and implementing policies to ensure women's participation in corporate management and governance.

6. Education, Training and Professional Development

Corporations will promote and strive to attain gender equality by adopting and implementing education, training and professional development policies benefiting women.

7. Business, Supply Chain and Marketing Practices

Corporations will promote and strive to attain gender equality by adopting and implementing proactive, non-discriminatory business, marketing and supply chain policies and practices.[34]

Companies were invited to adopt these as part of their business strategy. Implementing the actions would improve women's positions and provide markers to assess a company's progress toward achieving gender equity.

The CWP proved valuable for screening companies for inclusion in portfolios of socially responsible companies promoting gender equity in the workplace. However, getting corporations to adopt them was slow. Calvert, convinced that corporate adoption of the CWP would have a significant impact on advancing women in the workplace, began considering different avenues to increase adoption of them.

Actions to address gender inequities in the workplace were beginning to show signs of progress. For example, San Francisco wrapped up

---

34. Calvert Investments, *Calvert Women's Principles*, 1–7.

work with the Gender Equality Principles (GEP) Initiative.[35] "The GEP was one of the first comprehensive, free, data-driven approaches to help the private sector address issues facing women in the workplace and was a model replicated by the United Nations Global Compact Women's Empowerment Principles."[36] Progress—at an uneven pace and often incrementally—was being made. However, studies and reports at the conclusion of the MDGs and the twentieth anniversary of BPfA were clear: much more effort was needed.

The Equal Pay Act at Sixty

June 2023 marked the sixtieth anniversary of the Equal Pay Act. It was a catalyst for examining women's progress in gender equity, particularly in the workplace, and for assessing current conditions, identifying still existing barriers, and putting forth strategies for moving forward. The gender wage gap continued to narrow. In 2023, based on full-time, year-round workers, it was eighty-three cents on the dollar.[37] On the surface, it points to positive advances. However, it masks the fact the wage gap has remained virtually steady for more than twenty years; in 2002 women earned eighty cents on the dollar.[38]

In the US women now make up 47 percent of the overall workforce, up 30 percent since 1950.[39] However, in terms of increasing participation numbers and "getting more women into the workforce, the U.S. has fallen behind other countries with advanced economies."[40] Forecasts for 2032 indicate no expectation participation will grow even though in the over-twenty-five-year-old, college-educated workforce, women have been in the majority since 2019, making up 51 percent of that population.[41] However, it is not quite the achievement it seems, given women have been earning more degrees than men for close to forty years. According to the National Center for Educational Statistics, more women earned bachelor's degrees than men since 1982, more master's degrees since 1987, and

---

35. Sasco, *Director's Report*.
36. Aragão, "Gender Pay Gap."
37. Payscale, *2024 Gender Pay Gap Report*, 4.
38. Aragão, "Gender Pay Gap."
39. Schaeffer, "For Women's History Month."
40. Peck, "U.S. Has Fallen Behind," para. 1.
41. Schaeffer, "For Women's History Month."

more doctoral degrees since 2006.[42] Educational attainment and greater participation in the workforce do not necessarily translate into equal pay and/or the narrowing of the gender wage gap.

THE GLASS CEILING AND LEADERSHIP PIPELINE

Though there have always been some, like Peterson, concerned with the plight of women at all levels of the workforce, the attention and research on women in the workplace focused mostly on professional women. Traditional measures of progress often concentrated on the number of women at senior management levels, in the C-suite, and on corporate boards. There is some indication of positive movement in senior management levels. "An analysis of 86,000 executives from 7,300 US firms over 12 years found that women could reach parity in senior leadership positions between 2030 and 2037, among companies in the Russell 3000."[43] However, progress in the C-suite and on boards is slower in coming.

By 2023, the total number of individual women appearing on the list, which began in 1972, stood at 116. In addition, 2023 saw a record number of women CEOs on the list with 52 or 10.4 percent of Fortune 500 CEOs.[44] The number is unchanged on the 2024 Fortune 500 list.[45] S&P Global Market Intelligence research indicates "gender parity in the C-suite remains elusive . . . [and] suggests collective C-suite parity may not occur until mid-21st century, while parity at the highest levels in CEO and CFO positions could take even longer."[46]

The dearth of women in senior positions was for decades attributed to the glass ceiling, a term coined in the 1970s, which is "a metaphor describing the invisible barrier women and other marginalized groups face when trying to reach higher levels of professional success."[47] An articulation of three levels of barriers—societal, internal structural, and governmental—is found in a report of the Federal Glass Ceiling Commission.[48]

---

42. National Center for Education Statistics, "Table 318.10."
43. Laidlaw and Sandberg, *Breaking Boundaries*, 3.
44. Catalyst, "Historical List of Women CEOs."
45. Hinchliffe, "Share of Fortune 500 Companies."
46. Laidlaw and Sandberg, *Breaking Boundaries*, 7.
47. Reiners, "What Is the Glass Ceiling?," para. 1.
48. For a summary of the Glass Ceiling Act, see "Civil Rights Act of 1991." For more detail on the barriers, see Federal Glass Ceiling Commission, *Good for Business*, 7–8.

It is interesting to note that societal barriers include educational opportunity and attainment even though when the research was conducted women were completing bachelor's and master's degrees at higher rates than men. In part, it was a result of women choosing majors in disciplines which prepared them for jobs and careers in lower waged sectors, still often the case. The commission also considered other barriers including racism, lack of access to quality secondary education, and lack of financial means to attend college.

Researchers found a disconnect between the views of corporate leaders, who welcomed inclusion and the opportunity to eliminate barriers, and perceptions and experiences of women and minorities in the workplace. Studies found "upper- and middle-level white male resistance"; white men at these levels felt threatened by women and minorities, unlike CEOs and other corporate leaders who did not. The research suggested "the glass ceiling exists because of the perception of many white males that as a group they are losing—losing the corporate game, losing control, and losing opportunity. Many middle- and upper-level white male managers view the inclusion of minorities and women in management as a direct threat to their own chances for advancement."[49] Such zero sum thinking persists.[50]

There are many variations of the glass ceiling. Among them are the glass escalator, the glass cliff, and the labyrinth of leadership which impact women generally. There are also the maternal wall, which affects pregnant women and working mothers, the concrete ceiling, which impacts women of color, and the bamboo ceiling, which refers to the barriers Asian and Asian Americans face.[51] The practical results of these barriers are many, including earning wages that are lower than men's wages.

It is worth noting here that recognizing both the choices of individuals and the complexities found in workplace systems and structures impact women's advancement and economic empowerment. They also echo Finn's research on social structures. He is quite clear.

> Just as there are no persons who are *only* sinful or *only* virtuous, the same is true for social structures. No social structure is only virtuous. Because a social structure is a system of relations among social positions, different positions face different restrictions and opportunities. Inevitably, persons in some positions

---

49. Federal Glass Ceiling Commission, *Good for Business*, 31.
50. See Kerr and Pollack, *Engaging Men*.
51. For a full description of each of these, see Reiners, "What Is the Glass Ceiling?"

are privileged in some way, and others are at a disadvantage. There can be morally defensible reasons for privilege, but even among virtuous persons, privileges are too often excessive and disadvantages too often unjust. At the same time, no social structure is only sinful.[52]

Whether it is the educational focus a woman selects or the resistance of some white males to women's advancement in the workplace, the analysis presented above indicates personal choice is a contributing factor to either the attainment of or the lack of progress in women's advancement in the workplace. Likewise, social structures can contribute to progress or be a barrier to it.

The Broken Rung

For years breaking the glass ceiling and ensuring sufficient numbers of women in the pipeline to do so were seen as major correctives to the gender wage gap. A 2019 release of a McKinsey and Lean In report changed that. A detailed analysis of five years of wage data revealed imbalances do not begin at the mid-management level or when a woman takes time off after having a child. Imbalances begin at the first rung of promotion up the corporate ladder, a phenomenon called the "broken rung," now considered the most significant barrier women face.[53] "For the ninth consecutive year, women face their biggest hurdle at the first critical step up to manager. This year, for every 100 men promoted from entry level to manager, 87 women were promoted. And this gap is trending the wrong way for women of color: this year, 73 women of color were promoted to manager for every 100 men, down from 82 women of color last year. As a result of this broken rung, women fall behind and can't catch up."[54] The inability to catch up can be very costly for women. The National Women's Law Center (NWLC) indicates the national median amount of wages women lose over a lifetime due to the wage gap is $399,300; to reach the same lifetime income of a sixty-year-old man, a woman needs to work until she is sixty-eight years old. The state of Vermont has the lowest lifetime loss at $258,000 while New Hampshire the highest at

---

52. Finn, *Faithful Economics*, 15.
53. Huang et al., *Women in the Workplace 2019*, 3.
54. McKinsey and Company and LeanIn.Org, *Women in the Workplace 2023*, 14.

$721,760.⁵⁵ "Women are losing tens of thousands of dollars annually due to the wage gap, with Black, Latina, and Native women suffering from the largest gaps. This harms not only women, but the families who depend on their income."[56]

While the broken rung contributes to the gender wage gap, data from the National Association of Colleges and Employers paints an even bleaker picture. "Early data from NACE's 2023 Student Survey indicate that Class of 2023 male graduates had a median starting salary of $72,500; for women, the median starting salary falls at $52,500. This equates to a gap of 72%—widening more than 10%."[57] Some of the difference might be explained by graduates' area of study: 26 percent of men and 18 percent of women were business majors; for those in STEM fields 45.8 percent were men and 32.6 percent were women. In liberal arts 20.5 percent were men and 31.4 percent were women. Finally, for those in public service majors the breakdown was 7.6 percent of the men and 17.9 percent of the women.[58] However, the differences in graduates' majors do not explain away all the gap. Gatta and Gore are clear, "even when women go into gender nontraditional majors, they are still facing a wage gap within that major."[59] Their study reveals the median salary for business majors is $72,500 for men and $52,500 for women. For STEM majors the gap is smaller at $72,500 for men and $62,500 for women. For many college-educated women, the gender wage gap begins with the first job after graduation, not at the first broken rung.

There are also differences in the gender wage gap related to income group. "The wage gap is smallest [87.2 cents on the dollar] among lower-wage workers, in part due to the minimum wage creating a wage floor."[60] Even in the 20 most common occupations for women there is a wage gap with women making 86.5 cents on the dollar. Cashiers, who earn almost 97.7 cents on the dollar, come the closest to achieving parity, while receptionists earn slightly over 97.3 cents on the dollar with general office clerks at 95 cents.[61] The wage gap is highest for women in the high wage

55. National Women's Law Center, "Lifetime Wage Gap."
56. Javaid, "Wage Gap Robs Women."
57. Gatta and Gore, "What Can Be Done," para. 3.
58. Gatta and Gore, "What Can Be Done," fig. 2: Gender Distribution inMmajor.
59. Gatta and Gore, "What Can Be Done," fig. 1: Salary by Gender in Majors.
60. Gould, "Gender Wage Gap Persists," para. 4.
61. Hegewisch and Gartner, "Women Earn Less."

group at 77.4 cents on the dollar.[62] As for women in leadership positions, Emma Burleigh reports, "Women managers and supervisors earn 83 cents, directors make 82 cents, and executives make only 72 cents on the dollar."[63]

UNCLEAR FUTURE

Women are not expected to reach pay equity with men until 2059. But even that slow progress has stalled in recent years. If change continues at this century's slower rate, pay equity will not be reached until 2106.[64] Though the pace of progress is discouraging for many, it should not come as a surprise. As Finn notes, "People should have employment at an adequate wage. This is a difficult challenge in a market economy, where no one business firm bears this responsibility for any one worker or family."[65] Despite the difficulty of the challenge, business leaders and practitioners, academic researchers, and advocacy groups have all put forth suggestions and strategies to address many of the barriers women face in the workplace. These fall into three broad categories: structural changes in the conduct and/or regulation of business; changes in attitudinal or cultural perspectives, particularly gender stereotypes; and calls for individual companies to change policies and procedures and organizational culture.

CALLS FOR CHANGE

Some call for structural change focusing on legislation and regulatory oversight at local, state, and federal levels, for example, the Paycheck Fairness Act, reintroduced in March 2025 by Senator Patty Murray.[66] There are also calls for federal pay transparency legislation based on legislation passed by some cities and states.[67] These would apply not only to deal-

---

62. Gould, "Gender Wage Gap Persists."
63. Burleigh, "Gender Pay Gap Actually Increases."
64. Miller and Vagins, *Simple Truth*, 5.
65. Finn, *Faithful Economics*, 48–49.
66. For more information, see Murray, "On Equal Pay Day."
67. Grissom, "HR, Take Note." For information on pay transparency legislation currently in place or planned, see Berkshire Compensation Team, "Mid-Year Update"; Hendrickson, "U.S. Pay Scale Transparency." For charts detailing state-by-state pay equity laws, see Littler, "50-State Pay Equity Chart"; or World at Work, "Pay Equity Law by State."

ings with current employees but also to hiring processes. Other efforts call on Congress to appropriate sufficient funding for oversight groups like the Equal Employment Opportunity Commission and the Justice Department's Employment Litigation Section, though this is unlikely in the current environment. There are also efforts to strengthen the right to unionize and calls to raise the minimum wage.[68]

Gender stereotypes, explicit and implicit bias, and organizational cultures persist as barriers to wage parity and women's advancement. These include beliefs that women are more emotional than men, are more nurturing and compassionate than men, and are not as committed to careers as men. The latter is even more pronounced when considering women with children. These and other prejudices and stereotypes play into the leadership bias which holds that "men are inherently better leaders than women."[69]

Strategies for a Business Response

Examining commonly proposed strategies for change at the individual business level provides a microcosm for understanding the complex nature of effecting changes needed to achieve gender equity in the workplace. Those advocating for individual businesses to change often present the business case for doing so. They also believe having a critical number of corporations successfully eliminating—or at least severely reducing—barriers to gender equity in the workplace will make it more likely others will follow.

The procedural changes recommended are more extensive than those ordinarily used to address compliance issues. Regardless of the issue—hiring practices, performance reviews, career advancement processes, work-life balance policies, or other areas of company life—the call is for clear policies and procedures including transparent, measurable outcomes and continual assessment to reinforce policies and procedures which work and modify those which do not.

Successful companies give consideration to a number of areas. For example, moving away from gendered language in job descriptions and titles. As Heilman et al. explain, "Most jobs have components that

---

68. See, for example, Khattar, "Closing the Gender Pay Gap"; Ton, "Equality in the U.S."; and Gould, "Gender Wage Gap Persists."

69. Gopal, "Overcoming Gender Stereotypes." See also Celestine, "How Do Stereotypes."

embody both communal and agentic elements, configuring job descriptions and advertisements to balance these features provides a way to undercut the masculine gendering of jobs that promotes bias and discrimination against women."[70] There are also shifts in language used in policies focusing on work-life balance, such as shifting to "parental leave" or gender-neutral dress codes. Increasingly, workplace flexibility policies use gender-neutral terms, reflecting recent data showing a growing desire among all employees for greater work-life balance.[71]

Concerns have also been raised about the ways women are evaluated, whether applying for positions, participating in performance review, asking for raises, requesting promotions, or seeking sponsorship in company professional development opportunities.[72] "Gender bias in evaluations at each of these key points in career progression has been found to result in discriminatory actions that hinder women's advancement, with women being given less access, poorer performance evaluations, and fewer organizational rewards compared to equivalently qualified men."[73] Heilman et al. argue, "It is critical to keep evaluation criteria uniform by creating a predetermined set of criteria that is applied for everyone."[74] While these and similar strategies are necessary correctives, they are not sufficient. Efforts are needed to overcome social norms which permeate a firm's culture, particularly norms arising from prescriptive gender stereotypes.

Changing Corporate Culture

Until recently, many companies have addressed deep-seated biases and prejudices about gender through their diversity, equity, and inclusion (DEI) training programs. Results of these programs—now under threat—are not uniform for various reasons. Some are compliance oriented, "used not to reduce discrimination, but to shield against litigation."[75] Some are poorly designed or not supported by leadership. Others lack transparency and accountability. In some instances, the reasons for and impact of such

70. Heilman et al., "Women at Work," s.vv. "Altering Job Descriptions." See also International Labour Organization, *Breaking Barriers*.
71. McKinsey and Company and LeanIn.Org, *Women in the Workplace 2023*, 12, 23. See also Deloitte Global, *Gen Z and Millennial Survey*.
72. Heilman et al, "Women at Work"; and Bailin, "IWD2022."
73. Heilman et al, "Women at Work," 167.
74. Heilman et al, "Women at Work," 176.
75. *Economist*, "This Is an Intervention."

programs have not been effectively communicated to employees. Finally, many DEI programs meet with employee resistance because of feelings of loss of status and/or control, a sense of diversity fatigue, or as noted above, feelings that the problem of inequality in the workplace has been resolved.[76]

CONCLUSION

Further study into the potential of any of these strategies to promote human flourishing and foster positive change in the workplace in ways that are compatible with CST will benefit from the work Finn and others have done over the years. Of particular interest in this regard is his recent volume *Moral Agency Within Social Structures and Culture: A Primer on Critical Realism for Christian Ethics.*[77] The essays in that volume provide an approach not only to addressing the challenges of removing structural and cultural barriers which impede women's advancement and economic empowerment but also to understanding the ways in which the women and men who shape and are shaped by their workplaces exercise their moral agency in this process.

BIBLIOGRAPHY

Aragão, Carolina. "Gender Pay Gap in U.S. Hasn't Changed Much in Two Decades." Pew Research Center, Mar. 1, 2023. https://www.pewresearch.org/short-reads/2023/03/01/gender-pay-gap-facts/. Link discontinued.

Arbinger Institute. "Why Most DEI Training Programs Don't Work." Arbinger Institute, n.d. https://arbinger.com/blog/why-most-dei-training-programs-dont-work/#where-most-dei-programs-fall-short. Link discontinued.

Bailin, Jen. "IWD2022: How to Transcend the Stereotypes of Women at Work." *Forbes Newsletters*, Mar. 7, 2022. https://www.forbes.com/sites/sap/2022/03/07/iwd2022-how-to-transcend-the-stereotypes-of-women-at-work/.

Benedict XVI. *Caritas in Veritate*. Vatican, June 29, 2009. https://www.vatican.va/content/benedict-xvi/en/encyclicals/documents/hf_ben-xvi_enc_20090629_caritas-in-veritate.html.

Berkshire Compensation Team, The. "Mid-Year Update on State and Federal Pay Transparency Laws." Berkshire, June 24, 2024; updated July 17, 2024. https://www.berkshireassociates.com/blog/mid-year-update-on-state-and-federal-pay-transparency-laws.

---

76. For more detail, see Arbinger Institute, "Why Most DEI Training Programs Don't Work"; Park and Grensing-Pophal, "Why DEI Backlash Exists"; *Economist*, "This Is an Intervention"; and Yoshino and Glasgow, "DEI Is Under Attack."

77. Finn, *Moral Agency*.

Brady, Bernard V. "From Catholic Social Thought to Catholic Social Living: A Narrative of the Tradition." *Journal of Catholic Social Thought* 15 (2018) 317–52.

Brady, Diane, and Ira Sager. "Is Your Company up to Code?" *Business Week* (July 5, 2004) 16.

Burleigh, Emma. "The Gender Pay Gap Actually Increases as Women Climb the Corporate Ladder." *Fortune*, Feb. 22, 2024. https://fortune.com/2024/02/22/gender-pay-gap-increases-with-career-level-payscale-report/.

Calvert Investments. *The Calvert Women's Principles*. Bethesda, MD: Calvert Investments, 2005.

Catalyst. "Historical List of Women CEOs of the Fortune Lists: 1972–2023." Catalyst, June 22, 2023. https://www.catalyst.org/research/historical-list-of-women-ceos-of-the-fortune-lists-1972-2023/.

Catholic Transcript. "Untitled Photo." *Catholic Transcript* 66 (Oct. 17, 1963) 8.

Celestine, Titania. "How Do Stereotypes of Women in the Workplace Impact Their Career?" Girl Power Talk, Apr. 18, 2024. https://girlpowertalk.com/stereotypes-of-women-in-the-workplace/.

"Civil Rights Act of 1991." Congress, Nov. 21, 1991. https://www.congress.gov/bill/102nd-congress/senate-bill/1745#:~:text=Title%20II%3A%20Glass%20Ceiling%20%2D%20Glass,experiences%20of%20women%20and%20minorities.

Coleman, John A. "Neither Liberal nor Socialist." In *One Hundred Years of Catholic Social Thought: Celebration and Challenge*, edited by John A. Coleman, 25–42. Maryknoll, NY: Orbis, 1991.

Deloitte Global. *The Deloitte Global 2022 Gen Z and Millennial Survey*. Deloitte Global, 2022. https://www2.deloitte.com/content/dam/Deloitte/global/Documents/deloitte-2022-genz-millennial-survey.pdf.

Dorr, Donal. "Themes and Theologies in Catholic Social Teaching over Fifty Years." *New Blackfriars* 93 (2012) 137–54.

Economist. "This Is an Intervention." *Economist* 444 (Aug. 27, 2022) 73.

Federal Glass Ceiling Commission. *Good for Business: Making Full Use of the Nation's Human Capital; The Environmental Scan*. Washington, DC: U.S. Government, 1995. https://files.eric.ed.gov/fulltext/ED407540.pdf.

Finn, Daniel K. *Christian Economic Ethics: History and Implications*. Minneapolis: Fortress, 2013.

———. *Faithful Economics: 25 Short Insights*. Minneapolis: Fortress, 2021.

———. "Human Work in Catholic Social Thought." *American Journal of Economics and Sociology* 71 (2012) 874–85.

———, ed. *Moral Agency Within Social Structures and Culture*. Washington, DC: Georgetown University Press, 2020.

———. "Social Structures." In *Moral Agency Within Social Structures and Culture*, edited by Daniel K. Finn, 29–41. Washington, DC: Georgetown University Press, 2020.

———. "What Is a Sinful Social Structure?" *Theological Studies* 77 (2017) 136–64.

Gates Foundation. "Women in Leadership." Gates Foundation, n.d. https://www.gatesfoundation.org/our-work/programs/gender-equality/women-in-leadership.

———. "Women's Economic Empowerment." Gates Foundation, n.d. https://www.gatesfoundation.org/our-work/programs/gender-equality/womens-economic-power.

Gatta, Mary, and Anika Gore. "What Can Be Done to Shrink the Widening Gender Pay Gap?" National Association of Colleges and Employers, Aug. 23, 2023. https://www.naceweb.org/diversity-equity-and-inclusion/trends-and-predictions/what-can-be-done-to-shrink-the-widening-gender-pay-gap/.

Gopal, Jayanti. "Overcoming Gender Stereotypes to Build an Inclusively Diverse Workplace." *BWPeople*, Jan. 10, 2024. https://bwpeople.in/article/overcoming-gender-stereotypes-to-build-an-inclusively-diverse-workplace-505480.

Gould, Elise. "Gender Wage Gap Persists In 2023." Working Economics Blog, Mar. 8, 2024. https://www.epi.org/blog/gender-wage-gap-persists-in-2023-women-are-paid-roughly-22-less-than-men-on-average/.

Grissom, Andrew. "HR, Take Note: Employees Want Pay Transparency. Smart Companies Are Listening." Catalyst, Feb. 27, 2024. https://www.catalyst.org/2024/02/27/pay-transparency-is-necessary/.

Hegewisch, Ariane, and Hannah Gartner. Institute for Women's Policy Research. "Women Earn Less Than Men Whether They Work in the Same or Different Occupations." Institute for Women's Policy Research, Mar. 2024. IWPR #C521. https://iwpr.org/wp-content/uploads/2024/03/Occupational-Wage-Gap-2024-Fact-Sheet-1.pdf.

Hehir, J. Bryan. "John Paul II: Continuity and Change in the Social Teaching of the Church." In *Co-Creation and Capitalism*, edited by John Houck and Oliver Williams, 124–40. Washington, DC: University Press of America, 1983.

Heilman, Madeline E., et al. "Women at Work: Pathways from Gender Stereotypes to Gender Bias and Discrimination." *Annual Review of Organizational Psychology and Organizational Behavior* 11 (2024) 165–92.

Hendrickson, Christine. "U.S. Pay Scale Transparency Legislation Cheat Sheet." Syndio, July 29, 2025. https://synd.io/blog/us-pay-transparency-legislation-cheat-sheet/.

Hinchliffe, Emma. "The Share of Fortune 500 Companies Run by Women CEOs Stays Flat at 10.4% as Pace of Change Stalls." *Fortune*, June 4, 2024. https://finance.yahoo.com/news/share-fortune-500-companies-run-113000264.html.

Hollenbach, David. "Human Rights in Catholic Social Thought: A Living Tradition and Some Urgent Challenges Today." *Irish Theological Quarterly* 84 (2019) 259–67.

———. *Justice, Peace, and Human Rights*. New York: Crossroad, 1988.

Huang, Jess, et al. *Women in the Workplace 2019*. McKinsey and Company, Oct. 2019. https://www.mckinsey.com/~/media/McKinsey/Featured%20Insights/Gender%20Equality/Women%20in%20the%20Workplace%202019/Women-in-the-workplace-2019.pdf.

Hymowitz, Carol, and Michaele Weissman. *A History of Women in America*. New York: Bantam, 1978.

International Labour Organization. *Breaking Barriers: Unconscious Gender Bias in the Workplace*. ILO, Aug. 2017. ACT/EMP Research Note. https://www.ilo.org/sites/default/files/wcmsp5/groups/public/%40ed_dialogue/%40act_emp/documents/publication/wcms_601276.pdf.

———. *A Quantum Leap for Gender Equality: For a Better Future of Work for All*. Geneva: ILO, 2019.

Javaid, Sarah. "The Wage Gap Robs Women Working Full Time, Year-Round of Hundreds of Thousands of Dollars over a Lifetime." National Women's Law

Center, Mar. 2024. https://nwlc.org/wp-content/uploads/2024/03/EPD-FS-2024-3.1.24v2.pdf.

Just Wage Tool, A. https://socialconcerns.nd.edu/just-wage-tool/.

Kennedy, John F. "Remarks on Signing Equal Pay Act of 1963, 10 June 1963." John F. Kennedy Presidential Library and Museum, June 10, 1963. https://www.jfklibrary.org/asset-viewer/archives/jfkpof-045-001#?image_identifier=JFKPOF-045-001-p0002.

Kerr, Geoffrey T., and Alixandra Pollack. *Engaging Men: The Journey Toward Equity.* Catalyst, 2022. https://www.catalyst.org/research/engaging-men-equity/.

Khattar, Rose. "Closing the Gender Pay Gap." Center for American Progress, Mar. 14 2024. https://www.americanprogress.org/article/playbook-for-the-advancement-of-women-in-the-economy/closing-the-gender-pay-gap/.

Laidlaw, Jennifer, and Daniel J. Sandberg. *Breaking Boundaries: Women Poised for Milestone Achievement in Parity amid Otherwise Bleak Outlook.* S&P Global Market Intelligence, Aug. 2023. Quantamental Research. http://www.spglobal.com/marketintelligence/en/documents/breakingboundaries_research_v5.pdf.

Littler. "50-State Pay Equity Chart." Littler, Mar. 2025. https://www.littler.com/sites/default/files/2025-03/50-state-pay-equity-chart.pdf?lec6tn7bd.

McKinsey and Company and LeanIn.Org. *Women in the Workplace 2023.* McKinsey, Oct. 25, 2023. https://www.mckinsey.com/featured-insights/diversity-and-inclusion/women-in-the-workplace-2023.

Miller, Kevin, and Deborah J. Vagins. *The Simple Truth About the Gender Pay Gap.* American Association of University Women, Fall 2018. With Anne Hedgepeth et al. https://www.aauw.org/app/uploads/2020/02/AAUW-2018-SimpleTruth-nsa.pdf.

Murray, Patty. "On Equal Pay Day, Senator Murray Leads Entire Senate Democratic Caucus in Reintroducing Paycheck Fairness Act to End Wage Discrimination, Close Gender Pay Gap." Murray, Mar. 25, 2025. https://www.murray.senate.gov/on-equal-pay-day-senator-murray-leads-entire-senate-democratic-caucus-in-reintroducing-paycheck-fairness-act-to-end-wage-discrimination-close-gender-pay-gap/.

National Center for Education Statistics. "Table 318.10: Degrees Conferred by Postsecondary Institutions, by Level of Degree and Sex of Student: Selected Years, 1869–70 Through 2031–32." *Digest of Educational Statistics,* 2023. https://nces.ed.gov/programs/digest/d23/tables/dt23_318.10.asp.

National Women's Law Center. "Lifetime Wage Gap Losses by State for Women Overall." NWLC, Mar. 2024. https://nwlc.org/wp-content/uploads/2023/03/Lifetime-Losses-State-by-State-Women-Overall-3.1.24.pdf.

Nell-Breuning, Oswald von. "The Life of the Political Community." In *Commentary on the Documents of Vatican II,* edited by Herbert Vorgrimler, 5:290–327. New York: Crossroad, 1989.

Park, Lauren, and Lin Grensing-Pophal. "Why DEI Backlash Exists and What to Do About It." SAP, Aug. 30, 2023. https://www.sap.com/resources/why-dei-backlash-exists.

Payscale. *2024 Gender Pay Gap Report.* Payscale, 2024. https://www.payscale.com/content/report/2024-gender-pay-gap-report.pdf.

Peck, Emily. "The U.S. Has Fallen Behind When It Comes to Women in the Work Force." *Axios,* May 10, 2023. https://www.axios.com/2023/05/10/american-women-workforce-participation-chart.

Peterson, Esther E. "Oral History Interview." John F. Kennedy Presidential Library and Museum, Jan. 20, 1970. Interview by Ann M. Campbell. https://www.jfklibrary.org/asset-viewer/archives/jfkoh-eep-03.

Reiners, Bailey. "What Is the Glass Ceiling? A Guide to Understanding the Glass Ceiling Metaphor and How It Affects Employees." Built In, Nov. 7, 2023; updated by Abel Rodriguez, Oct 21, 2025. https://builtin.com/diversity-inclusion/glass-ceiling.

Ryan, John A. *A Living Wage: Its Ethical and Economic Aspects.* New York: Macmillan, 1906.

Sasco, Carol. *Director's Report.* City and County of San Francisco Department on the Status of Women, Oct. 28, 2020. https://www.sfgov.org/dosw/sites/default/files/DOSW%20Directors%20Report%2010-28-2020%20Final.pdf.

Schaeffer, Katherine. "For Women's History Month, a Look at Gender Gains—and Gaps—in the U.S." Pew Research Center, Feb. 27, 2024. https://www.pewresearch.org/short-reads/2024/02/27/for-womens-history-month-a-look-at-gender-gains-and-gaps-in-the-us/.

Schuck, Michael. *Social Catholicism in Europe: From the Onset of Industrialization to the First World War.* New York: Crossroad, 1991.

Ton, Zeynep. "Equality in the U.S. Starts with Better Jobs." *Harvard Business Review*, Aug. 17, 2020. https://hbr.org/2020/08/equality-in-the-u-s-starts-with-better-jobs.

United Nations. "Beijing Declaration and Platform for Action." In *Report of the Fourth World Conference on Women*, 1–132. Sales No. 96.IV.13. https://www.un.org/en/conferences/women/beijing1995.

U.S. Bureau of Labor Statistics. "Women's Earnings 76 Percent of Men's in 2000." TED: The Economics Daily, Sept. 5, 2001. https://www.bls.gov/opub/ted/2001/sept/wk1/art02.htm.

Williams, Oliver F. "The UN Global Compact: The Challenge and the Promise." *Business Ethics Quarterly* 14 (2004) 755–74.

———. "The United Nations Global Compact: What Did It Promise?" In *Leadership and Business Ethics*, edited by Gabriel Flynn, 327–43. 2nd ed. Issues in Business Ethics 60. Dordrecht: Springer, 2022.

Wolfe, Regina Wentzel. "The Calvert Women's Principles: Catalyst for Promoting Gender Equity and Empowerment of Women in the Workplace." In *Leadership and Business Ethics*, edited by Gabriel Flynn, 313–26. 2nd ed. Issues in Business Ethics 60. Dordrecht: Springer, 2022.

———. "John Ryan and Women's Wages: Still a Radical Stance?" In *Religion and Public Life: The Legacy of Monsignor John A. Ryan*, edited by Robert G. Kennedy et al., 165–78. Lanham, MD: University Press of America, 2001.

World at Work. "Pay Equity Law by State—Are You in Compliance?" World at Work, n.d. https://worldatwork.org/tools/pay-equity-laws-by-state-are-you-in-compliance.

Yardley, Rosemary. "U.S. Women Still Undervalued\Pay Gap Continues." *Greensboro News and Record*, July 1, 1993; updated Jan. 25, 2015. https://greensboro.com/u-s-women-stillundervalued-pay-gap-continues/article_93785361-45f1-565c-a55b-1ccf7f17184e.html.

Yoshino, Kenji, and David Glasgow. "DEI Is Under Attack. Here's How Companies Can Mitigate the Legal Risks." *Harvard Business Review* (Jan. 5, 2024) 1–7. https://hbr.org/2024/01/dei-is-under-attack-heres-how-companies-can-mitigate-the-legal-risks.

Reflecting on Finn's "Altruism and Self-Interest" and the Need for Humility Ten Years Later

Joseph Kaboski

BACK IN 2007, THE late Thomas Levergood, who had founded the Lumen Christi Institute a decade prior, asked me if I thought economists would be interested in a conference and conversation with Catholic bishops on the topic of the economy and ethics. An assistant professor with a growing family and veering closer to the "perish" side of the "publish or perish" route, I politely responded, "No." Thomas was persistent, however, and eventually lured me in by having the late Francis Cardinal George repeat the same request. I couldn't say no to the leading thinker in the American Catholic hierarchy, so I said an Our Father and dove in. Thomas and I got to work inviting academics we thought might be interested in these conversations (many of whom are writing for this Festschrift), and Thomas suggested Dan's name. These Lumen Christi conferences on economics and Catholic social thought had a profound impact on my own thinking and became a source for new friendship and community, and this community of economists became formalized as the Catholic Research Economists Discussion Organization (CREDO).

It was through these conferences that I got to know and appreciate Dan Finn. Cross-disciplinary conversation can be a challenge, especially when the topic of conversation is economics, ethics, and society. This was especially true in the early years, as economists, theologians, and other scholars often came to the conversations with very different perspectives, languages, and, too often, axes to grind. It was on this front that I found Dan's participation to be extremely helpful. He is one of the few theologians writing on these matters whom I have come across who has put in the effort to really understand the economic concepts and economic language, even obtaining a master's degree in economics from the University of Chicago. Still he maintained his fidelity to the faith and values of Christ and his church, and he caused me to reconsider my own thinking on matters regularly at these meetings. I have enjoyed materials and writings that he has shared with me, but most of all I enjoyed our conversations, especially at these conferences.

FINN'S "ALTRUISM AND SELF-INTEREST"

To my memory, Finn only formally presented once at these conferences. Back in 2014, he gave a highly insightful presentation entitled "Altruism and Self-Interest," where he surveyed the thoughts of various economists over the years on the role of self-interest and psychology. It exemplified Finn's deep understanding of the state of economics today and what is at stake.

Finn began with a history of economic thought explaining its evolution along the path from a political economy clearly rooted in the humanities (indeed, Adam Smith was formally a professor of *ethics* after all) to its current standing as a social science, with a keen eye on its implications for the role of human self-interest in the analysis. Finn started with John Stuart Mill, who used a narrative approach but already viewed economics as borrowing from the "pure science of mind."[1] He defined economics as a scientific approach to studying humankind as "occupied solely in acquiring and consuming wealth," but although the field studied this as the individual's primary motive for the questions of interest, Mill acknowledged that such an assumption was a necessary simplifying assumption, "absurd" as a full description of man but "a mode in which science must necessarily proceed." Mill's approach was nonetheless narrative.

A generation later, the marginalists introduced a mathematical approach including marginal utility theory, a substantial step forward toward modern day economics. Quoting the British economist Stanley Jevons, Finn emphasized that economists still viewed their approach as only capturing the basest of human desires and so subordinate to ethics.

---

1. Mill, "Definition of Political Economy."

"A higher calculus of moral right and wrong would be needed to show how a man may best employ his wealth for the good of others as well as himself," and yet economics was still useful for normative guidance for "when that higher calculus gives no prohibition, we need the lower calculus to gain us the utmost good in matters of moral indifference."[2]

Finn emphasized, however, that by the mid-twentieth century, economics had both broadened and narrowed its perceived territory. On the one hand, quoting economic historian Lionel Robbins's definition of the discipline, economists now claimed that economics covered "human behavior" more generally, not simply an aspect of human behavior. This approach is perhaps most famously exemplified by Nobel laureate Gary Becker, who won his Nobel Prize for expanding the field and applying the tools of economics to thinking about social phenomena such as crime, marriage, fertility, and discrimination.

On the other hand, the claims of economists were now narrower, in that the methods of economics themselves no longer claimed to say anything about the deeper psychology of humanity, only the decisions of individuals and how they responded to incentives and budgets. The classical utility theory of Nobel laureate Paul Samuelson, the dominant approach to economics even today, simply defined "rationality" as an internally consistent set of preferences, themselves defined by human actions that satisfied the criteria of consistency, completeness, and transitivity (i.e., people's preferences are stable and rankable; if a person prefers A to B and B to C, they prefer A to C). And yet, the theory can be agnostic as to the origins of such preferences, or even the process of deliberation. Samuelson links the utility theory to empirics using his "revealed preference approach." It assumed that among feasible (think "affordable") options agents reveal their underlying preferences in the decisions they make: if you chose a Cadillac when a Ford and Chrysler were affordable, you must prefer the Cadillac (at its price) to the others (at their prices).

The talk was insightful on a number of fronts. As I have already mentioned, Finn understands the predominant claims of modern economics, which already put him in rare territory among theologians, even those who think they understand economics. He cites the most influential writers, and among them their most influential methodological writings, and those ideas which have remained accepted practice or latent methodological or philosophical assumptions. I could quibble about some fine

---

2. Jevons, *Theory of Political Economy*, 32.

points, and I believe I did afterward, but those are the quibbles of intellectual conversation that I might also have with a practicing economist. Finn also pointed out genuine inconsistencies and limitations in the approach of most economists, many of which the practicing economist is not always conscious of.

To emphasize the first, Finn particularly critiqued Nobel laureate Milton Friedman, whose class he took at the University of Chicago, as an economist whose approach lacked internal consistency. In particular, throughout his writings Friedman seems to genuinely believe that human behavior reflects self-interested motives and consistently argues so. On the other hand, in his famous essay on positive economics, Friedman states that realism is not a criterion for good theory. "Truly important and significant hypotheses will be found to have 'assumptions' that are wildly inaccurate descriptive representations of reality."[3] And yet, the lack of a needed rationale or human behavior beyond the narrow rationality in economics flies in the face of the assumption of self-interested motivated individuals, or even the idea that economists model goal-oriented individuals.

As an example of a limitation, economists draw the distinction between positive economics (i.e., economics that is merely "descriptive" or "predictive" of what *would* happen under a given policy) and normative economics (i.e., economics that is "prescriptive," making value judgments about what policy *should* be enacted). We claim in positive economics that preferences simply describe the individual's behavior. A corollary is that this renders interpersonal comparisons meaningless. I can say that a person prefers bananas to apples, but the logic of utility theory does not extend well to comparing people's behavior, since preferences are merely ordinal. What does it mean to say one person maximizes their utility better than another person does?

Things like "willingness to pay" are often used to evaluate policies, but these rely only on how an individual trades off between alternatives in their practice. Interpersonally, people intuitively appreciate that a wealthy person's willingness to pay more for a luxury car than a poor person largely reflects their higher income rather than a difference in the objective underlying benefit of the car to the different individuals, or a norm that says society is better off with rich people having luxury cars. The fact that rich people buy luxury cars merely says that the poor person

---

3. Friedman, "Methodology of Positive Economics," 14.

would need to give up more than they are willing to in order to buy the car, whereas the rich person need not.

In practice, economists are typically uncomfortable explicitly weighting, or at least taking strong stances on, the gains of some groups of people relative to the losses of others, for example, because the social science of economics offers little guidance. Normative economics generally introduces some sense of diminishing marginal utility of wealth, which was something that Bentham and the utilitarians incorporated into their ethical school of thought. However, this requires moving beyond the social science approach of simply attending to observable human behavior onto the shakier ground of cardinal utility functions, the ethical foundations of which cannot be evaluated empirically.

And yet, Finn correctly points out that an inability to make interpersonal comparison is a serious limitation. So powerfully and clearly, he stated, "Any discipline that cannot make a distinction between Mother Teresa and the felon based on some conception of what is good for human beings is on thin ice when claiming authority in public policy discussions."[4] It is the line that has stuck with me the most from his talk, and for the past ten years I have kept a version of it in my undergraduate course.

The key running point behind Finn's talk was clear, and it was a very forceful one. Economics' inability to ground human behavior in any deeper sense of life purpose or even inner psychology and its inability to make interpersonal comparisons severely limit the contributions that it can make in public discussion of ethical issues. Economics can give very useful insights, but given these two limitations, economists should not hold the sole or perhaps even the primary position in policy discourse.

EXTENDING FINN'S CRITICISMS

I fully agree with the essence of Finn's talk as laid out above, but I would like to extend it in various directions. The first direction involves the methodological approach of economics and addressing the larger tension between appropriately answering the broader question of "what economics is about" and recognizing and fully appreciating, for better or worse, the tools at economists' disposal.

---

4. Unfortunately, I do not have a copy of Finn's text: I recall his remark from memory.

I think the first tension involves the role of the economist. It is a tension in both Friedman's essay and Finn's talk. As my colleague (the saintly) Tim Fuerst was known to say, "Economics is an advice-giving profession." The key part of that advice giving, economists' comparative advantage (to use our own lingo) is in predicting the consequences of a policy, not the ethics of the policy. Good economics is simply useful economics that can be helpful for guiding policy by helping understand and predict its impacts. Modern day economists are not philosophers or ethicists, and that is evident by the limited appreciation of the philosophical presuppositions laden in the work of most economists. Moreover, most are not even big picture thinkers, but simply technicians concerned with, for example, how the Fed should handle interest rate policies in order to limit inflation and unemployment. Yes, economics differs from engineering in its primary focus on human phenomena and has far-reaching consequences on human beings, but both are ultimately about designing policy that "works."

Friedman's "The Methodology of Positive Economics" is an example to me that economists are bad philosophers. It has been critiqued for its philosophical approach, influenced in some way by logical positivism, but not fully fitting into a clear category.[5] It captures something important about the pragmatic nature of economic modeling, and yet its problematic nature was apparent to me even upon reading it as a first-year graduate student at the University of Chicago. The point about unrealistic assumptions is a reasonable defense against the criticism that economic models lack realism. Models are by their nature gross simplifications. Unnecessary realism is not a feature of a model but a bug. We already have the real world; what we need is a drastically less real world that is understandable and useful. Any theory is necessarily an abstraction and therefore unrealistic on many fronts. An advice-giving economist's job is to get at the core forces at play—individual, market, and institutional—behind the phenomenon of interest, especially those core forces most important for the design of policy.

And yet, the flippancy of Friedman that Finn quotes is indeed a problem, and a well-known one. The second influential paper on a methodology of economic science that we read as first-year graduate students at Chicago was the famous "Lucas Critique," by Nobel laureate (and one of my advisors) Robert E. Lucas Jr. Lucas took the baton from Friedman in

---

5. Caldwell, "Positivist Philosophy of Science."

macroeconomics becoming (in my opinion) the most influential economist since Keynes in the methods of how macroeconomists think about and, more importantly, do the business of economic modeling.[6] The core of his argument was almost exactly the opposite of Friedman's argument: it is not simply enough to make unrealistic assumptions as long as they fit the data. Without realistic assumptions about human behavior, we could not reliably expect such patterns to hold under different circumstances, unless our theories were "micro-founded" on the behavior of actual people. In practice, today's micro-founded models appear no less self-interested than the models of Friedman, but the practical issues of policy design leads to at least an acknowledgment that we need to think about not only how people behave but *why* they behave in those ways.

And yet, the ethical evaluation of what constitutes "good policy" is often just as important as knowing the consequences of policy. This is especially evident given that Christians are not pure consequentialists in their ethics. Even when it comes to ethics, I think economics has important insights, but it is important to understand the limitations of those insights.

The overwhelming ethical consideration that economists consider in their normative analysis is "efficiency." Yet if it is to be at all honest and useful for normative policy guidance it is important to appreciate the term's field-specific meaning and thus its limitations. Just as "rational" has a narrow and technical meaning within economics, so too does "efficiency." When economists speak of efficiency or inefficiency, they generally use the term in the sense of Pareto efficiency, named after Wilfredo Pareto.

The definition of Pareto efficiency is a situation of optimality in which no more costless gains are possible—that is, in which giving someone an allocation they prefer more (i.e., higher utility) requires taking away something, or giving someone else an allocation they prefer less (lower utility). It is typically viewed as a minimum standard of desirability for this reason. The usual use of the concept does not prohibit circumstances in which redistribution is done, taking something desired by one person in order to give it to another person (from rich to poor, for example), but it does say that all mutually agreed-upon exchanges should be exhausted first. It is therefore a sense of efficiency or optimality in that it doesn't allow for wasted opportunities in which a reallocation could lead to someone getting an allocation they prefer without someone else

---

6. Lucas, "Critique."

getting something they prefer less. When I teach this in my course, I use the restaurant orders of our class party as an illustrative example. If the waiter brings out the orders to the wrong people, efficiency is a minimum criterion that would require allowing them to trade to the meal they prefer (or are at least indifferent about).

In his talk, Finn addressed the minimum wage as an example in which economists can have difficulties judging aggregate trade-offs between, for example, increased earnings and lost jobs. Before judging trade-offs, it is important to understand the efficiency argument against the minimum wage, which goes beyond simple aggregates. The argument goes something like this: If markets are free, competitive, and efficient, banning wages below a certain amount will result in people willing to work at a wage below the minimum not being hired, and people willing to hire at that wage not being able to hire. Theory predicts that the amount of total labor hired will decrease (an aggregate prediction). There will be a surplus of unhired labor at the higher minimum wage, and firms may decide to substitute capital for workers, hiring even fewer workers, and creating an even greater shortage of jobs. But at the individual level, the people who eventually get jobs will not in general be the ones most willing to work. People who were quite willing, even desperate, to work may not be the people eventually employed, but instead it may be new workers that are now encouraged to seek jobs at the higher wage. The point is that it may not only be the number of jobs and the average wages to consider, but the identities of those getting jobs may now shift away from those the most willing to work (perhaps because they are in most need of work) because mutually agreed-upon exchanges have been prohibited.

Pareto efficiency has a close connection with free exchange, which allows for mutually agreed-upon exchanges. Indeed, some of the most powerful results in economics speak to this concept of efficiency. The First Welfare Theorem, perhaps the most important result in economics, provides the theoretical circumstances under which market economies lead to such outcomes. Though the theorem itself is precise, it roughly states that in a competitive economy, in which all goods have a market, and all prices and goods are well known, the free market is Pareto efficient. In many ways, it can be viewed as a mathematical formalization of Adam Smith's invisible hand, and a theoretical justification for much of why economists like markets, but it is not an ideologically driven result. Instead, it gives economists insight into when markets "work well" and when they don't, highlighting problematic situations like market power, other price distortions (including those caused by the government), informational asymmetries (think used cars or insurance as examples), externalities, or poorly defined property rights that lead to the tragedy of the commons. For example, the welfare theorem clearly shows why unfettered markets lead to levels of pollution that are inefficiently too high, even if every single person could agree that lower levels were preferable.

Although not referencing any inner psychology, an ethical limitation that Finn notes, the relationship between free exchange and Pareto efficiency is consistent with human behavior being rational and goal-oriented. Moreover, free exchange is generally a good thing, even from the vantage of Catholic social teaching. It is not top down and therefore consistent with individual freedom, subsidiarity, etc. Indeed, the terminology typically used is "mutually beneficial" exchange.

However, my language of "mutually agreed-upon" exchange is chosen to better emphasize an important subtlety that prevents a Catholic from swallowing Pareto efficiency as desirable in all circumstances. First, even if the exercise of freedom is subjective, we know that moral truth is objective. People are sinful and intentionally decide to "agree to," even mutually, all sorts of exchanges that benefit only one party or neither party. Examples include many of the things that have recently become legalized and socially accepted under libertarian persuasion, such as recreational drugs, prostitution, sports gambling, gay marriage, pornography, and the like. Further, many of these involve clearly addictive behaviors, and so in no way promote growth in what the Catholic tradition considers true liberty. Indeed, their promotion reflects a narrow conception of human freedom that is divorced from both objective truth and human reason. The push for these policies further highlights the limitation of the economic approach that Finn identified: (1) assuming that all behaviors and interior attitudes are morally equal (or being agnostic on this front), and (2) taking preferences as given, rather than asking how culture may create and interact with interior passions to either promote or undermine virtue or vice.

Second, and related, we know that a good ethical approach cannot be purely consequentialist. Indeed, ethics necessarily relates to virtue, vice, and thus to the interior intention of the moral actor. This is something that economics, properly done, can say nothing about. At worst, it can assume that these issues are somehow irrelevant.

A related, perhaps clearer, point is the limits of using efficiency as the sole ethical consideration. It simply leaves out too much that is important to the "higher calculus." Most obviously, "efficiency" in no way addresses considerations of inequality. Returning to the example of our class meal, if the waiter had somehow given all the meals to one person who was selfish, we would still have a situation where no agreeable trades could be made, but we would also have the majority of the class going hungry while the selfish person either overate or simply threw the meals away. More strongly, it leaves out any consideration of justice itself, solidarity, a preferential option for the poor, peace, or any other virtue or Catholic social value.

At the deepest level, efficiency completely omits any reference to intention. Finn criticizes the Smithian idea that narrowly pursuing one's self-interest always serves the common good when markets are free. If one's intention is only to serve one's self (perhaps consumed by vices like greed, sloth, gluttony, and pride) how can it be morally praiseworthy, regardless of the outcomes?

ADDRESSING FINN'S CRITICISMS

As an economist, a practical question is what is the best approach from within the discipline given the strength of Finn's critique. Finn's most explicit call is for "greater humility" in economics about public policy recommendations.

I think the first lesson toward this end is returning to a position in which we acknowledge that economics captures only a certain dimension of human life and society, however important this may (or may not!) be. By virtue of having chosen a particular discipline, there is some "revealed preference" that the approach of our discipline fits our own personal approach. Still, we should be aware of our field's limitations.

A thrust of Finn's own prescription, however, is that more voices are needed in policy conversations. At some level, in a democracy there are always many voices in any possible conversation. And there is a tendency for every discipline to believe that it should have more weight in policy conversations. My sense is that other disciplines can view economists as calling the shots, when economists often feel like we have surprisingly little influence on policy, especially those policies where we have the most consensus knowledge. Yet, it is true that each president has their own Council of Economic Advisors, and there is no corresponding Council of Theological Advisors or Sociological Advisors. That probably has more to do with economics being an advice-giving discipline and the technical expertise that economists provide.

How might economists better invite other considerations into policy discussion? My own experience is that it is challenging for everyone. Those with the clearest and simplest policy prescriptions tend to get heard the most, in the same way that the simplest sound bites are the most influential. The fact is that my own policy influence is probably minimal.

Instead, I am one player in a broader profession producing academic work of policy relevance. Certainly, within the research profession, academic integrity necessitates that we nuance our policy prescriptions and flesh out the various impacts. In my own work, I often give the cost benefit analysis (which might come from a utility-based analysis of tradeoffs), but I also emphasize that these valuations can be different for different people (even within the utility-based analysis), and I emphasize that impacts can be multidimensional. I present a wider set of results of outcomes. In my empirical work, I have tried to collect a broader set of outcomes all of which might be of interest. In my teaching, I often describe a policy prediction, but then I ask my class, "Why might the real world not give the same result that the model predicts?" Here the idea is to emphasize the difference between actual human beings and the (necessarily) simple caricatures of them in our theories. Similarly, I describe a policy that would be efficient (according to theory), but then ask the class what other things they might consider when evaluating the policy. The standard answers involve inequality concerns, but occasionally insightful students will go so far as mentioning things like the impacts on culture. In my course on economics and Catholic social thought, we spend entire units discussing issues that go beyond those typically considered by economists. We delve into these things in more depth in the CREDO/Lumen Christi summer seminar on Catholic social thought for economists, which is mainly targeted toward young research economists.

How does one make progress influencing a profession? One approach is to simply do one's own thing or, more ambitiously, to create one's own economics, perhaps even a Catholic economics. Doing something that is too distinct from professional trends is daunting for a young economist trying to make tenure. At the larger level, it bears the additional risk of merely building an intellectual ghetto at best, and a second-rate, mistrusting group unable to discern the good and true in secular disciplines at best.

The more productive approach is also the more Catholic approach of finding the intermediate space between polemic and syncretistic, and acknowledging what is good in the secular thought of the ages but not acquiescing to what is problematic. It is an approach of planting seeds that may bear fruit in the future.

Let me discuss three relatively recent developments relevant to Finn's criticisms: (1) the hegemony of economics in policy decisions, (2) the role of psychology in economics, and (3) the integration of broader ethical concerns into economics proper.

The first is the simplest and is in my own area of development economics. In 2019, three economists, Abhijit Banerjee, Esther Duflo, and Michael Kremer, won the Nobel Prize in Economics "for their experimental approach to alleviating global poverty."[7] It was a unique prize, since the three economists had not developed the experimental approach for which they won. The methods of randomized, controlled trials (RCTs)—where you evaluate a program by comparing ex post a treatment group that gets the program with a control that does not, and randomization guarantees that the two groups were ex ante identical—had already been used for decades in medicine to evaluate drugs, and even within economics to evaluate policies. Instead, Banerjee et al. won the prize for spreading the use of these programs to fight poverty, and a large part of this contribution was institutional, through their founding of the Jameel Poverty Action Lab, which has funded and promoted this work throughout the economics profession and the global development community (including nonprofits and governmental actors).

The idea was that much policy was designed without any evidence of whether it worked as intended, and we needed evidence about the impacts of policies before judging them. However, over the past ten to fifteen years, the original language of "evidence-based" policy has been slowly replaced by "evidence-informed" policy as a nod to the fact that policy needs to take more than just evidence into account. One needs a normative lens through which to evaluate policy, and this is distinct from evidence and not the expertise of experimentalists.

The second development worth highlighting is a subfield of economics that merges psychology and economics. Behavioral economics, as it is called, was a bit of an outsiders' club thirty to forty years ago but has had heavy influence on the discipline. Two economists have won the Nobel

---

7. Nobel Prize, "Sveriges Riksbank Prize."

Prize in Economics (Daniel Kahneman in 2002 and Richard Thaler in 2016) for their contributions to behavioral economics. One novel element that behavioral economics brings up is the idea of internal conflict. People can be time inconsistent, which means that what they plan today for tomorrow is no longer what they wind up doing when tomorrow comes along (think cheating on a diet or exercise routine, continually promising oneself to quit smoking, or procrastinating on work). This brings up a challenge even within the narrow normative sense of Pareto optimality because with respect to which person's decisions (today's or yesterday's) should one try to optimize? It also begins to show the limitations of a narrow definition of "rationality," since often our behavior doesn't meet that minimal bar.

Work emerging at the intersection of psychology and economics opens up other interesting lines of inquiry as well. A friend, Bruce Wydick (together with Paul Glewwe and Laine Rutledge, the first two of which I know are dedicated Protestant Christians), evaluated the impact of child sponsorship programs on child outcomes across six developing countries: Bolivia, Guatemala, India, Kenya, the Philippines, and Uganda.[8] He found sizable impacts on children's educational attainment and the adult jobs. Wydick attributed these impacts to the theological virtue of hope, transmitted through the love that children felt from having been sponsored. However, rather than preaching Christian doctrine to the secular economics discipline, he instead decided to convey his words in a way that worked within the existing structure of the field but expanded it. He referred to "aspirations," a new concept in economics but one that is only a stone's throw from the concept of "expectations," which is central to economics. I think this is the way to make progress. This paper was published around the time of Finn's critique, and since then others have now studied the impact of depression on economic outcomes, the impacts of therapy and antidepressants, expanding the consideration of psychology. Economists now even participate actively in the measurement of "subjective well-being," in which people are surveyed about how happy or satisfied with their lives they are. Again, this largely represents not only learning but progress on the dimension of ethics, but it is largely imperfect. I think when confronting the secular world, progress is what you shoot for. One shouldn't make the perfect the enemy of the good.

---

8. Wydick et al., "Does International Child Sponsorship Work?"

The last example represents both elements of progress together with a clear sense of how far we still have to go and the continuing relevance of Finn's critique. The role of population growth has a long history in economics, dating back to Thomas Robert Malthus, the Anglican priest-cum-economist and father of demography. In his essay on the principle of population, Malthus famously argued that population growth would always outstrip economic growth, keeping the mass of people's income levels equilibrating at subsistence poverty.[9] In the mid-nineteenth century after Malthus had passed, Stanley Jevons expressed similar worries in his essay on the coal question.[10] This population concern has continued with Neo-Malthusian influences arguing that a quality-quantity trade-off (people having fewer children but investing more, e.g., education, in them) is important for economic growth. Indeed, these fears and theories have spurred a great number of population control policies, spanning from Draconian policies (such as forced sterilizations in 1970s India and the One Child Policy in China, which spanned from the 1980s to the 2010s) to softer policies like contraception subsidies or advertising propaganda about responsible family sizes.

The ethics of population control have never been a part of economics proper, which lacks the ability to deal with normative questions about fertility and population for the reasons that Finn highlighted. Bentham's famous maxim, "the greatest good for the greatest number of people," sounds like a nice slogan, but should the greatest number of people include a growing population? Economists like Becker thought about fertility in terms of utility theory and Pareto efficiency, where children were choices that parents made, just as any other economic decision. Under such an idea the value of a child is the value the parent places on him or her, and the decision of when to then value the child's decision independently is a further challenge to that approach. Those who espoused true utilitarianism as a school of ethics had different takes. Bentham himself felt that fertility decisions should largely be left outside the purview of the government. The nineteenth-century utilitarian ethicist Sidgwick argued that for any given level of happiness, i.e., utility, a greater number of people means more happiness and is thus desirable.[11] But if the additional people lowered the *average* happiness of others, a calculation would be needed to see whether *total* utility increased. Over

---

9. Malthus, *Principle of Population*.
10. Jevons, *Coal Question*.
11. Sidgwick, *Methods of Ethics*.

one hundred years later, Parfit came upon his "repugnant conclusion" that population ethics valuing total utility could say that a society with a huge population of miserable people was preferable to a society with a moderate population of happy people.[12] In contrast, one that valued only average utility might value a population of ten extremely happy individuals. What to do? Despite his conclusion, Parfit maintained confidence that an amenable solution was possible. Practically, however, within the economics discipline, typical measures of welfare still focus on average living standards, and therefore any value on population is only implicit and instrumental. My own view is that the conclusion demonstrates the absurdity of the calculus itself, not to dimension the assumed scenarios.

Regardless, Malthusian fears and policies have dominated economic discourse on demography. The dominant economic theory was that population growth was bad for economic growth, bad for the environment, and unsustainable. It must be underscored that many of these promoted policies run contrary to Catholic social teaching and ethics in many ways, including doctrine on human dignity, contraception, abortion, the role of the family, and the necessity of the state respecting subsidiarity. And yet, many of these governments and populations have now changed their tunes as the cause of their fears have changed. The recent reality of fertility rates well below the 2.1/women needed to maintain populations is an economic concern for many countries who now see their countries drastically shrinking, with too few young people to care for the old, and rural ghost towns. There is both theory and evidence, mostly from the 1990s, that larger populations lead to greater rates of innovation, and so reduced innovation is another concern.

The tables are turning in stunning fashion. In the past month, I have seen presentations of working papers on population with angles that would have been inconceivable even ten short years ago when Finn wrote. The first was a paper by Chinese economist Anzon Zhou, who showed that government efforts to increase fertility have been much less effective than government efforts to decrease fertility.[13] He therefore argued that a rational government would err on the side of a higher fertility level. The second is a paper by Adhami et al. that argued that, if we value the years of lives of others in the same way that we value the years of our own lives, then population growth has been a huge boon for welfare,

---

12. Parfit, *Reasons and Persons*.`
13. Engle et al., "Asymmetric Fertility Elasticities."

and many countries with low growth like Mexico have higher growth in population-adjusted "welfare" than growth miracles like China.[14]

Again, part of me views this as encouraging that "more people" is valued (especially as a father of five). But the truth is that all of this is instrumental, and none of it overtly reflects a value of the dignity of every human being. It may well be that these papers are taking a well-evaluated strategic tack, as Wydick's use of "aspiration." Perhaps policies and attitudes will improve because of this, and this constitutes real progress. But, at least for the time being, the general approach continues to suffer from all the shortcomings that Finn identified.

MOVING FORWARD

In the ten years since Finn's critique, some progress has clearly been made on the side of economics. Moreover, there are some excellent writers who, following in Finn's footsteps, are carrying the torch in thinking seriously about these questions. The works of Andrew Yuengert and Mary Hirschfeld come to mind.[15] Economists are slower moving, but at least one additional economist has grown to increasingly appreciate an even greater need to be humble in the face of complex moral questions. Thank you, Dan!

BIBLIOGRAPHY

Adhami, Mohamad, et al. "Population and Welfare: Measuring Growth When Life Is Worth Living." Pete Klenow, Apr. 15, 2025. Version 4.0. http://klenow.com/Population_and_Welfare.pdf.

Caldwell, Bruce. "Positivist Philosophy of Science and the Methodology of Economics." *Journal of Economic Issues* 14 (1980) 53–76.

Engle, Samuel, et al. "Asymmetric Fertility Elasticities." Anson Zhou, Mar. 2025. https://ansonzhou.github.io/MyWebsite/asymmetry.pdf.

Friedman, Milton. "The Methodology of Positive Economics." In *Essays in Positive Economics*, 3–43. Chicago: University of Chicago Press, 1953.

Hirschfeld, Mary. *Aquinas and the Market: Toward a Humane Economy*. Cambridge, MA: Harvard University Press, 2018.

Jevons, William Stanley. *The Coal Question: An Inquiry Concerning the Progress of the Nation, and the Probable Exhaustion of Our Coal Mines*. London: Macmillan, 1867.

———. *The Theory of Political Economy*. London: Macmillan, 1871.

---

14. Adhami et al., "Population and Welfare."

15. Hirschfeld, *Aquinas and the Market*; Yuengert, *Approximating Prudence*.

Lucas, Robert. "Econometric Policy Evaluation: A Critique." In *The Phillips Curve and Labor Markets*, edited by Karl Brunner and Allan Meltzer, 19–46. New York: American Elsevier, 1976.

Malthus, Thomas Robert. *An Essay on the Principle of Population*. London: Johnson, 1798.

Mill, J. S. "On the Definition of Political Economy; and on the Method of Investigation Proper to It" (1836). In *Essays on Some Unsettled Questions of Political Economy* (1844), 120–26. 3rd ed. London: Longmans Green & Co., 1877.

Nobel Prize. "The Sveriges Riksbank Prize in Economic Sciences in Memory of Alfred Nobel 2019." Nobel Prize, 2019. https://www.nobelprize.org/prizes/economic-sciences/2019/summary/.

Parfit, Derek. *Reasons and Persons*. Oxford: Oxford University Press, 1984.

Sidgwick, Henry. *The Methods of Ethics*. London: Macmillan, 1874.

Wydick, Bruce, et al. "Does International Child Sponsorship Work? A Six-Country Study of Impacts on Adult Life Outcomes." *Journal of Political Economy* 121 (2013) 393–436.

Yuengert, Andrew. *Approximating Prudence: Aristotelian Practical Wisdom and Economic Models of Choice*. Perspectives from Social Economics. Palgrave Macmillan, 2012.

Analysis and Practical Dialogue
The Moral Ecology of Markets

Andrew M. Yuengert

Even in 2006, before the intractable polarization of the last nineteen years, competing arguments over markets seemed unresolvable. Daniel Finn disagreed:

> Everyone involved engages a common set of issues. . . . But to understand those different answers . . . we must recognize that a moral argument is entailed when addressing any of the four elements of this moral ecology. Too many of the current participants in the debate over markets leave such moral arguments largely implicit.[1]

Finn is confident that a framework encompassing all of the relevant moral questions about the effects of markets on society (each of the elements of his *moral ecology of markets*) will force parties on all sides of the debate to grapple with the moral claims of the other side, instead of implicitly ignoring those claims:

> This book proposes a common framework of issues on which all perspectives, from right to left, about the morality of markets already take a position. Although a common framework will not by itself resolve the disputes, it can make possible a conversation, a dialogue, about strengths and weaknesses of market institutions and their moral context.[2]

---

1. Finn, *Moral Ecology*, 107–8.
2. Finn, *Moral Ecology*, 5.

Finn does not expect miraculous agreement from his common framework, just a conversation based on mutual comprehension:

> The most fundamental conviction behind the argument in this book is that all participants in the debate about the justice of markets are already addressing the same four problems of economic life and taking positions on the same four elements of the moral ecology of markets. In spite of significant differences of perspectives, because we have common problems to face and a common framework in play, what we need is a common conversation.[3]

By opening up the analysis of markets to a greater range of moral judgments, Finn makes possible a more transparent dialogue on the purpose of market institutions and the trade-offs involved in the constitution and regulation of markets. He is confident that much of the disagreement is due to differences in moral evaluation.[4] By bringing these differences out into the open, debates about markets can be more productive, resulting in real disagreement and agreement, not just confused misunderstanding and vexation.[5]

Although Finn does not give us a list of the participants to the debate, in what follows it will be useful to identify three groups: free market defenders, market skeptics, and radicals (who treat markets as integral to a system of oppression). Each of these groups brings to the debate about markets a distinct system of analysis—each with its own value system and claims about what is practically possible.

The analytical framework of *The Moral Ecology* is compelling; I find little in his *analysis* to improve, and enthusiastically recommend the book. Nonetheless, Finn seeks more than a common *analytical* understanding of the empirical and moral issues. The implicit but urgent purpose of this common dialogue is *practical*. In the three quotations above, Finn points beyond his framework to decisions about *what to do* about the economy. The "common set of issues" and "common problems" we face are practical problems. We must better understand "the strengths and weaknesses of market institutions" in order to better constitute and regulate them.

To get from the analysis of a problem to concrete action to address the problem, we need more than analysis. First, we need a *moral*

---

3. Finn, *Moral Ecology*, 154.
4. Finn, *Moral Ecology*, 7.
5. Finn models the dialogue he proposes: e.g., "Nine Libertarian Heresies"; "Private Property, Self-Regulation, and Just Price."

commitment to act on the understanding that analysis provides. Second, we must *evaluate the practical shortcomings* of the analysis—the distance between the general analytical constructs and the messy, chaotic environment in which we must act. Neither of these extra elements is analytical. The thesis of this essay is that if we frame our practical disagreements as if these elements do not exist, we will mischaracterize those disagreements and make them more difficult to resolve.

An alternative account of reasoning about practical matters, the neo-Aristotelian philosophy of human action, preserves a crucial role for analysis.[6] At the same time, it integrates the two other elements of practical decision-making. A comparison of purely analytical approaches with the neo-Aristotelian account allows us to speculate about the distortions in practical reasoning that result from relying too heavily on analysis alone to resolve practical disagreements. There is little previous research into the consequences of relying so heavily on analysis to resolve practical disagreements, so my thoughts here are preliminary, speculative, and tentative.

Section 1 summarizes the analytical achievement of *The Moral Ecology*. Section 2 describes the practical insufficiency of analysis. Section 3 explores the neo-Aristotelian account of decision-making, emphasizing the integration of analysis, moral commitment, and contingent judgment throughout the structure of human action. Section 4 offers several conjectures about the distortions that ensue from purely analytical treatments of practical matters. Section 5 concludes with tentative advice about how to improve practical dialogue about the place of markets in a flourishing society.

THE ANALYTICAL FRAMEWORK OF *THE MORAL ECOLOGY*

The Moral Ecology of Markets tackles a dismaying problem: mutual incomprehension between market defenders and market skeptics. This mutual incomprehension originates in the claims of market defenders that their arguments are morally neutral. This odd claim has roots in twentieth-century positivism and in the aspiration of economics to the

---

6. The *neo-Aristotelian approach* includes Aristotle, Thomas Aquinas, and their modern interpreters: Aristotle, "Nicomachean Ethics"; Aquinas, *Summa Theologiae*; Stump, *Aquinas*; MacIntyre, *Ethics in the Conflicts of Modernity*.

rigor and objectivity of natural science.[7] The second chapter of *The Moral Ecology* critiques the claims of moral neutrality in the work of Milton Friedman, James Buchanan, and Friedrich Hayek.[8]

The analytical heart of the book is chapters 5 through 7, in which Finn lays out his moral ecology as an organizing scheme for the various moral commitments that affect the evaluation of markets. Chapter 5 sets the stage, outlining "The Four Problems of Economic Life." The first two involve the classic functions of markets: solving the *allocation problem* and the *distribution problem*. The third, the *problem of scale*, addresses the environmental impact of markets, which goes beyond externalities to explore our proper relationship to the natural order. The fourth problem is *the quality of social relations*. Anonymous exchange may undermine individual character and the quality of human community, both of which are crucial to well-functioning markets.

Finn notes that these four problems are closely related, both positively and negatively.[9] Consequently, we cannot insulate arguments that emphasize one of the problems (say allocational efficiency) from concerns raised by the other problems. There are trade-offs among all four problems. Moral judgment is necessary to sort out the trade-offs.

In chapters 6 and 7, Finn builds on this framework to develop a *moral ecology*, constructed around four elements, or four relevant moral contexts. The justice/desirability of market institutions depends on these four elements taken together. The first element raises the question of *freedom*. We all value freedom, but no market is entirely free (if we define freedom as utterly unconstrained action). Markets are constituted by restrictions on freedom—at the very least, on what can be sold, on how things can be sold, and on how disputes are adjudicated.[10] The second element is the provision of *essential goods and services*: Does everyone have access to goods considered crucial to human flourishing? A third element is *the morality of individuals and groups*. An economy of trustworthy and generous workers and employers is morally preferable to an economy in which each individual is indifferent to the fortunes of others—or worse, cruelly predatory to the poor and vulnerable. The fourth element is the health of *civil society*: the network of voluntary associations between the individual and the state. Civil society produces social goods that are

7. Schliesser, "Separation."
8. Finn, *Moral Ecology*, 11–33.
9. Finn, *Moral Ecology*, 91–97.
10. Finn, *Moral Ecology*, 119.

poorly described in individualistic terms, is a setting for the formation of individual character, and counters the individualizing effects of markets.

Finn's Achievement and Its Practical Limits

The four-part moral ecology provides an expanded framework within which a wide range of moral judgments finds a place. The arguments of market defenders—the value of individual and group freedom, and the productive and innovative efficiency that results when individuals are free to pursue their interests in markets—belong in the ecology, but they are only one element. Claims about efficiency and wealth production share analytical space with the claims of market skeptics and radicals—about which goods are essential, and whether markets deliver them broadly enough. Concerns about whether markets undermine or increase trust and generosity, and whether moral judgments on individual behavior are relevant to the moral evaluation of the system, also find a place in the moral ecology. Finally, the moral ecology opens up space for a discussion of the key role played by the many communities of civil society, which produce social goods and cooperation of every sort.

Once you embrace the moral ecology, it is difficult to insulate the analysis of any one element in it from interaction with the others. Market defenders cannot automatically dismiss arguments for state intervention in the economy because they spring from concerns about essential goods or civil society. Market skeptics and radicals cannot automatically dismiss arguments against state intervention in the economy simply because they arise from concerns about liberty and efficiency. This is an undeniable contribution of the framework.

Finn asks the partisans of each of the various analytical systems—market defenders, market skeptics, and radicals—to *suspend judgment* about their analytical frameworks and policy positions. When you suspend judgment, you create a distance between your analysis, your moral motivations and judgments, and your emotions. This distance allows you to consider and understand the differences and the similarities between competing frameworks and policy positions. This essay argues that an overreliance on analysis to resolve practical disagreements may make the suspension of judgment more difficult. To see why this is so, in the next section we will contrast the partial nature of analysis with the synthetic judgments necessary for action.

ANALYSIS: INDISPENSABLE BUT INSUFFICIENT

Modern scholars are experts at analysis of every kind.

- In *theoretical analysis*, we carefully define terms, specify relationships between terms, and investigate the logical implications of our assumptions. For example, under what theoretical assumptions will a minimum wage result in higher employment?

- In *empirical analysis*, we investigate past relationships in data, conforming our measures and inquiry to developed standards of investigative method and statistical evidence. For example, what are the effects of past minimum wages on employment?

- In *moral analysis*, we employ precisely defined ethical principles (rights, duties, justice, benevolence, the calculus of consequences) to evaluate outcomes in the social order. For example, when is a freely contracted wage unjust?

Each of the three general positions on markets (market defender, market skeptic, and radical) draws on theoretical and empirical analysis (with some overlap) to make its case. *The Moral Ecology* adds moral analysis to theoretical and empirical inquiry, in order to make the role of moral principle clear to all parties to the market debate.

I have argued elsewhere that one of the uncomfortable truths of the modern age is that analysis can never by itself result in a practical decision—in a decision about what to do.[11] There is a gap between analysis and any practical decision—a gap that analysis itself cannot bridge. To achieve analytical precision, one must neglect much that is necessary to decision-making in messy, chaotic reality. Three aspects of analytical simplification explain its practical insufficiency. First, analysis is *abstract*. There is an unavoidable trade-off between descriptive accuracy and analytical precision. Precise empirical measures and theoretical categories necessarily do damage to the more complex underlying realities that are practically relevant. Second, analysis is *conditional*: the conclusions of analysis are valid only to the extent that its assumptions and measurements describe current circumstances accurately. When theoretical and empirical assumptions do not hold in the context of application, decision-makers must adjust the precise analytical guidance, or perhaps even reject it. Third, analysis is *technical*. It employs agreed-upon canons of

---

11. Yuengert, *Catholic Social Teaching*, ix–xi.

practice to produce its results. Technical experts (PhDs) have mastered the technique and been certified as proficient in the production of analytical artifacts.

In contrast to analysis, action is *unconditional*. To apply analysis to a particular situation, one must evaluate the distance between the precise categories of analysis and the circumstances that analysis necessarily excludes. Practical decisions require *synthesis*; they bring multiple partial analytical perspectives together, along with discernment of contingent circumstance and a commitment to the ends/values/goods that motivate action. Practical action does not have the luxury of conditional conclusions. Moreover, there is no *analytical* guidance for moving from the conditional abstractions and general statements of analysis to practical decisions. Actual decision-making is neither abstract, conditional, nor technical. Practical decisions require a different kind of reason—the virtue of practical wisdom.[12]

Finn's goal of mutual comprehension within a common analytical framework is necessary and laudable, particularly when mutual incomprehension and recrimination are ubiquitous. Nevertheless, even a commonly accepted and shared analytical framework that includes the category of moral analysis can only partially explain and resolve differences in *practical* judgments about markets. The *goal* of dialogue about practical matters cannot be purely analytical. None of us will be fully satisfied if market defenders and skeptics agree on a common analytical framework, understand their differences, rise from their seminar table, and celebrate their analytical achievement over a meal in the faculty club. The goal of productive disagreement about markets is ultimately practical: How should we establish and regulate markets? What should our policies be, in the United States in 2025? What concrete policies should other countries pursue?

To get from analysis to the synthesis of practical action requires two additional steps:[13]

1. *Motivation*: Analysis is conditional on judgments of moral goodness. *If* we evaluate social outcomes in a Rawlsian framework, certain conclusions follow. *If* we accept human dignity as a moral standard, it imposes certain hard limits on market exchange. An

---

12. See Yuengert, *Catholic Social Teaching*, ch. 2.

13. See Yuengert, "Economics and Interdisciplinary Exchange." See also Yuengert, *Catholic Social Teaching*, ch. 6.

actual decision, however, is unconditional. One might *understand* the implications of Rawlsian justice or personalism and still be unmoved to act on the principles of Rawlsian justice or personalism.

2. *Judgments about contingency*: Effective action is conditional on the applicability of our analytical concepts to concrete, unpredictable circumstance.[14] Contingencies of every sort (culture, political feasibility, configurations of power, the virtues and vices of decision-makers) affect what is possible in a particular society at a particular time. They introduce an openness into our deliberations that resists analytical precision.

The central concern of this chapter is the effect of using analysis as a guide to practical action without regard to the necessity of making moral commitments and contingent judgments. The analyst may simply ignore these practical elements. More often, he assumes that they are separable from the analysis itself; these elements are tasks for others. Analysis may organize our thoughts about action and then gesture toward these tasks, but it must necessarily do so in an analytical way.

The deeply moral purpose of *The Moral Ecology* is to provide a framework which clarifies the role of moral judgments in the debate over markets, in order to encourage readers to acknowledge their own moral judgments. Moral considerations and judgments of contingency appear in Finn's analytical framework, but their presence does not motivate particular actions or evaluate the particular circumstances of action. One may understand the role of moral judgment in the *analysis* without committing to instantiating those moral judgments in *action*. It is even more difficult to incorporate contingent judgment about present circumstances into analysis; the best one can do is to review empirical analyses of the effects of past policies.[15]

The separation of analysis from morals and contingent judgment is characteristic of modernity. Analysis separated itself from moral commitment in order to avoid seemingly unresolvable moral disagreements. Moreover, analysis considers moral commitment to be a threat to objective method. To maintain its objectivity and authority, analysis depends on shared appeals to the tools of analytical reason. Even when we admit that analysis itself stops short of practical decision-making, we hope that better analysis will promote good action somehow.

14. Aquinas, *Summa* II-II, q. 47, a. 3.
15. Finn, *Moral Ecology*, 3, refers to the past success of the Social Security program.

Because moral commitment and contingent judgment are resistant to analysis, the action-oriented analyst will often assume that they are the responsibilities of other people. We leave motivation to rhetoric and public relations. We leave contingent judgment to practical people who know how to get things done. Even if the analyst himself engages in rhetoric and contingent judgment, these tasks are strictly separable from analysis.

Implicit in much analysis is the hope that the tasks of moral motivation and contingent judgment application follow in an unproblematic way from competently realized analysis. For example, one might expect that, by cataloguing moral questions about productive efficiency and wealth, essential goods, human character, and the goods of civil society in one place, *The Moral Ecology* makes the last three more salient and potentially compelling to market defenders, and the first more salient and potentially compelling to market skeptics. It does not effect the resolution of these competing values for the decision-maker, but by listing the values and the potential trade-offs it sets the stage for the task of moral motivation.

However hopeful we are that a comprehensive account of moral questions will encourage openness to the full range of the moral ecology, the account is still analytical, and has the weaknesses of a purely analytical treatment. When analysis proceeds as if it is sufficient for practical judgment, ignoring the entanglement of analysis-motivation-circumstantial judgment, it presents a distorted picture of practical decision-making and can lead to an incomplete understanding of what drives practical disagreement—even disagreement at the analytical level. I will argue in section 4 that the distortions occur at the levels of both motivation and contingent judgment.

An understandable response to my criticism is: What else might Finn have done? Why not seek broader analytical agreement, and then rely on others to provide motivation and contingent judgment? Is there any viable alternative to this? I am arguing here that analysis cannot be insulated from motivation and contingent judgment without consequence for our understanding. Analysis is not fully neutral; it often proceeds from moral motivations. Analysis which does not explicitly acknowledge its practical limits often downplays the role of contingent judgment in practical disagreement.

An alternative to heavy reliance on analysis is the neo-Aristotelian account of human action. By its nature, deciding what to do is synthetic, not analytical. The neo-Aristotelian account of human action describes the challenge of reasoning about concrete decisions. Within this alternative account, we can discern the place of all three elements—analysis, motivation, and contingent judgment—in human action and begin to speculate about what happens when analysis attempts to be practical without regard to the other two elements.

AN ALTERNATIVE TO PURE ANALYSIS

In the neo-Aristotelian account, practical decision-making is governed by the virtue of practical wisdom. Since our subject is the place of markets within a flourishing society, we are particularly interested in the species of political practical wisdom: practical wisdom exercised in governing a state. I will first outline the exercise of practical wisdom in governance as Aquinas specified it. Aquinas's treatment was premodern, predating by six centuries the dominance of social science in public policy deliberation. When we add social science to Aquinas's account, the dominance and potential distortions of analytical social science become more evident.

The Structure of the Human Act

The neo-Aristotelian account of practical reason integrates all three of the elements of a practical decision (analysis, motivation, and contingent judgment), but within a different schema: the structure of the human act.[16]

Before outlining the act itself, Aquinas discusses the human goods that motivate action. The neo-Aristotelian account is a natural law theory; it roots the human good in human reasoning about natural inclinations. Human beings flourish when they live life in a characteristically human way. Human flourishing includes the exercise of reason, which (imperfectly) evaluates and directs human desires. The exercise of practical reason in the service of our flourishing is crucially different from analytical reason. First, in practical reasoning, reason and will find their way to certain basic goods, which are basic human inclinations. The first principle of practical reason is the person's orientation toward her good (often, her perceived good). According to Aquinas, components of

---

16. Aquinas, *Summa* I-II, q. 1–20. An incisive summary of the structure is Stump, *Aquinas*, ch. 9.

this good are life, procreation, friendship, and truth.[17] The goodness of these is self-evident. To understand them, we require no reference to any further good they might promote.[18] They are also quite general; no one realizes *truth* or *friendship* in general. Humans specify and realize them through concrete action.

A second aspect of practical reason is that it is self-reflective, capable of developing what Jean Porter describes as "a sense of what it means to be human, to live a properly human life, and to relate rightly to others."[19] This self-reflective sense develops in community and within a culture. Even radically different cultures and ethical systems invoke the most basic human goods in a characteristically human way: through an account of what it means to live well as a human being in community.

Even before Aquinas outlines the structure of the human act, he has already begun his account with the prior principles of human action, discerned in basic human inclinations. In contrast to analytical accounts, in which analysis is separable from motivation toward the good and contingent judgment, in Aquinas's account the human good organizes all human action.

Although Aquinas lays out the structure of the human act in eight stages,[20] we can profitably reduce it to three:

1. *The discernment and choice of ends.* In Aquinas's account, the acting person begins by perceiving his environment and discerning the possibility of realizing some good in the circumstances as they present themselves to his perception. The primary virtue in this first stage is the ability to see what is going on in front of you, to discern the landscape of action and conform yourself to it. This evaluative perception answers questions like: "What is actually going on here? What human goods are at stake? What good might my action accomplish, or what harm should it avoid?"[21] This stage is itself integrative.

2. *Deliberation and choice of means.* When the acting person perceives that there is some human good achievable through action, he must then decide which course of action will best realize that

---

17. Aquinas, *Summa* I-II, q. 94, a. 2.

18. Finnis, *Natural Law*, chs. 3 and 4, enumerates a longer list of ultimate goods: life, truth, beauty, justice, friendship, religion, play, and practical reasonableness.

19. Porter, *Justice*, 29.

20. Stump, *Aquinas*, ch. 9.

21. Yuengert, *Catholic Social Teaching*, 265.

good. Because of contingency, he might achieve any particular good in multiple ways. The act of deliberation sorts through the various avenues of action, evaluating their relative effectiveness. Deliberation of this sort requires the insights of both analysis and contingent judgment. The integration of analysis and contingent judgment rules out any purely analytical account of either of these first two stages.

3. *Action itself.* Once an acting person perceives some good achievable through her action, and deliberates about and chooses a best course of action, the final stage is to carry out the act itself.[22] Although the prospect of a failure to act in the third stage can proactively affect the first two stages, we will not explore this final stage in this essay.

This account of the structure of the human act differs from the pure-analysis-plus-motivation-plus-contingent-judgment account in two significant ways. First, motivation and contingent judgment are integrated with analysis in each of the first two stages. To determine which goods are achievable in a certain context, and to evaluate the various possible ways of achieving them, requires both analysis and contingent judgment acting together. Second, no purely analytical account of action conceived of in this way is possible. Analysis cannot tell you what to want, and analytical method excludes the contingencies that decision-makers must confront. The virtue of practical wisdom orders motivation, analysis, and contingent judgment throughout the structure.[23]

The Effect of the Social Sciences on the Structure of the Human Act

Aquinas's outline takes into account neither modern social science analysis nor modern moral analysis. Both of these developments alter the structure of the human act substantially, by changing how we perceive and pursue the human good in politics, the nature of perception employed in evaluating the possibility of achieving the good, and deliberation among alternative courses of action.

The neo-Aristotelian account of the human act relies on a direct perception of both the human good and the contours of the decision-making

---

22. Aquinas, *Summa* II-II, 47.8.
23. Yuengert, *Catholic Social Teaching*, ch. 2.

environment. Before the rise of modern social science, political decision-makers apprehended both the good to be achieved and the means to achieve directly, by means of their own observations and those of their advisors. Modern public policy presents a radically different challenge to those who govern and regulate. This change affects every part of the structure of human action, including the goods that motivate action. The modern policymaker still must directly perceive the "local" political realities that affect what is achievable, but much of her attention is absorbed by abstract social theories: markets, evolving social norms and meaning, systems of oppression, for example. These precisely defined social phenomena are reified abstractions. At best, they are sketches of reality. Although we may attribute what we observe to abstractions like "the market" or "systemic oppression," none of us directly observes these realities as a whole. They exist outside of our everyday experience. By means of them, we interpret what is in front of us. Indeed, they teach us to be suspicious of our commonsense apprehensions of "what is really going on."

The fact that we filter the world through abstract social constructs ("the market," "culture," "public opinion," "structures of oppression") affects every stage of the structure of the human act. First, it affects the description of the human good that frames neo-Aristotelian action. Modernity offers competing accounts of the good—expressive individualism, Kantianism, utilitarianism, the capabilities approach, for example—that are themselves analytical products. Some of these (utilitarianism, expressivism) pair comfortably with competing analytical frameworks. The fact that these accounts of the good are themselves products of analysis creates an additional layer of difficulty for practical dialogue. We will return to this connection and its implications for productive dialogue in the next section.

The social sciences likewise transform the first two stages of the human act. In the first stage (discernment and choice of ends), the possibility of achieving the good is conditioned by how one sees the world. How one sees the world depends on the social science lens one adopts. This has two practical effects. First, two different social science frameworks will bring to the attention of the policymaker different aspects of the social order, highlighting different goods. For example, market defenders, skeptics, and radicals will see the policy possibilities differently. Second, to the extent that social science models dominate the vision of policymakers, policymakers will overlook contingencies that are relevant to policy. Analysis derives its power by simplifying, and contingencies disappear in the abstractions of models.

In the second stage of action (evaluation and choice of means), debates over the best way to achieve a preferred social goal become conflicts over competing social analyses. The policymaker must judge between dueling experts, each perhaps utilizing a different analytical model. Moreover, each "neutral" model may reflect a different set of moral commitments. To the contingencies that normally attend political judgment are added contingencies relevant to the judgment of competing public policy analyses, each of which overlooks practically relevant circumstances.

When we incorporate modern analysis into the structure of the human act, the practical dominance of analysis becomes clear. The developed analyses of social science are the primary lens through which we discern value, and the primary methods of determining which ends are possible. We organize our practical thoughts around analysis instead of around the goods that motivate us.

In modern policy discussions, the good is itself plural. It is expressed not in terms of human inclinations but in analytical categories. Analysis cannot motivate us toward one account of the good, although we may analyze the effects of different moral commitments in competing analytical accounts of policy. *The Moral Ecology* attempts just this kind of analytical comparison. Still, there are no analytical rules for how to choose a motivation to act among the many options available to us.

The dominance of analysis also reframes contingency. Contingency no longer requires an appreciation for differences in culture, for the existing matrix of power and influence, for the mood of the people. To the extent that analysis recognizes contingency at all, contingency becomes a concern about the "empirical fit" of models—the extent to which past experience is a valid guide to current policy.

ANALYTICAL DISTORTIONS TO PRACTICAL DISAGREEMENT

It goes without saying that good decision-making needs careful analysis. Nonetheless, it is possible to grant *too great* a role to analysis in decision-making. Both motivation and contingent judgment are also necessary, but these are not analytical, so analysis fails to consider them with the seriousness they deserve.

When we try to understand the source of our practical disagreements in purely analytical terms, we distort our understanding of that disagreement and may even make mutual understanding less likely. The distortions occur both at the levels of motivation and contingent judgment.

Motivational Distortions

In modern decision-making, the standard of goodness which is supposed to motivate us, and by which we evaluate our practical options, is itself often a product of analysis. What motivates us to choose among competing frameworks and policies? If motivation is separable from analysis, then the goal of motivation need not include analytical understanding. The separation of motivation from reason fueled the classical Greek suspicion of rhetoric, defined as the art of persuasion. According to Aristotle, individuals are persuaded by the character of the speaker (ethos), by appeals to emotions (pathos), or by the strength of the argument itself (logos).[24] Only the last depends on the truth of the proposition. Consequently, the task of motivation, when it focuses on appeals to emotion or on the character of the speaker, may obscure mutual understanding.

In the case of *The Moral Ecology*, market defenders may draw motivation from an emotional commitment to freedom, admiration for the independent man, or a high opinion for the kinds of cooperation that result in mutual benefit, mutual respect, and increased wealth. In addition, an acceptance of the authority of (and loyalty to) those who introduced them to free market principles may make it difficult to suspend judgment and consider countervailing arguments. Market skeptics may feel a similar set of supportive sentiments, associating love for the poor and marginalized with particular analytical arguments. They may associate certain analytical approaches with the authority of prominent market skeptics, through whom they encountered the arguments they support. For every Friedrich Hayek, Milton Friedman, or Thomas Sowell on the right, there is a John Maynard Keynes, Joseph Stiglitz, or Jeffrey Sachs on the left.

---

24. Aristotle, "Rhetoric" 1.2.

This is not to suggest that competing motivations do not have analytical content. Ideally, motivations to act will be rooted in logos, and not just pathos or ethos. However, one may be motivated to act without regard to the logos of the analysis itself. Slogans like "The right doesn't care about the poor and marginalized" and "The left cares more about doing something, whether it helps the poor or not" obscure relevant analytical differences and make intellectual exchange more difficult, even among scholars. If analysis is separate from motivation, it is unsurprising that motivation based on emotion or loyalty may distort analytical openness. Motivations based on logos offer a common ground for intellectual exchange about markets; motivations based on ethos or pathos make the suspension of judgment more difficult.

Distortions from Ignoring Contingent Judgment

In the face of the practical insufficiency of analysis, it is tempting to treat partial analysis as if it is sufficient for practical deliberation. Lacking an account of the whole, they promote a partial view to a task beyond its practical competence. John Cardinal Newman, in *The Idea of a University*, points out this danger, using the nascent social science of political economy as an illustration. In the inaugural lecture for the Oxford chair in political economy, Nassau Senior acknowledged that the new field analyzes only a part of social reality (wealth creation), and has no disciplinary competence to claim that wealth-getting is either good or bad. Nevertheless, in the same lecture Senior exceeds his self-imposed disciplinary limits to make claims about the moral goodness of wealth. According to Newman, Senior makes this claim because political economy recognizes no comprehensive inquiry into the whole of society.[25] He attributes the temptation to view partial analysis as the whole to a basic human hunger for intelligible, complete narratives: "Though it is no easy matter to view things correctly, nevertheless the busy mind will be ever viewing. We cannot do without a view, and we put up with an illusion, when we cannot get a truth."[26]

There is no shortage of recent examples of this temptation. Alasdair MacIntyre asserts that the inability of educated elites to see the whole, and the concomitant presumption that their limited perspective *is* the

25. Newman, *Idea of a University*, 65–69.
26. Newman, *Idea of a University*, 57.

whole, led to many of the disastrous blunders of the twentieth century. These elites "acted decisively and deliberately without knowing what they were doing."[27] The reliance on body counts during the Vietnam War, the neglect of necessary preconditions for market success in post-communist Russia, and the adoption of Covid death rates as the primary policy metric in the recent pandemic (to the exclusion of measures of social stress and economic disruption) all attest to the tendency of analysis to rely on its partial view as a guide to policy when a vision of the whole is lacking.

When analysis loses sight of the moral motivations and contingent judgments necessary for effective action, it can become ideological, assuming a role in explanation and practical guidance for which it is ill equipped. This can be true of the market defenses of Hayek, Friedman, or Buchanan, and the market-skeptical analyses of Stiglitz or Keynes. I can think of two consequences of this tendency to entrust a practical task to analysis, each of which makes dialogue between competing analyses more difficult. First, a partial analysis pretending to be sufficient for practical judgment becomes a vehicle for the moral judgments most closely associated with its narrow focus. Those devoted to personal freedom adopt analyses that focus most intensely on free markets. Those who care about the poor or the oppressed are more likely to attach this sentiment to analyses in which this care is most obviously expressed.

A second consequence of partial analyses pretending to practical adequacy is a demand for purity. Attempts to pursue Finn's open dialogue, to combine the insights of one partial analysis with the competing insights of another, may appear to compromise analytical principles. Those who put analysis into messy practice—to realize human goods insofar as it is possible in the circumstances—may appear to their allies (and to themselves) to be betraying values that are closely identified with the model itself.

These two consequences make it difficult to suspend judgment about one's analysis in order to put it into a larger analytical conversation of the sort Finn proposes. If analysis is closely tied to the values that motivate it, to the extent that those values seem self-evident, it will be more difficult to enter into dialogue. To defend your analysis is to defend the values you (implicitly or explicitly) hold dear. Suspension of judgment may itself seem to be a compromise.

---

27. MacIntyre, "Very Idea of a University," 361.

Finn's use of Albert Hirschman's *Rhetoric of Reaction* is itself evidence that questions of prudential application can be interpreted as evidence of a lack of commitment to the model, or evidence of bad faith.[28] Partisans of a particular analytical approach might view questions about feasibility as a kind of reaction instead of an exercise integral to practical wisdom. The three theses of Hirschman's *Rhetoric*—perversity, futility, and jeopardy—are in fact common considerations in the exercise of prudential application. In light of the circumstances, one might argue that a proposed policy might have *perversely* opposite effects from those the policymaker intends; that a proposed policy is *futile* and ineffective; or that the proposed policy *jeopardizes* other important outcomes. In practical application, these three theses can be exercises of wise statesmanship. When we downplay contingency, we are more likely to treat them as evidence of bad faith and overlook prudential judgments against our position.

The demand for analytical purity is evident in explanations for why a particular analysis fails. When the Big Bang in Russia resulted in a corrupt, lawless oligarchy, market defenders were inclined to blame Russia for the failure of the market opening, instead of asking how a less pure "free market" analysis might have been appropriate in the specific circumstances of a Russian culture with a long communist past. On the other extreme, failures of socialist experiments are often blamed on the impurity of the effort; if "real socialism" had been tried, it would have succeeded. When analysis pretending to be practical fails, the tendency is to blame either those who applied the models imperfectly or the hapless subjects of the failed policy. This results in a kind of antihumanism: human beings are deficient because they fail to live up to the behavioral expectations laid out in the analysis. In the worst cases, the practical failure of analysis-driven policy results in attempts to create a new kind of human, instead of serving human beings in all their imperfections.

SOME TENTATIVE ADVICE

To enter into dialogue about markets with those whose perspectives are quite different, one must exercise a crucial intellectual skill: the suspension of judgment. To step away from your own position, to consider how it compares with very different approaches, and to give critiques of your

---

28. Finn, *Moral Ecology*, 73–74, cites Hirschman, *Rhetoric of Reaction*.

position a fair hearing makes dialogue possible. In *The Moral Ecology*, Dan Finn attempts to bring together partisans of competing analytical approaches to markets. He invites each of them to suspend judgment—to recognize in other approaches different moral judgments on a common set of economic questions. I have great respect for Finn's accomplishment in this book, but am skeptical that it will overcome the resistance to dialogue.

We might blame this recalcitrant resistance on recent polarizing trends in politics and culture, or on the bullheadedness of ideological rivals, but there is another possibility: we rely too much on analysis as a basis for understanding and resolving our practical disagreements. The analysis of social science and ethics cannot tell us *what to do*, but we nonetheless rely heavily on analysis to understand our practical disagreements. To decide well requires careful analytical thought, but it also requires nonanalytic elements: a commitment of the will to the ends of action (morals), and contingent judgment about phenomena that exceed our analytical grasp.

When we rely on analysis to carry the weight of our decision-making, it increases the importance of any particular analysis beyond its value in ordering our thoughts about the causes and effects of alternative policies. First, particular moral judgments may become more deeply associated with the analytical systems that compete for influence. These competing systems (free market, market skeptic, and radical) are each built around a system of values. Moreover, the task of motivation does not always rely on appeals to reason. The resulting moral motivations may rest not on reason, but on ethos or pathos. It is harder to suspend judgment when your attachment to an analytical system rests on something other than reasoned judgment.

The neglect of contingent judgment in action leads to a persistent temptation to assume that contingency does not matter and that a partial analysis is in fact an adequate description of the practical landscape. This makes the practical compromises that are necessary when one analysis meets another, or when analysis meets contingent reality, appear traitorous. Those who engage in dialogue in good faith, or who must put policy analysis into messy practice, are morally suspect when analysis presumes to be a comprehensive guide to good policy.

This essay is heavy on diagnosis, but light on treatment. If the dominance of analysis in practical matters is a real problem as I have described it, then the solution lies in restoring analysis to its proper place. A simple acknowledgment of the practical limits of analysis may avoid many of the distortions pointed out above.

Whenever possible, we should consciously separate the task of moral commitment from the task of analysis. In doing so, we are not repeating the insupportable claim of moral neutrality. When we carry out our social analyses without reference to the need for moral commitment, the analysis itself takes on moral overtones. Suspension of judgment becomes morally fraught, and thus more difficult. Finn's analysis can help the parties to disagreements about markets to see their common concerns more clearly and trace out the effects of their different moral judgments. Nevertheless, we should take greater care to separate moral commitments from analysis, to make it easier to suspend judgment.

Similarly, we should keep the need for contingent judgment in mind even as we focus on differences in social science analysis. When analysis takes contingency seriously, the necessary compromises in application of the model are not betrayals of the model—they are wise adjustments made in pursuit of the goods that motivate the model. The compromises made necessary by contingency draw attention away from the model and its purity and toward the ends of the analysis—the human goods that should motivate analysis in the first place. This will draw attention to Finn's purpose in writing *The Moral Ecology*—to focus the dialogue about the justice of markets on differences in judgment about what is humanly good.

BIBLIOGRAPHY

Aquinas, Thomas. *Summa Theologiae*. Translated by the Fathers of the English Dominican Province. Cincinnati: Benziger Brothers, 1948.
Aristotle. "Nicomachean Ethics." In *The Basic Works of Aristotle*, edited by Richard McKeon, 935–1112. Translated by David Ross. New York: Random House, 1941.
———. "Rhetoric." In *The Basic Works of Aristotle*, edited by Richard McKeon, 1325–450. Translated by W. Rhys Roberts. New York: Random House, 1941.
Finn, Daniel K. *The Moral Ecology of Markets: Assessing Claims About Markets and Justice*. Cambridge: Cambridge University Press, 2006.
———. "Nine Libertarian Heresies Tempting Neoconservative Catholics to Stray from Catholic Social Thought." *Journal of Markets and Morality* 14 (2011) 487–503.
———. "Private Property, Self-Regulation, and Just Price: A Response to Philip Booth and Samuel Gregg." *Journal of Markets and Morality* 15 (2012) 325–28.
Finnis, John. *Natural Law and Natural Rights*. Oxford: Clarendon, 1980.
Hirschman, Albert O. *The Rhetoric of Reaction: Perversity, Futility, Jeopardy*. Cambridge, MA: Harvard University Press, 1992.
MacIntyre, Alasdair. *Ethics in the Conflicts of Modernity: An Essay on Desire, Practical Reasoning, and Narrative*. Cambridge: Cambridge University Press, 2016.

———. "The Very Idea of a University: Aristotle, Newman, and Us." *British Journal of Educational Studies* 57 (2009) 347–62.

Newman, John Henry. *The Idea of a University*. Notre Dame, IN: Notre Dame University Press, 1982. First published 1852.

Porter, Jean. *Justice as a Virtue: A Thomistic Perspective*. Grand Rapids: Eerdmans, 2016.

Schliesser, Eric. "The Separation of Economics from Virtue: A Historical-Conceptual Introduction." In *Economics and the Virtues: Building a New Moral Foundation*, edited by Jennifer A. Baker and Mark D. White, 141–64. Oxford: Oxford University Press, 2016.

Stump, Eleonore. *Aquinas*. Arguments of the Philosophers. New York: Routledge, 2003.

Yuengert, Andrew M. *Catholic Social Teaching in Practice: Exploring Practical Wisdom and the Virtues Tradition*. Cambridge: Cambridge University Press, 2023.

———. "Economics and Interdisciplinary Exchange in Catholic Social Teaching and *Caritas in Veritate*." *Journal of Business Ethics* 100 (2011) 41–54.

The Social Teaching of the Church in the Last Quarter of a Century

Stefano Zamagni

A PERSONAL PREAMBLE

DANIEL FINN IS AN honest intellectual. He has never compromised on intellectual integrity and never worked on any issue for the sake of "fashion," academic, societal, or political. He possesses a strength of belief that he has arrived at with scholarship, sympathy, and genuine compassion for every kind of underprivileged minority. The acuteness and sensitivity with which he has been an observer of the socioeconomic scene convinced him to devote great attention to the ethical foundations of economic discourse. Indeed, Daniel has never lost sight of the ultimate aim of economics: the betterment and improvement of the human condition.[1]

This volume celebrates Finn's work as a leading researcher and scholar in the area of the ethical and spiritual dimensions of economic life. Of specific relevance is Finn's contribution to the understanding of the modern company not simply as a money making machine, but as a "political agent" contributing to the transformation of the context in which it operates. The final goal of Finn's work is to move ahead toward a different kind of economy, one that is inclusive and not exclusive, human and not dehumanizing, one that cares for the environment, not despoiling it. In Finn's scholarship, economic life once again becomes a humane

---

1. See Finn, *Moral Ecology*.

activity where interpersonal relations and ethical values occupy the center of the stage. Needless to say, I am particularly happy to contribute to Finn's Festschrift with the essay that follows.

INTRODUCTION

The focus of the present note is on the development of the social teaching of the church (STC) over the past quarter of a century. The specific reference is therefore to the work of the three most recent pontiffs: John Paul II, Benedict XVI, and Francis. In order not to burden the text, I will omit the apparatus of quotations, limiting myself to pointing to references to the various texts.

"The world suffers for lack of thought": this statement from Paul VI's *Populorum Progressio* (no. 85), subscribed to and taken up several times by Benedict XVI and Pope Francis, is the one that most captures the present of church theology in the twenty-first century. The world, especially the advanced West, with the end of the millennium has changed so profoundly and rapidly that this change calls for an updating of a large part of the previous reflection of the STC, still rooted in a theology inadequate to come to terms with postmodernity—just think of the macro-themes of family, work, finance, management, bioethics, the future of capitalism. It is against this background that the truly remarkable contributions of the three aforementioned pontiffs should be read and interpreted, the ultimate aim of which is to suggest a viable way to arrive at ethical commonality (the *Koinotes* of the Greeks) in pluralistic society in the properly socioeconomic sphere.

It is now well known that among the many open questions that modernity has left us is that concerning the unresolved disagreement between the lines of thought that, in order to bring to light important dynamics of our societies, have ended up dissolving subjectivity in the collective (think of neo-Marxism or neo-structuralism), on the one hand, and those lines of thought that have indeed exalted subjectivity, but at the price of reducing the social to a mere aggregation of individual desires, on the other hand. The way suggested by the STC is to make a weld between these two polarities, showing how, in today's historical conditions, it is false to dichotomize the following dyads, as if one comes at the expense of the other: independence-belonging; freedom-justice; efficiency-equity; self-interest and solidarity as alternative. That is, it is wrong to think that any strengthening of the sense of belonging should be seen as requiring a reduction in the independence of the individual; any progress on the efficiency front as a threat to fairness; or any improvement due to self-interest as a weakening of solidarity.

JOHN PAUL II AND THE ETHICS OF THE COMMON GOOD

A point on which the Polish pope's magisterium has dwelt with uninterrupted insistence since *Centesimus Annus* is what needs to be done to arrive at ethical consensus in sociopolitical matters. In his address to the United Nations on Oct. 5, 1995, the pope had insisted on the point that it is possible to agree on sociopolitical issues on a shared common basis because "the universal moral law written on the human heart is precisely that kind of 'grammar' which is needed if the world is to engage this discussion of its future."[2] And addressing the members of the Congregation for the Doctrine of the Faith in February 2004, John Paul II, after recalling the suitability of the natural moral law to be an instrument of dialogue with all, noted as the main cause of why this does not in fact happen: "the spread among believers of a morality of a fideistic character" and the consequent lack of "an objective reference for legislation, which is often based only on social consensus."[3] This is a position that will continue, with renewed strength, with Benedict XVI. Moreover, already in his *God and the World*, Ratzinger had written, "Natural law reveals to us that nature also contains within itself a moral message. The spiritual content of creation is not only mechanical-mathematical in nature.... But there is an overlay of spirit, of 'natural laws' in creation, which bears imprinted within itself and reveals to us an inner order."[4]

The condition that must be met for STC to be visualized not as an additional moral theory to the many already available in the literature, but as a "common grammar" to all of them, is that it announces that its point of view is to care for the human good. Indeed, where the various ethical theories in vogue today place their foundation either in the search for rules (as is the case with the multiple versions of positivistic naturalism, according to which ethics is borrowed from the juridical norm), or

2. John Paul II, "Address to the United Nations," no. 3.
3. John Paul II, "Address to Biannual Plenary," no. 5.
4. Ratzinger, *God and the World*, 142.

on the subject of action (think of utilitarian and contractualist theories), STC accepts as its Archimedean point the idea of "being with." Ethics, even before being concerned with enunciating principles and suggesting rules, is an abode, a "home" in which one cares for oneself and for others; in a word, for the human good. The hallmark of the ethics of the common good, which has always been the *proprium* of STC, is that in order to grasp the identity of human action, it is necessary to place oneself in the perspective of the person who acts[5] and not in the neutral perspective of the third person or in the perspective of the impartial spectator (as Adam Smith had proposed). Aquinas had already observed that the moral good, being a practical reality, is known primarily not by the one who theorizes it, but by the one who practices it: it is he who can identify it and thus choose it with certainty whenever it is in question.[6]

What does it mean to embrace the point of view of the ethics of the common good? To answer, it is worthwhile to start from the consideration that socioeconomic action cannot be reductively conceived in merely terms of the institutions, rules, instruments that ensure social *coexistence*, but also (and especially) *life in common*. Aristotle had already understood the profound difference between life in common and the mere communal grazing that is characteristic of animals. If, therefore, communal life is the context within which individual, ethically sensitive life plans are realized, then that context must also be recognized as having, itself, an ethical dimension. Otherwise, one would fall into an obvious pragmatic contradiction.

But what lies behind the expression "common good"? A simple but effective way to grasp the proper meaning of *common good* is to place it in comparison with the concept of *total good*. While the latter can be metaphorically rendered with the image of a summation, the addends of which represent the goods of individuals (or of the social groups of which society is made up), the common good is rather comparable to a product, the factors of which represent the goods of individuals (or groups). Immediate is the meaning of the mathematical metaphor: in a summation some of the addends can be canceled out, while the total sum still remains positive. Indeed, it may even be the case that if the goal is to maximize the total good (e.g., national GDP) it is convenient to "cancel out" someone's good (or welfare) provided that someone else's welfare

---

5. See John Paul II, *Veritatis Splendor*, no. 78.
6. This paragraph is adapted from Zamagni, "Catholic Social Thought."

gain increases sufficiently to more than compensate for it. Not so, on the other hand, with a product, because nullifying even one factor resets the entire product to zero. Thus, the logic of the common good does not allow for substitutability (i.e., *trade-offs*): one cannot completely sacrifice someone's good—whatever their life situation or social configuration—in order to improve someone else's good, and this for the fundamental reason that that someone is still a *human person*. For the dominant logic, on the other hand, that someone is merely an *individual*, i.e., a subject identified by particular interests, and these—as we know—can be safely added together (or compared), because they have no face, i.e., identity, or history.

Why does the category of the common good continue to be confused, as income grows, even among practitioners, generating quite a few misunderstandings and causing quite a few sterile and inconclusive disputes? The most convincing answer is that today's dominant culture is so steeped in philosophical utilitarianism that even those places that, at least in words, oppose it, end up suffering its practical conditioning. Indeed, bear in mind that it is with Jeremy Bentham's utilitarian ethics that the idea that the purpose of economic action is the maximization of total utility is affirmed and spread, with the result that the organization of the market (i.e., the economy) and public institutions must be such that it does not stand in the way of achieving such a goal.

Another consequence of the pernicious confusion between the common good and the total good bears mentioning. It poses a direct challenge to the frequent conflation and assimilation of the notions of charity and solidarity in Catholic thought. A few examples are worth mentioning. In the *Catechism of the Catholic Church*, the term "solidarity" is mentioned twenty-three times, and even sixty-three times in the *Compendium of the Social Doctrine of the Church*.[7] On the other hand, in the texts issued by the Second Vatican Council, the term in question occurs nine times only. It should be noted that *Gaudium et Spes* does not employ the former expression *doctrina socialis* to mean the social doctrine of the church, but rather that of *doctrina de societate*. This change of terms would not even have been noticed if M. D. Chenu had not intervened on the subject a few years later with his influential thesis that the STC is in fact a mere social teaching of the church that merely reads those *res novae* that "constitute

---

7. Catholic Church, *Catechism*; Pontifical Council for Justice and Peace, *Compendium*.

points of convergence for many people and express to some extent their expectation."[8]

This is a puzzling thesis, to say the least, that for the purpose—quite rightly—of averting the risk of making the STC an ideology, or even a political program, effectively empties it of both its own principled content and its practical-oriented function. The "dispute" would later be resolved in *Sollicitudo Rei Socialis* (1988), where John Paul II writes that STC "is not even an ideology, but the accurate formulation of the results of careful reflection on the complex realities of man's existence. . . . Its principal purpose is to *interpret* these realities, examining their conformity or dissimilarity with the lines of the Gospel's teaching on man and his earthly and at the same time transcendent vocation; to *orient*, therefore, Christian behavior. It belongs, therefore, not to the field of ideology, but to theology and especially to moral theology" (no. 41, emphasis added).

But there is more. In the *Catechism* (no. 2850), we read that the bond that unites us in the body of Christ is solidarity and not already charity. On the other hand, the October 2005 Synod of Bishops in Rome issued, at the conclusion of its work on the theme "The Eucharist: Source and Summit of the Church's Life and Mission," a message in which the concept of solidarity is treated three times (nos. 4, 5, 13) and that of charity only once (no. 20).[9] There is no one who does not see what risks the Christian message runs when charity and solidarity are understood as terms that are essentially equivalent to each other and therefore substitutable, or interchangeable.

POPE BENEDICT AND THE STC OF POSTMODERNITY

What is the figure of Pope Benedict XVI's contribution of thought to the deepening and expansion of the scope of the social doctrine of the church? The reference here is both to *Caritas in Veritate* (*CV*) and the so-to-speak preparatory encyclical, *Deus Caritas Est*, and to the messages that, on various occasions, have been published subsequently. The space available only allows me three highlights of central relevance. First, however, a general note. The great novelty of the pope's work resides in the method, that is, literally in the path traced to read the *res novae of* a time,

---

8. Chenu, *Social Doctrine of the Church*.
9. Synod of Bishops, "Living Bread for the Peace of the World."

such as the present, marked by two absolutely unprecedented events: the globalization of the economy, especially of finance (often confused with the internationalization of economic relations, which has existed for centuries) and the fourth industrial revolution, in which new technologies have fundamentally changed modes of production and, in particular, the organization of work in businesses. In the light of the four immutable principles of the STC, Pope Benedict reads today's economic and social reality by offering us a quite original interpretation: the STC cannot limit itself to denouncing a certain model of social order and offering suggestions to alleviate its sometimes devastating effects (though it still must do that). It must also indicate which alternatives, among those realistically possible, are capable of capturing the spirit, the soul of the Christian message. For do not forget that Christianity is an embodied religion, not a "wrapped" religion, that is, fixed on "paper."

A first point worthy of the greatest attention is the broadening of the notion of Christian justice, which cannot be restricted to judging the distributive moment of wealth, but must go as far as the moment of its production. That is, it is not enough to claim the "just reward to the worker"—as we read in *Rerum Novarum*. It is necessary to ask whether or not the production process is carried out with respect for the dignity of human labor; whether or not it accommodates fundamental human rights; whether or not it is compatible with the moral norm of the person. Already in *Gaudium et Spes* (no. 67) we read, "It is therefore necessary to adapt the entire productive process to the needs of the person and his forms of life," and not vice versa. Labor is not a factor of production that, as such, must adapt, indeed adjust to the needs of the production process in order to increase its efficiency. On the contrary, it is the production process that must be organized in such a way as to allow people their human flourishing and to make possible the harmonization of family and work life.

Pope Benedict tells us that such a project is feasible today, in the season of postindustrial society, as long as we want it. That is why *CV* urges insistently to find ways to apply fraternity in practice as the regulating principle of the economic order. Solidarity is not enough. *CV* speaks of fraternity, because a fraternal society is also one of solidarity, but the reverse is not true, as so many experiences confirm. Ultimately, the appeal is to remedy the fundamental error of contemporary culture that has led to the belief that a democratic society could progress by keeping the code of efficiency—which would suffice by itself to regulate relations within the sphere of the economic—and the code of solidarity—which would regulate inter-subjective relations within the sphere of the social. It is this dichotomization that has impoverished, for no objective reason, our societies.

A second point is worth noting. In *CV*, the terms "enterprise" and "entrepreneur" are the ones that recur most frequently. Nothing similar is found in previous encyclicals, where the term "enterprise" was evoked only in passing. Why? Benedict shows that he has grasped the *proprium* of entrepreneurial activity, which is to aim not at the maximization of profit, but of shared value, as we call it today. Profit is the measure, not the goal of doing business. This is why *CV* rejects the identification of the entrepreneur with the figure of the capitalist and thus recognizes that, alongside the capitalist form of enterprise, other forms of enterprise must be able to find a place in the market, from cooperative to social to communal to nonprofit. (This is the first time in an STC magisterial document that these types of enterprises receive official recognition.)

It is from the above that the pope goes so far, with uncommon audacity, as to affirm that the principle of gift as gratuitousness—not donation as gift—must enter into ordinary economic activity. This is the "blasphemy" that the strong market powers, especially the financial ones, did not forgive him at the outset. What does the dimension of the economic ever have to do with gift-giving? Is it not true that economic action is governed by the "iron" laws of the market? Is it not enough for business to practice philanthropy, corporate welfare, in order to call itself socially responsible? The pope, a refined theologian, in responding with a firm "no" to such questions, comes to reiterate that the logic of gratuitousness cannot be reduced to a purely ethical dimension, because gratuitousness is not merely a virtue. Justice is an ethical virtue, and its importance cannot be reiterated enough; gratuitousness is rather about the supra-ethical dimension of human action, because its logic is superabundance—while that of justice is the logic of equivalence. This is what makes the civil market economy a paradigm that is truly an alternative to those of traditional political economy and Marxian economics. (Note that paradigm means, literally, vision, a look at reality, and therefore should not be confused with either the term "theory" or "model.")

Finally, I would like to mention a third point, concerning the subtitle of *CV*: "For integral human development." The key word here is "integral." Human development is composed of three dimensions: material growth (still measured by GDP); the socio-relational dimension; and the spiritual dimension. Human development is integral when the three dimensions are taken together, that is, in a multiplicative and not additive form, as is commonly believed. This means that it is not legitimate, for the purpose of increasing growth, to sacrifice one or the other two dimensions. For example, laws or decrees that, in a short-lived attempt to increase GDP, cancel the holiday, the meaning of which is radically different from that of rest, are not legitimate. Or enacting measures that, in order to increase tax revenues, effectively sanction the legalization of gambling. Or again, to intervene in the labor market with measures that, for the very laudable purpose of improving women's participation in work, jeopardize the holding of the family's educational project. And so on.

Now, regardless of the fact that—as is shown—such measures achieve the desired effects only in the short term, the central issue Pope Benedict raises is that of freedom. Development, literally, means the absence of "viluses," the unwrapping or removing of impediments of various kinds. To strive for development then means to strive for the enlargement of the space of people's freedom: freedom understood, however, not only in the negative sense as freedom from impediments, nor even only in the positive sense as freedom of choice. One must add to it the freedom "for," that is, the freedom to pursue one's vocation. It is this perspective of discourse that, in the current historical conditions, while it allows us to overcome sterile diatribes at the cultural level and harmful contrasts at the political level, allows us to find the necessary consensus for a new path.

The fifteenth century was the century of early Humanism; at the beginning of the twenty-first century, the need for a new Humanism is increasingly felt. Then it was the transition from feudalism to city society that was the decisive engine of change; today, it is an equally radical epochal transition: that from industrial to postindustrial society. Migration; endemic increase in social inequalities; identity conflicts; environmental issues; problems of biopolitics and biolaw are just some of the expressions that tell of the current "malaise of civilization," in Freudian terms. In the face of such challenges, merely updating old categories of thought or resorting to refined techniques of collective decision-making do not serve the need. New ways must be dared. With respect to this, it will not be denied that the work and contribution of Pope Benedict XVI has been—and hopefully will continue to be—simply decisive.[10]

---

10. See Finn, *True Wealth of Nations*.

FRATERNITY AS A PRINCIPLE OF SOCIAL ORGANIZATION IN THE TEACHING OF POPE FRANCIS

With the apostolic exhortation *Evangelii Gaudium* and the encyclical *Laudato Si'* (*LS*), Pope Francis intended to shake consciences in the face of the scandal of a humanity that, while it has ever-increasing potential, has not yet been able to overcome some structural wounds that humiliate the dignity of the person.[11]

The functioning of the economic system is characterized by immense potential and rebalancing mechanisms that are not automatic, however, but work if activated with righteous intention and wisdom. The great historical contradiction is the staggering growth of prosperity in some areas of the world but not in those cut off and on the margins. Globalization has burst this contradiction by turning the misery of the last into a threat to the welfare of the first. With the transformation of markets from local to global and with the possibility of almost instantaneous transfer of "weightless commodities" (sounds, data, images, currency) from one place to another on the planet, the billion people living below the extreme poverty line are in fact competing, with their low labor costs, with workers in countries accustomed to living on much better wages and better protections, often progressively eroding those wages and protections. High-income countries therefore can no longer save themselves but must start with the last if they are to defend the welfare and jobs of young people threatened by offshoring and the erosion of the national productive fabric. That is why working for the last, striving to promote their dignity, today is no longer just the heroic choice of missionaries but the necessity and urgency of everyone to defend the rights and protections achieved. Globalization has the virtue of making us increasingly interdependent by uniting the rich, the emerging, and the poor of the planet in one destiny.

It is against this backdrop that the considerations of *LS* should be read, a masterful document of epochal significance destined to constitute, for many years to come, an indispensable point of reference vis-à-vis the ecological question for believers and nonbelievers alike. *LS* is not simply an alarm but a heartfelt invitation to reconsider the foundations of the market economy model in vogue today. It is thus an invitation to emerge

---

11. Material in this section of the essay is adapted from Zamagni: "Civilizing the Economy"; and "For an Integral Ecology."

from the "night of thought" in which the current passage of epoch forces us to remain. Markets are not all equal because they are the precipitate of cultural and political projects. There is a market that reduces inequalities and one that raises them. The first is called civil, because it dilates the spaces of *civitas* by aiming to include virtually everyone; the second is the uncivil market, because it tends to exclude and regenerate the "existential peripheries." In the current phase of the financial capitalism model, the second type of market has become hegemonic, and the results are before our eyes: social inequalities are increasing to an extent unknown in previous centuries; democracy is subjugated to the demands of the market; environmental degradation is advancing at a pace that is no longer sustainable. To this situation, not to hypothetical realities, the pope calls the attention of all, believers and nonbelievers alike.[12]

Contrary to what a hasty reading of the document might suggest, the pope is by no means against techno-science, nor against entrepreneurship. Nor is it his intention to demonize the market economy. And how could he do so when one considers that the market economy, as a socioeconomic institution, was formed in the fourteenth and fifteenth centuries within the framework of Catholic thought? The fact is that the pope's speech has a much more solid theoretical foundation than a certain mass-media narrative would have us believe. Its figure is that of historical realism, and its aim is to reconnect knowledge and experience of reality, to make thought become the practice of life. So, for Pope Francis, Christianity cannot be reduced either to orthodoxy alone—that would be the risk of rationalistic intellectualism—or to orthopraxis alone, to a kind of spiritual pathos for "beautiful souls" in search of consolation. Concretely, this implies that besides the *factum*, what man does, there is the *faciendum*, what man is capable of doing in view of a new historical project. The encyclical does not fall into the trap of biologism, naturalism, nor that of anthropocentrism. The pope does not identify himself with a "thin" theory of ethics, as is, for example, John Rawls's theory of justice. For Rawls, the task of politics is only to guarantee purely negative conditions, that is, to ensure freedom of choice for each individual. But the freedom to choose is not the same thing as the freedom to be able to choose: those who ignore, in fact, their abilities cannot even wish to realize them. This is why Pope Francis argues for a "thick" theory of ethics,

---

12. See Finn, "Unjust Contract."

that is, an ethics of the good aimed at realizing all the capacities of human beings in order to allow them to flourish fully.

The great theme of the encyclical is well rendered by its subtitle: "On Care for Our Common Home." It is integral ecology that is the cornerstone of the text. Precisely because the world is an ecosystem, one cannot act on one part of it without the others being affected. This is the meaning of the statement that "there are not two separate crises, one environmental and another social, but a single and complex socio-environmental crisis" (*LS* no. 139). Ecology and economy have the same root—*oikos*—which designates the common house inhabited by man and nature. But since the beginning of the Anthropocene—a term coined by Nobel laureate in Geology Paul Crutzen in the 1960s—that is, since the first industrial revolution in the second half of the eighteenth century, it has happened that, with gradually increasing intensity, the society of humans has thrown nature "out of the house." Its resources were savagely depleted without any regard either to their reproducibility or to the negative externalities that productive activity was generating. Grave, in this process of exploitation, is the responsibility of "official" economic science, which has never considered—except in very recent times—taking into account in growth models the ecological constraint. Not only that, the economic *mainstream* has made legions of unsuspecting scholars and naive managers believe that the goal of short-term profit maximization was the necessary condition to be met to ensure continued progress. Therein lies the legitimization—certainly not the justification—of the vice of *short-termism*, which was also one of the triggers of the 2007–8 financial crisis.

Well, it is in an attempt to straighten this "crooked wood" of modernity that Pope Francis spends strong words of denunciation against the prevailing growth model. Three main theses are argued and defended in *LS*. The first is that poverty alleviation and sustainable development constitute two sides of the same coin: "The human environment and the natural environment degrade together" (*LS* no. 48). This suggests that all those interventions based on the assumption of separation between poverty alleviation and environmental conservation are doomed to failure. Indeed, if poor countries fear collusive agreements between environmentalists and neo-protectionists in advanced countries aimed at limiting their market access—this is the eco-imperialist concern—the environmentalists in the North fear, on the contrary, that environmental protection measures may be swept aside by the WTO (World Trade

Organization) by fostering a race to the bottom in setting environmental standards. This follows from a lack of an integral vision that does not allow either side to understand that the degradation of the environment and that of society are like two sides of the same coin.

The second thesis is that the ecosystem is a global common good (*LS* nos. 23, 174), rather than either a private good or a public good. It follows that neither traditional market instruments nor publicizing interventions by national governments serve the purpose. As is well known, the *commons* are subject to the devastating consequences typical of situations known as the "prisoner's dilemma": each waits to see the other's moves in order to take advantage of them, with the result that no one moves first. The fact is that while there is still no global governance of the economy we are dealing with one climate system, one ozone layer, and so on. These are, precisely, global commons: one country's use of them does not diminish the amount available to other countries; on the other hand, no country can be excluded from using them. (Clearly, pollutant emissions represent global common "evils.")

The third thesis concerns Pope Francis's strenuous defense of economic biodiversity. A market economy that wants to strive for integral ecology cannot disregard the plurality of forms of enterprise; especially it cannot do so without leaving room for those subjects that produce value—and therefore wealth—by anchoring their behavior to principles such as that of mutuality and intergenerational solidarity. To deny or prevent this would irresponsibly mean giving up on integral human development, which, never let it be forgotten, includes three dimensions (material, i.e., growth; socio-relational; spiritual) among themselves in a multiplicative and not already additive relationship—as the economic *mainstream* goes on to preach.

Finally, a special mention cannot but go to that sort of "Rosetta Stone" of Francis's thought that is the encyclical *Fratelli Tutti*. Its great merit is to have clarified, in a definitive way, the meaning and scope of the principle of fraternity, which does not have the same meaning as brotherhood or, even less, as solidarity. Fraternity is a concept that tells of the belonging of a plurality of people to the same species or to a given community of destiny; it is a transcendent concept that lays its foundation in the recognition of a universal belonging. Brotherhood unites friends but separates them from non-friends; it makes partners and thus closes those who are united to others. Fraternity, on the other hand, is universal and creates brothers, not members, and thus tends to erase the natural and historical boundaries that separate. Cain's gesture suggests that fraternity is not derived from blood. There is no biological fraternity, as much as to mean that there is no fraternity without recognition of our responsibility to each other. While brotherhood has a naturalistic presupposition, fraternity has its presupposition in the reference to a bond, which makes us one another's keepers.

Fraternity, in the proper sense, is an invention of Christianity, although common opinion places it within the republican triad. But things are not in those terms. In the 1789 Declaration of the Rights of Man and of the Citizen, there is freedom and equality, but not fraternity, a word that would later be included but never receive much attention. We know the reason for this: it had not been forgotten that this word had served to justify and, even legitimize, the immense injustices of the ancien régime. Such an arrangement of the sequence by the French Enlightenment proved deleterious: freedom and equality, both conceived within individualism—the prevailing value of modernity—are themselves inherently divergent and conceptually contradictory values. It is fraternity that manages to keep freedom and equality in balance, that is, in harmony. Equality, without the consciousness that it is first and foremost for the other, becomes deadly loneliness. Freedom can be instituted and equality imposed. Fraternity, on the other hand, is not established by law; it comes from a personal experience of responsibility and must be practiced, *primarily* for the sake of the other, not because we feel obligated by some code.

Equally distant is fraternity from solidarity. It is a great merit of the Franciscan school of thought that it has been able to define, in both institutional and economic terms, the principle of fraternity by making it a cornerstone of the social order. There are pages from the Rule of Francis that help well to understand the proper meaning of the principle of fraternity. Which is that of constituting, at one and the same time, the complement and surpassing of the principle of solidarity. In fact, while solidarity is the principle of social organization that allows unequals to become equals, that of fraternity is the principle that allows already equals to be diverse—mind you, not different. Fraternity allows people who are equal in their dignity and fundamental rights to express diversity in their life plans, that is, their specificity. (Take care not to confuse difference with diversity: the former is opposed to equality; the latter is opposed to uniformity. That is why one can be equal and different; while one cannot be equal and unequal.) This co-presence of equality and singularity is what uniquely characterizes the principle of fraternity.

The eras we have left behind, the 1800s and especially the 1900s, were characterized by major battles, both cultural and political, in the name of solidarity, and this was a good thing; think of the history of the labor movement and the struggle to win civil rights. But the good society in which to live cannot be satisfied with the horizon of solidarity, because while the fraternal society is also a society of solidarity, the reverse is not true. What makes the difference? Gratuity. Where it is lacking, there can be no fraternity. Gratuity is not an ethical virtue, as justice is. It concerns the supra-ethical dimension of human action; its logic is that of superabundance. The logic of justice, on the other hand, is that of equivalence, as Aristotle already taught. We understand then why fraternity goes beyond justice. In a society with only justice and no gratuitousness there would be no room for hope. What could its citizens possibly hope for the future? Not so in a society where the principle of fraternity had succeeded in taking deep root, precisely because hope feeds on superabundance. It is in view of this that the authentic meaning of the Economy of Francis project, launched on May 1, 2019, by Pope Francis and aimed, *first and foremost*, at the younger generations, can be grasped. (More than ninety countries have so far seen this project transformed into a realized work.)

INSTEAD OF A CONCLUSION

To have forgotten the fact that a society of humans in which the sense of fraternity is extinguished and in which everything is reduced, on the one hand, to improving market transactions based on the exchange of equivalents and, on the other hand, to increasing transfers implemented by public and private welfare structures, gives us an account of why, despite the quality of the intellectual forces in the field, a credible solution to the trade-off between equity and freedom has not yet been arrived at. The society in which the principle of fraternity is dissolved is not capable of a future; that is, the society in which there is only "giving for the sake of having" or "giving for the sake of duty" is not capable of progress.

I would like to conclude with the wise words of John Paul II, specifically addressed to the economic profession:

> To subject everything to profit involves a real loss of freedom for the scientist. And those who would uphold scientific freedom by appealing to a "values-free science" prepare the way for the supremacy of economic interests. In a broader view, the

pre-eminence of the profit motive in conducting scientific research ultimately means that science is deprived of its epistemological character, according to which its primary goal is discovery of the truth. The risk is that when research takes a utilitarian turn, its speculative dimension, which is the inner dynamic of man's intellectual journey, will be diminished or stifled.[13]

The scientific work of Daniel Finn and his entire testimony of life offer a confirmation of the truth of this remarkable statement. So, also for this reason he deserves a special appreciation and sincere gratitude. *Ad majora*, Daniel!

BIBLIOGRAPHY

Catholic Church. *The Catechism of the Catholic Church*. 2nd ed. Huntington, IN: Our Sunday Visitor, 2023.

Chenu, M. D. *The Social Doctrine of the Church: Origin and Development*. Brescia: Queriniana, 1971.

Finn, Daniel. *The Moral Ecology of Markets*. Cambridge: Cambridge University Press, 2006.

———, ed. *The True Wealth of Nations: Catholic Social Thought and Economic Life*. Oxford: Oxford University Press, 2010.

———. "The Unjust Contract: A Moral Evaluation." In *The True Wealth of Nations: Catholic Social Thought and Economic Life*, edited by Daniel K. Finn, 143–64. Oxford: Oxford University Press, 2010.

Francis. *Evangelii Gaudium*. Vatican, Nov. 24, 2013. https://www.vatican.va/content/francesco/en/apost_exhortations/documents/papa-francesco_esortazione-ap_20131124_evangelii-gaudium.html.

———. *Fratelli Tutti*. Oct. 3, 2020. https://www.vatican.va/content/francesco/en/encyclicals/documents/papa-francesco_20201003_enciclica-fratelli-tutti.html.

———. *Laudato Si'*. Vatican, May 24, 2015. https://www.vatican.va/content/francesco/en/encyclicals/documents/papa-francesco_20150524_enciclica-laudato-si.html.

John Paul II. "Address to the Participants in the Biannual Plenary Assembly of the Congregation for the Doctrine of the Faith." Vatican, Feb. 6, 2004. https://www.vatican.va/content/john-paul-ii/en/speeches/2004/february/documents/hf_jp-ii_spe_20040206_congr-faith.html.

———. "Address to the United Nations." Vatican, Oct. 5, 1995. https://www.vatican.va/content/john-paul-ii/en/speeches/1995/october/documents/hf_jp-ii_spe_05101995_address-to-uno.html.

———. "Letter to H. E. Msgr. Josef Kowalczyk Participating in the International Conference on 'Conflict of Interest and Its Significance in Science and Medicine' (Warsaw, 5–6 April 2002)." Vatican, Mar. 25, 2002. https://www.vatican.va/content/john-paul-ii/en/letters/2002/documents/hf_jp-ii_let_20020411_conference-poland.html.

---

13. John Paul II, "Letter on 'Conflict of Interest.'"

———. *Sollicitudo Rei Socialis*. Vatican, Dec. 30, 1987. https://www.vatican.va/content/john-paul-ii/en/encyclicals/documents/hf_jp-ii_enc_30121987_sollicitudo-rei-socialis.html.

———. *Veritatis Splendor*. Vatican, Aug. 6, 1993. https://www.vatican.va/content/john-paul-ii/en/encyclicals/documents/hf_jp-ii_enc_06081993_veritatis-splendor.html.

Paul VI. *Populorum Progressio*. Vatican, Mar. 26, 1967. https://www.vatican.va/content/paul-vi/en/encyclicals/documents/hf_p-vi_enc_26031967_populorum.html.

Pontifical Council for Justice and Peace. *Compendium of the Social Doctrine of the Church*. Washington, DC: United States Conference of Catholic Bishops, 2004.

Ratzinger, Joseph. *God and the World*. Milan: San Paolo, 2001.

Second Vatican Council. *Gaudium et Spes*. Vatican, Dec. 7, 1965. https://www.vatican.va/archive/hist_councils/ii_vatican_council/documents/vat-ii_const_19651207_gaudium-et-spes_en.html.

Synod of Bishops. "Living Bread for the Peace of the World." Crossroads Initiative, Oct. 23, 2005. https://www.crossroadsinitiative.com/media/articles/living-bread-for-the-peace-of-the-world-synod-of-bishops/.

Zamagni, Stefano. "Catholic Social Thought, Civil Economy, and the Spirit of Capitalism." In *The True Wealth of Nations: Catholic Social Thought and Economic Life*, edited by Daniel K. Finn, 63–94. Oxford: Oxford University Press, 2010.

———. "Civilizing the Economy for an Integral Ecology." In *Eine Wirtschaft, die Leben fordert: Wirtschafts- und unternehmensethische Reflexionen im Anschluss an Papst Franziskus*, edited by Gabriel Ingeborg et al., 131–52. Ostfildern, Germ.: Matthias Grünewald, 2017.

———. "For an Integral Ecology." *Japan Mission Journal* 70 (2016). https://www.oriens.or.jp/jmj/jmj_back/jmj_back_2016.html.

Catholicism, Economics, and the Critical Realist Connection

Douglas V. Porpora

It is my honor and absolute pleasure to contribute to this volume commemorating the life and work of Daniel Finn. As my title suggests, Professor Finn is one of those for whom life and work are connected. Connected in particular are Finn's Catholic faith and his work as an economist. As a one-time president of, among other organizations, the Catholic Theological Society of America and the Association for Social Economics, Finn is not one of those who think social science is best practiced in a value-free way, a way detached from how those of us outside the ivory tower actually live our lives.

Finn's departure from value neutrality marks a break from the so-called positivist philosophy of science underlying standard disciplinary economics. Finn is more consistent with the post-positivist philosophy of science known as *critical realism* (CR) that Finn later came to embrace. Actually, however, as I will endeavor to show here, Finn was less a convert to CR than, like me, someone who had all along been practicing it even before learning of it.

CR is not only in my opinion a more tenable philosophy of science than positivism but also in several ways much more congruent with a Catholic perspective. From its start, CR has always held particular appeal for both Catholics and humanist Marxists and for those like me who happen to be both. In contrast with the postmodern poststructuralism more popular in the humanities, CR shares Catholicism's and Marxism's commitments to truth and philosophically underlies a more humanist conception of causality and the human person than either positivism or poststructuralism.

In CR furthermore, there are philosophical grounds for a structural critique of capitalism absent from both positivism and poststructuralism. Although it may come as a surprise to many American Catholics and their bishops, Catholic social teaching, while not altogether opposed to capitalism, is not altogether uncritical of it either. We find Finn navigating the Catholic "third way" between capitalism and communism in the first volume of an initiative sponsored by the Institute of Advanced Catholic Studies (IACS) at the University of Southern California. Titled *The True Wealth of Nations*, the volume re-explores from a Catholic perspective the relationship between "market-driven wealth creation" and the common good.

> For a long time thinkers in the mainstream Christian traditions have viewed economic activity, especially that left to private initiative, with suspicion or even antagonism. Since the Industrial Revolution, the economic system known as capitalism has been blamed for the poverty of the poor and for injustices committed toward them. . . . A significant shift in that tradition was signaled within the Catholic tradition by several encyclicals of the late Pope John Paul II, notably *Centesimus Annus*, published in 1991. It argued that the creation of wealth in a market-driven economic system, could, in the right conditions, promote the common good. It offered general criteria drawn from Catholic social thought for judging whether it actually did so.[1]

Do our actual market-driven economic systems unequivocally serve the common good? The first IACS volume, edited by Finn, brought together Catholic theologians and economists to discuss the question. That volume included no critical realists nor any mention of CR or its proponents in the index. When four years later, a second IACS volume appeared, *Distant Markets, Distant Harms*, also edited by Finn, three critical realist sociologists were included. All happened to be Catholic. I was among them.

As I will argue here, both before and after he explicitly embraced it, the substance of CR has served Finn as a philosophical bridge between Catholicism and a humanist approach to economics. In what follows, I want to summarize what positivist mainstream economics looks like;

---

1. Finn, *True Wealth of Nations*, 5.

how CR approaches things differently; and how Finn's work looks before and after his formal embrace of CR.

MAINSTREAM POSITIVIST ECONOMICS

The word *positivism* was coined by Auguste Comte in the 1830s—along with the word *sociology*. The French Enlightenment we associate with Voltaire, Diderot, and Rousseau was largely a philosophical critique of received views and, as critique negates, could be considered negative. In opposition to that philosophical negativity, Comte called for a new positive orientation that would not be based on the purely conceptual analysis of philosophy but on the empirical analysis of science.

Specifically, what Comte sought was a social physics—the application to the social sphere of the same approach physicists apply to the natural sphere. Like many philosophers even today, Comte conceived of physics as a closed system of inviolable Humean laws.

In the classical view of philosopher David Hume, laws are essentially what philosopher Roy Bhaskar termed *event-regularities*, that is, empirical regularities among events. If one thing happens (Event A), then, because of that first happening, something else happens (Event B). The form of such regularities among events is a conditional of the form *If A then B*.[2]

Positivism conceives of causality as such lawlike regularities among events. Thus, just as physicists seek the laws of nature, social scientists are empirically to search out the laws governing society. The positivist conception of causal explanation is the *covering law model*. If someone asks, for example, why event B happened, the positivist answer would be to cite a law covering the occurrence of B—*If A then B*—and the prior occurrence of A.

Ultimately, the law *If A then B* can be represented mathematically as an equation: $B = mA$, where m represents some constant parameter applied to A. A itself might be a compound event made up of a whole string of simultaneous events, $A_1, A_2, \ldots A_n$, in which case, the mathematical equation would be expanded to $B = m_1A_1 + m_2A_2 + \ldots + m_nA_n$, and we have what is called a regression equation.[3]

---

2. Bhaskar, *Realist Theory of Science*.

3. For a fuller account of the covering law model of causality, see Porpora, *Reconstructing Sociology*.

With the exception of anthropology, which remains defiantly narrative in method, all of the social sciences have been influenced by positivism and its idea of causality with the consequent embrace as well of the foregoing kind of mathematical expression. That influence and mathematical embrace is nowhere as strong as in economics, where mainstream economists believe they can actually pin down the exact values of the parameters and thus deliver the world invariant laws of economic activity.

There is more to positivism than just this ultimately mathematical view of causal explanation. For one thing, it is realist. It believes in an objective reality independent of what we think about it, and it believes that our thoughts or theories about that objective reality are easily separated from the reality itself.

Of course, to maintain that separation, positivism enjoins the scientific researcher to avoid personal value judgments. In this respect, positivism holds onto a rigid fact/value distinction, according to which only facts are real, and values are just in our heads. Thus, like Detective Joe Friday in the 1950s television show *Dragnet*, positivists want "just the facts, ma'am." In other words, social scientific researchers ought to be value neutral, and this value neutrality is another key element of the positivist approach to social science.

CRITICAL REALISM

Widely associated with Roy Bhaskar's seminal texts,[4] CR actually began with an entire progressive community of scholars that included other philosophers like Andrew Collier, Peter Manicas, and Christopher Norris; heterodox economists like Tony Lawson; and social scientists like Ted Benton, Margaret Archer, Andrew Sayer, and Petter Naess.

As its name implies, like positivism, CR is realist, but critically so. From the CR perspective, the positivist approach is naively realist. Thomas Kuhn's *The Structure of Scientific Revolutions* dropped a bombshell on positivism's naïve realism. It documented how there are no uninterpreted or untheorized facts. Putative facts are instead always identified via the conceptual framework of one or another theory.

At the close of the twentieth century, postmodernism was one powerful reaction to the seemingly fatal blow Kuhn had delivered to positivism. According to postmodernism, survived now as poststructuralism,

---

4. Bhaskar: *Realist Theory of Science*; and *Possibility of Naturalism*.

reality is always a social construction, and claims to truth are always a power play by the holders of one possible construction of reality against its rivals. On this view, largely influenced by French deconstructionists, the job of social scientists is merely to show how claims to truth—about race, gender, colonialism, etc.—can be flipped to show the opposite in a never-ending play of language.

CR emerged as an alternative to both positivism and postmodernism (including its poststructuralist successor). In the first place, as noted, in contrast with postmodernism and poststructuralism, CR is realist. The first premise of CR, ontological realism, means that reality is not all socially constructed, that there exist things in the world independent of our consciousness or our efforts. The world itself, CR affirms, existed before we ever arrived on the scene.

As also noted, however, if CR is realist, in contrast with positivism, it is critically realist. That means CR agrees with postmodernism and poststructuralism that there are no uninterpreted observations and that theory cannot be separated from empirical observations. At the same time, in contrast with postmodernism and poststructuralism, CR also expressly affirms what it calls judgmental rationality—that rival theoretical perspectives can always be judged comparatively on their merits and that however we linguistically describe things, the referents identified by those descriptions can—and in practice—very often exist independently of those descriptions. Atoms, for example, are presumed by CR to exist whether they are as described by the ancient Greek Democritus or quantum physicist Niels Bohr.

And with CR's recovery of an ontologically objective world, CR also recovers from postmodernism and poststructuralism the important concept of truth as a match between what we claim or believe and the ontologically objective reality. Indeed, CR holds against postmodernism and poststructuralism that their critical postures toward power structures hold purchase only if the bases of their critiques are true.[5]

Also like postmodernism and poststructuralism, CR rejects positivism's rigid fact/value distinction, believing instead that values are always undergirded by facts and that many facts—like whether or not there has been a murder—are inherently valuative. Thus, against positivism and like postmodernism and poststructuralism, CR denies that research need be value neutral and in fact maintains that when two sides are

---

5. See, e.g., Porpora, *Reconstructing Sociology*.

epistemically and morally unequal, a stance of neutrality actually departs from objectivity into false equivalence.

Most centrally, however, whereas postmodernism and poststructuralism remain unclear about their understanding of causality, CR rejects positivism's covering law model in favor of a "powers" view of causality. In effect, the covering law model saps causal power from the things of the world and relocates it in causal laws. The laws on this view are what has power.

Adopting the so-called *powers view*, CR says, in opposition to positivism, that there is more to reality than events. There are also things with their own causal powers. Cars, for example, have the causal power to transport people. Volcanos have the causal power to erupt. Water has the causal power to dissolve salt.

Once causality is detached from lawlike regularities, quantitative statistics lose their privileged methodological status. As all these causal powers can be mitigated or overcome by things with contrary causal powers, in the causally open world, no lawlike regularities are expected. Although non-lawlike regularities can be evidence of some causal power at work, it is the causal power and how it works rather than any kind of law that does the explaining.

Lastly, in contrast with positivism, CR is emergentist rather than reductionist in nature. As Bhaskar argued, if one thinks of causality in terms of inviolable laws relating events before inviolably to events after, then the motions of the most elementary particles composing everything else become determinative of the behavior of everything else.[6] Thus, in principle if not in practice, our human choices become determined by our brain chemistry, which is determined by molecular laws, which is determined ultimately by quantum phenomena. That is reductionism.

When we move from the covering law model of causality to a powers view, there are no inviolable laws at any level, just things exhibiting causal powers at different levels, always interacting and interfering with each other so that nothing is predetermined, with the action of higher-level powers enjoyed by human persons irreducible to lower-level powers. That view is called emergentism, and it is embraced by all critical realists.

So much for CR in general. As Finn was especially influenced by one critical realist in particular, however, a few words need be said about

---

6. Bhaskar, *Realist Theory of Science*.

her, that is, the late Margaret Archer, my dear friend and the one who connected me to the projects of the IACS and Finn. As a critical realist, Archer certainly embraced all the above premises of CR. Her major contribution has been threefold: affirming the broadest social ontology on offer (SAC); offering a general morphogenetic/morphostatic model that ties together how the different categories of social being relate; and championing a humanist conception of human actors.[7]

SAC is the acronym Archer coined to stand for structure, agency, and culture. Viewing them as separate categories comprises the broadest social ontology available. Anthony Giddens and later William Sewell famously redefined structure in cultural terms—as rules and schemas, effectively collapsing structure into culture, and, insofar as Giddens thought rules exists only in rule-following, ultimately into agency.[8] Following on such logic, the so-called cultural turn and practice theories likewise narrowed what constitutes the social: All is culture or all is practice. Against this ontological narrowing, Archer's SAC affirmed the distinctness of the three different categories, and she wrote extensively on each.

Another of the most important contributions of Archer is the morphogenetic/morphostatic (M/M) model.[9] I have always considered that model a reprise of Marx's dictum from the eighteenth Brumaire of Louis Napoleon that people make their own history but not under circumstances of their own making. In line with that Marxian understanding, the M/M model is historical. In it, both culture and structure figure as initial conditions in which actors find themselves. Having, in line with CR, causal powers of their own, culture and structure exert effects on actors. Not being lawlike, however, the causation exerted on actors is not deterministic. Actors have their own causal powers and can respond to the causal effects of their circumstances in creative and unpredictable ways. Thus, their actions may preserve the circumstantial status quo (morphostasis) or change them (morphogenesis).

Implicit in the M/M model is a humanist conception of human action. Historically, for Catholics and fellow humanists, a big problem with the positivist account of causality is that it implies a deterministic vision of the universe that precludes all free will and human moral responsibility. If all events are caused by inviolable causal laws connected to past

---

7. Archer, "Social Morphogenesis."

8. See, e.g., Giddens: *Central Problems in Social Theory*; and *Contemporary Critique of Historical Materialism*.

9. Archer, *Realist Social Theory*.

events, then so are human choices, which are events as well. Given the past events that cause them, none of us can choose other than we do. Even today, as a result of the still hegemonic covering law model of causality, most professional philosophers remain determinists.[10] Breaking away from the covering law model in favor of a powers view of causality frees the whole world, including human decision-making, from determinism. Among others as well, including me, Archer gave strong support to a humanist understanding of the human actor.[11]

DANIEL FINN'S WORK AS A CATHOLIC ECONOMIST

In this final section of my chapter, I want to examine Finn's affinity with CR before he knew about it and how it has affected his work afterward. To begin, we can identify two features right off that Finn has always shared with CR. First, as a Catholic, Finn believes that God exists independent of our belief or disbelief in that existence. Thus, consistent with Catholic doctrine, Finn has always been an ontological realist. That ontological realism likewise extends to social justice; it too exists or does not in a society regardless of what people think.

Social justice is a value-laden term. It is what is called a thick descriptor.[12] I have likewise referred to such descriptors—murder, rape, genocide—as moral facts.[13] That is, although value-laden categories, whether a case fits one of them is an empirical question. To answer that question, one may maintain an open mind, but the question itself remains value laden and so neither it nor the answer will be value neutral. As noted, with his abiding concern for market harm and social injustice, even before coming across CR, Finn rejected positivism's call for value-neutral social science.

We can see further prior affinities Finn shared with CR by examining work Finn authored just before encountering CR. In an article on method in the journal *Markets and Morality*, he replies to fellow Catholic Gregory Gronbacher, who argued for a "synthesis of free market thought with Catholic social thought." Against Gronbacher, Finn argues that

10. Bourget and Chalmers, "What Do Philosophers Believe?"
11. Archer, *Being Human*.
12. Appiah, *Experiments in Ethics*.
13. Porpora, *Reconstructing Sociology*.

free-market thought is incompatible with Catholic theology. Finn himself uses the word *positivism* as a target of critique and likewise as below uses the word *reductionism*, both targets of critique by CR.

> The point, however, is that theologians who extend their conversation into the discipline of economics ought not take for granted whatever reductionisms that particular mainstream economists have come to accept as the price for "good" science.[14]

Admittedly, what Finn criticizes as reductionist is not directly a commitment of economists to philosophical physicalism (i.e., the reduction of mind to brain, etc.), but to the economists' reduced concept of a person, often known as *homo economicus*. We see below what Finn has to say about it.

> In the Chicago and Public Choice Schools, individual actors appear as utility maximizers, a model that falls far short of any adequate sense of a personal identity, within which an individual's emotional and intellectual capacities and inclinations can help shape that person's behaviors and beliefs. It is hard to imagine how these two schools "can take subjectivity seriously on all levels." Let us be clear that the objection here is not simply theological dissatisfaction concerning the limitations necessitated within social science, even though Gronbacher makes this argument in defense of the free-market schools of economics. The history of criticism regarding narrow individualism and one dimensional maximization in mainstream economics is far too broad and deep to summarize here.[15]

There are two pertinent features to notice in the above excerpt. First, the attack on *homo economicus* shows Finn, consistent with Catholicism, supporting a fuller, more humanist conception of the actor. People are not just utility maximizers. Instead, they should, and many do, temper their own self-interest with calls to something morally greater. With morality and ultimately religion, Finn is again already before encountering CR implicitly incorporating along with agency or the A of CR's SAC, but also the C or cultural category as well.

But along with a humanist understanding of persons and an implicit incorporation of culture evident in the above extract, we see something else. We see in the last sentence that Finn wants to fight the fight against

---

14. Finn, "On the Choice of Method," 225.
15. Finn, "On the Choice of Method," 227.

reductionism not just by appeal to Catholic theology but on social science's own terrain. He is actively seeking secular, scientific grounds to oppose reductionism. And, although Finn already finds such sources, CR's humanism and Archer's particularly will come much more comprehensively to ground Finn's perspective.[16]

Most centrally, Finn criticizes the methodological individualism of mainstream economics. Methodological individualism is a perspective that sees no causality in the social sphere beyond what individual people think and do. That is, the focus is always on individuals, either alone or in concert. Emergent social constructs, like the market or social structures, are denied having any causal effects. It is this denial of the causal effects of the cultural and structural artifacts that humans produce that Finn criticizes.

> Nonetheless, even the Austrian School rejects a third element in Gronbacher's version of methodological individualism. This concerns his statement that "the person is a more substantial reality than any collective or group." Gronbacher clearly understands groups, nations, and other collections of persons to be real in a way that Friedrich Hayek, for example, has quite explicitly denied. Because Hayek considers only individuals to be real, he thinks the very notion of social justice is a charade, which is incompatible with the analysis of economic life provided in the personalism of John Paul II.[17]

What Finn is saying here is that although not being individual human actors, social structures like the market and inequality nevertheless have causal effects that cannot be ignored. If markets had no effects beyond the effects of individual people's actions, there would be no call to regulate them. And if Hayek, focusing only on individuals, considers social justice a charade, it is because he fails to recognize how economic inequality, for example, produces in myriad ways unequal life chances for those unequally positioned. Even though Finn does not here use the words, in his opposition to "unfettered 'free' markets," Finn sees that emergent forms created by individuals carry their own causal powers. With that recognition, Finn incorporates the final element of SAC, the S element, signifying structure.

On the other hand, still without the concept of causal powers attaching to things such as structures, Finn can come close but not fully to the CR position on the matter. "Markets themselves," Finn says, "do not

---

16. Archer: *Being Human*, as well as *Reflexive Imperative in Late Modernity*.
17. Finn, "On the Choice of Method," 228.

'do' anything in a literal sense.... Markets, by themselves, create situations for the realization of virtue or vice; they cannot directly cause such realities."[18] Situations or circumstances have long been a standard consideration in Christian ethics. Critical realists share that consideration but go on to add that structured situations are not always just neutral occasions for different actions. Structured situations often positively dispose actors to act in certain ways. As Adam Smith observes, "It is not from the benevolence of the butcher, the brewer or the baker, that we expect our dinner, but from their regard to their own interest."[19] In other words, the mutual threat that capitalists pose to each other is a structural situation that affects the interests of each capitalist, motivating each to behave in certain ways. Motivating behavior by affecting interests is a species of causation. Adopting CR will better enable Finn to make that point.

As mentioned, the first IACS volume Finn edited was *The True Wealth of Nations*. It continues an interest in the moral evaluation of market economies. Among a range of participants specializing in theology and/or economics, there were no sociologists or critical realists. While there is much talk of capitalism, there is little mention of structure or even of causality.

Four years later, the second volume appeared, titled *Distant Markets, Distant Harms: Economic Complicity and Christian Ethics*. This time, the colloquium convened to discuss this issue included several sociologists, among them, three of us CR sociologists: Margaret Archer, Pierpaolo Donati, and myself.

From the index alone, it is readily apparent that we critical realists had an impact. There, we find Bhaskar listed once with Archer, Donati and me listed many times beyond our own contributions, indicating influence on other contributors. We likewise now find multiple references to causality; competition; CR; and social structure.

And we find the influence of CR now clearly on Finn as in the following extract from the introduction.

> Mainstream economics has been notoriously individualist in its conception of economic life, and as a result, social structures of all kinds—whether firms, families, government, or markets—are undertheorized within economic science. Sociology is the discipline where there has been a consistent and careful analysis of social structures and their impact on people's lives. Thus,

18. Finn, "On the Choice of Method," 230.
19. Smith, *Wealth of Nations*, 26–27.

Christian economic ethics has much to gain from a conversation with sociological colleagues.[20]

The passage embodies the thesis of my entire chapter. CR, adopted from sociology, becomes the philosophical bridge through which Finn now comes to connect economics with Catholic moral thought. The adoption shows up especially in relation to social structure.

> Understanding social structures as relationships among preexisting social positions, Douglas Porpora cautions that simply putting more virtuous managers in place of CEOs will not make much difference, because the constraints and incentives implicit in the role of CEO will lead the next person to hold that position to make largely the same decisions.[21]

I am of course humbled to have Finn largely adopt my own conception of social structure or at least the conception of social structure that, against current trend, I have championed (for I hardly originated it). Finn then goes on to give one of the best renditions ever of the CR account of social structure—including my own.

> Sociologist Margaret Archer addresses the process by which the market, like all social structures, provides "structural conditioning." In critical realist sociology, only persons are agents, but structures have a causal impact on those agents, often unintended by the persons whose actions caused those structures to emerge in the first place. That causal impact occurs not by some "hydraulic pressure" but by shaping the situation in which people find themselves. Whether CEOs, elementary school teachers, or college students, the social position that an agent takes on influences what they do by means of the vested interests, opportunity costs, and "situational logics" of action.[22]

We see two important things in the above account. First, we see that adopting CR, Finn now can speak more effectively of the causal powers of market systems. But second, we see how, in the CR understanding, that causal power of a social structure does not vitiate a humanist conception of human agency.

Two years later, we see Finn applying his newfound perspective in a paper for *Theological Studies*. The keywords include "critical realism";

---

20. Finn, *Distant Markets*, xi.
21. Finn, *Distant Markets*, xii.
22. Finn, *Distant Markets*, xii.

"critical realist sociology"; "emergence"; and "sinful social structure." He begins with a quote from Pope Benedict XVI in *Caritas in Veritate*: "The Church's wisdom has always pointed to the presence of original sin in social conditions and in the structure of society."[23] As he does in much of his work, Finn then proceeds carefully to take us through Catholic social teaching to show an abiding concern with but also a lack of clarity about social sin and especially sinful structures.

> It is exceedingly difficult to present a rationally coherent explanation of social sin. Things are quite different with the idea of sinful social structures. Of course, structures are not conscious agents and thus don't sin. But the adjectival form "sinful" performs a helpful task, as does the word "evil" in phrases such as "an evil plan." And yet Catholic social thought has no coherent account of what a social structure is, presumably a prerequisite for considering what it means to apply the descriptor "sinful" to one. This article sets out to accomplish both these goals.[24]

Given this aim for this important article, Finn contributes to Catholic thought by applying the concept of structure that I and other critical realists have struggled to offer. As a fellow Catholic, I am honored to contribute even indirectly to that effort, but the point relative to this chapter is that with this piece Finn has become a critical realist himself, using it to connect better economics and Catholic social thought.

CONCLUSION

My final statement above contains the basic thesis of this chapter. My argument has been that Daniel Finn is less a convert to CR than, like myself, someone whose work was implicitly on board with it even before knowing about it. I remember how I first discovered CR. I had submitted an article to the journal I now co-edit, *Journal for the Theory of Social Behaviour*. It was a critique of the covering law model in sociology, and the editors of the journal liked it so much as to devote an entire issue to it with replies from sociology's major proponents of the model. As I waited for these replies to arrive, the editors suggested I read some of the seminal texts of CR.[25] I concluded that I was a critical realist and replied to the replies as

---

23. Finn, "What Is a Sinful Social Structure?," 136, quoting Benedict XVI, *Caritas in Veritate*, no. 34.

24. Finn, "What Is a Sinful Social Structure?," 138.

25. Bhaskar, *Realist Theory of Science*; and Harré and Madden, *Causal Powers*.

such. I imagine Finn having a kindred experience. In any case, as I hope to have shown in this chapter, CR better articulates for Finn the connection his work has always tried to draw between economic conditions and Catholic social thought. I am grateful for his effort toward that end.

BIBLIOGRAPHY

Appiah, Kwame Anthony. *Experiments in Ethics*. Cambridge, MA: Harvard University Press, 2010.
Archer, Margaret S. *Being Human: The Problem of Agency*. Cambridge: Cambridge University Press, 2000.
———. *Realist Social Theory: The Morphogenetic Approach*. Cambridge: Cambridge University Press, 1995.
———. *The Reflexive Imperative in Late Modernity*. Cambridge: Cambridge University Press, 2012.
———. "Social Morphogenesis and the Prospects of Morphogenic Society." In *Social Morphogenesis*, edited by Margaret S. Archer, 1–22. Dordrecht: Springer, 2013.
Benedict XVI. *Caritas in Veritate*. Vatican, June 29, 2009. https://www.vatican.va/content/benedict-xvi/en/encyclicals/documents/hf_ben-xvi_enc_20090629_caritas-in-veritate.html.
Bhaskar, Roy. *The Possibility of Naturalism: A Philosophical Critique of the Contemporary Human Sciences*. New York: Routledge, 2014.
———. *A Realist Theory of Science*. New York: Routledge, 2013.
Bourget, David, and David J. Chalmers. "What Do Philosophers Believe?" *Philosophical Studies* 170 (2014) 465–500.
Finn, Daniel K., ed. *Distant Markets, Distant Harms: Economic Complicity and Christian Ethics*. Oxford: Oxford University Press, 2014.
———. "On the Choice of Method in Economics: Options for Humanists." *Journal of Markets and Morality* 3 (2000) 224–38.
———, ed. *The True Wealth of Nations: Catholic Social Thought and Economic Life*. Oxford: Oxford University Press, 2010.
———. "What Is a Sinful Social Structure?" *Theological Studies* 77 (2016) 136–64.
Harré, Rom, and Edward H. Madden. *Causal Powers: A Theory of Natural Necessity*. Malden, MA: Blackwell, 1975.
Giddens, Anthony. *Central Problems in Social Theory: Action, Structure, and Contradiction in Social Analysis*. Berkeley: University of California Press, 1979.
———. *A Contemporary Critique of Historical Materialism*. Berkeley: University of California Press, 1981.
Kuhn, Thomas S. *The Structure of Scientific Revolutions*. Chicago: University of Chicago Press, 1997.
Porpora, Douglas V. *Reconstructing Sociology: The Critical Realist Approach*. Cambridge: Cambridge University Press, 2015.
Smith, Adam. *An Inquiry into the Nature and Causes of the Wealth of Nations*. Vol. 2 of *The Glasgow Edition of the Works and Correspondence of Adam Smith*. Edited by R. H. Campbell and Andrew S. Skinner. Indianapolis: Liberty Classics, 1979. First published 1776.

Emergents and the Problem of Collective Economic Responsibility

Albino Barrera, OP

Dan Finn brought sociology and critical realism into conversation with theology and economics to account for sinful social structures.[1] He strengthened Christian social thought's long-standing teachings on sinful social structures by showing how they develop and evolve using conceptual tools and language drawn from the social sciences, such as the notion of "emergents," that is, newly formed substances or phenomena that are real and not merely conceptual. This is an important contribution to the field.

In this chapter, I propose that the usefulness of the notion of emergents goes beyond sinful social structures. This insight from sociology and critical realism can also be used to deal with the problem of collective economic responsibility. Many social philosophers are skeptical about the conceptual coherence of what we call "collective responsibility." They claim that the latter is nothing more than an aggregation of individual responsibilities. I submit that the notion of emergents provides us with a conceptual tool to convince skeptics that there is such a thing as collective economic responsibility.

NEED FOR COLLECTIVE ECONOMIC RESPONSIBILITY

The debate among social philosophers on the social coherence of collective responsibility cannot be ignored, especially not in the economic

---

1. Finn: *Moral Agency*; "What Is a Sinful Social Structure?"

realm because of the phenomenon of socialization. Recall that as early as *Mater et Magistra* in 1961, John XXIII had already observed that individuals were increasingly no longer able to do what they used to accomplish by themselves. Society had gotten to be so complex that ever-larger circles of people need to collaborate to accomplish what individuals used to single-handedly achieve on their own.

US economist John Maurice Clark saw the same phenomenon even earlier at the turn of the twentieth century when he noted the changing basis of economic responsibility in response to the transformation of American business at that time.[2] Building on Clark's insight a century later, Michaela Haase described this shift as a move away from what she calls the classical personal model of responsibility to the modern model of collective responsibility.[3]

Consider the contrast between these two models of responsibility. The classical model of responsibility is based on metaphysical assumptions involving intentionality and causality. Its concern is to establish responsibility for harms based on the axiom that "whoever causes it is responsible for it." It is retrospective, that is, backward looking in tracking down who is responsible for the damage. It is deemed to be the older version of ethics as imputation.[4] Thus, this model of responsibility has also been called the "liability model."[5] This is a responsibility that deals mostly with face-to-face relationships.

In contrast, the modern model of responsibility's scope extends well beyond face-to-face relationships to include the larger community/society that may not be within the person's immediate circle. There is a palpable shift in focus, to wit: the creation of social value and the prevention of harm compared to the liability model's interest in establishing blameworthiness and liability for incurred harms (referred to as the classical model). Thus, it can be said to be prospective rather than retrospective, that is, forward looking rather than backward looking. The goal is to bring about the desired state of affairs.

The shift from the classical model of responsibility to the modern model of responsibility was a result of increased complexity of socioeconomic life. Causality has become much more complex because of tighter

2. Clark, "Changing Basis."
3. Haase, "Economic Responsibility Revisited," 218–20.
4. Haase, "Marketing Theory," 131; Paulson, "Hans Kelsen's Doctrine"; Eshleman, "Moral Responsibility."
5. Young, *Responsibility for Justice*.

and more complicated interdependency. This in turn leads to many more externalities which also turn out to be far more consequential. We are no longer dealing with simple linear causality or face-to-face transactions but with a web of interrelationships.

Creating social value for the community or preventing harm in such a complex socioeconomic terrain is properly the task of groups rather than individuals working singly or independently of each other. It is the phenomenon of socialization. Thus, the shift from the personal model of economic responsibility to the modern model of responsibility brings the need for a clear conception of collective economic responsibility front and center. Creating social value for the community and preventing harm become the overarching responsibility of the community. This is the modern model of collective economic responsibility.

In sum, we have a shift from the classical model of responsibility (causality and liability; ascription of praise or blame) to a modern model of responsibility (creation of social value; bringing about desired state of affairs). We have an increasing reliance on collective responsibility and not merely on disparate or aggregated personal responsibilities. We witness this shift in practice. Note how extra-market interventions are largely collective endeavors. Social safety nets, such as unemployment insurance, social security, food stamps, etc., are government efforts. Moreover, the public expects such government interventions. In the EU social democratic form of capitalism, the people willingly pay the necessary taxes for such national safety nets. Civil society, in general, also makes up for market failures through nongovernmental organizations (NGOs), social enterprises, corporate social responsibility, socially responsible investing, advocacy groups, and numerous grassroots initiatives. These are all examples of the community or parts thereof acknowledging that (1) there is something awry in the marketplace that needs to be corrected, and (2) that we as a community can and should do something to rectify or mitigate such ills.

HURDLES TO COLLECTIVE ECONOMIC RESPONSIBILITY

Despite the centrality of collective economic responsibility in the modern economy, there are at least two conceptual hurdles that must be overcome:

- Is there such a thing as collective economic responsibility?
- If so, is it merely a matter of social or legal convention or is there a real basis for such collective responsibility?

We examine each of these in what follows.

Philosophical Problem: Collective Responsibility as a Coherent Conceptual Construct

Does it make sense to talk of collective responsibility? Is there even such a phenomenon as collective responsibility? Is the notion of collective responsibility a coherent conceptual construct? These questions are central for socioeconomic life because it is collaborative by nature, especially in the modern era. Specialization and division of labor, accumulative harms and benefits, bounded rationality, and network effects are key market characteristics that give rise to economic responsibilities. These market characteristics are collective in nature, both in how they arise and in their resulting requirements. Thus, we must find a solution to social philosophers' disagreements on the conceptual coherence of collective responsibility.

Collective responsibility can be understood in two senses, namely, as an aggregative or as a conglomerative phenomenon. Aggregative collective responsibility is merely the sum of the individual responsibilities of the group's membership. Such collectivity merely refers to a "collection of people."[6] There is not much disagreement among philosophers on aggregative groups or aggregative responsibilities.

In contrast, conglomerative collective responsibility refers to the responsibility of the entire group separate from the individual moral responsibility of the members that comprise it. In other words, the conglomerate takes an identity of its own, one that is distinct from that of its membership. Conglomerative collective responsibility is a whole much greater than the sum of the individual responsibilities of its membership. One could thus describe it as a synergy. A conglomerative collectivity has been described as an "organization of individuals such that its identity is not exhausted by the conjunction of the identities of the persons in the organization."[7] The debate among philosophers revolves around

---

6. French, *Collective and Corporate Responsibility*, 5.
7. French, *Collective and Corporate Responsibility*, 13.

the coherence of conglomerative collective responsibility as a conceptual construct and as a real existent.

The debate centers on the question of group morality. Can a group be treated as a distinct moral agent on its own separate from the moral agency of its constituent members? Can a group take a moral identity of its own?

The main argument against collective responsibility as an existent is that a group is not a moral agent; only individuals can be moral agents. After all, moral agency rests on the dual faculties of reason and will. Does a group have these? Can a group have these?

There is an important distinction between behavior and moral action.[8] Collective behavior is the outcome of group activity without any group intention. For example, people go shopping on the Friday following Thanksgiving Day, and retail stores tout their deep discounts. This has become a modern ritual for a sizable segment of the US population. Together, the collective behavior of these shoppers and retailers makes for what has come to be known as Black Friday. In contrast, collective (moral) action is the outcome of a group intention as drawn from its desires or beliefs. To be more than just a mere group behavior, group moral action must be the result of a group intention. But what does a group intention mean? How does that come about? And even if we were to assume, for the sake of argument, that there is such a thing as a group intention, such a group intention presupposes a shared will and a shared mind.

Critics of collective responsibility hold that only individuals, not groups, have moral agency,[9] and therefore only individuals, not groups, can have and pursue an intention.[10] It follows that only individuals can bear moral responsibility.[11] References to group mind or group intention are properly viewed merely as derivative constructs or analogous terms because they are derived from the individual mind and intention.[12]

---

8. Corlett, "Collective Moral Responsibility," 575.

9. For example, see Lewis, "Collective Responsibility"; Watkins, "Methodological Individualism"; Sverdlik, "Collective Responsibility"; Corlett, "Collective Moral Responsibility"; and Narveson, "Collective Responsibility."

10. Other arguments against conglomerative responsibility include the problem of blaming an individual for the action of others. Why should I be responsible for the actions of others (Lewis, "Collective Responsibility"; Duff, "Responsibility," 8:293)? Moreover, collective responsibility would mean that members of that group can be blamed and be held liable for harms they did not directly cause or intentionally cause (Sverdlik, "Collective Responsibility," 68).

11. Narveson, "Collective Responsibility," 179.

12. Sosa, "What Is It Like to Be a Group?," 215.

In the absence of a mind and a will, a group cannot be the bearer of moral responsibility, and consequently, it cannot be praised or blamed for a moral action. A group cannot be treated as a moral subject of a moral action.[13] Thus, for critics, it is unclear what it means to hold the group accountable since the group is not a moral agent per se.

Proponents of collective responsibility present varied arguments in support of their contention that groups can be proper bearers of moral responsibility. Some argue that group intention is a coherent moral construct. "Plural subjects" are a common occurrence in life. A "plural subject" emerges whenever people band together with "joint commitments" to pursue a specific course of action with a particular aim in mind. Such a group is not a mere random crowd. These are people who voluntarily bind themselves to one another in a common cause. In this case, there is a group intention as evidenced by their joint commitments. Thus, we do not have a mere individual as a subject, but we have a "plural subject" comprised of those who have committed themselves to a particular course of action in pursuit of a shared aim.[14] An example of a "plural subject" is the thirteen colonies that bound themselves to one another in a joint commitment to pursue a clearly defined aim (Declaration of Independence) and to follow through with joint action (the American Revolution).[15]

Regarding group action, some argue for two conditions that make for collective rather than individual action.[16] First, the actors are related to one another, and such a relationship leads them to act in a manner they would not or could not have acted as individuals. Second, there is a representative who can claim to speak or act for the group. This includes actions by the person who claims to have the authority to represent the group through such action. Clearly, both conditions are readily met in many instances in economic life. Note, for example, partnerships, limited

---

13. See Weber's discussion of methodological individualism in his *Economy and Society*, vol. 1.

14. Gilbert: *On Social Facts*; and "Who's to Blame?"; Bratman: "Shared Cooperative Activity"; "Shared Intention"; and "Dynamics of Sociality"; Velleman, "How to Share an Intention."

15. Tuomela makes the same point on joint commitments ("we-intentions") leading to joint action, but instead of calling this a plural subject, he calls it a representative subject. The collective intention and action supervene constituent individual actions or intentions comprising the group ("Actions by Collectives"; "We-Intentioned Revisited"; and "Joint Intention"). This approach of a representative subject has been likened by some to Hobbes's *Leviathan*—a collective subject. See Smiley, "Collective Responsibility."

16. May: *Morality of Groups*, 55; "State Aggression."

liability corporations, and social enterprises. This is not even to mention political entities, such as nations.

Proponents of collective responsibility caution that not all groups can be viewed as moral agents in their own right and therefore considered proper bearers of moral responsibility. They identify certain conditions that must be satisfied for a group to be deemed capable of intending and acting as a group, as a conglomerative collectivity. For example, they must have a well-organized and functioning structure and procedures for decision-making and action. There must be a clearly identified group that is capable of making self-conscious deliberations and decisions (e.g., a board). There is a well-established mechanism for pursuing action on behalf of the group or for implementing the governing body's decision. There are standards of conduct to which members are held to account. There must be a structure that specifies lines of authority and accountability within the group.[17]

Practical Problem: Impact on the Study of Economic Responsibility

How does the philosophical debate on the notion of collective responsibility affect our study of economic responsibility? What are its implications for our theological understanding of economic responsibility? To begin with, our shared economic life is neither merely an aggregative nor a conglomerative collectivity. Our common economic life is not merely an aggregation of people pursuing varied economic activities and conducting a wide variety of transactions in the marketplace. Market activity is indeed spontaneous in the way it has arisen and evolved. Nevertheless, economic life, especially market exchange, is an iterated process. It is not merely a one-time or a sudden or a random gathering of economic agents. Moreover, it has structures and underlying institutions that took a long time to build and that are constantly reinforced or developed further through the community's customs, law, and usage. It is governed by formal and informal rules of thumb that govern people's expectations and transactions in the public square (bounded rationality). Indeed, common economic life is not merely a random, ad hoc collection of individuals.

At the same time, our common economic life is not a conglomerative collectivity either because it is not a moral agent on its own. Take the

---

17. French, *Collective and Corporate Responsibility*, 13–14.

case of intentionality. Despite their common goal of satisfying their basic needs, market participants cannot be said to intend and pursue in unison the market's resulting processes and outcomes. The butcher, baker, and brewer did not collectively intend to ensure a stable supply of provisions for the entire community. They were each bent on pursuing their own economic interest. There are at least two minimum conditions that must be satisfied to warrant blaming a conglomerative collectivity, namely: there must be a bad intention, and such intention must be shared. Neither of these applies to the marketplace and its participants.

In talking of market harms, there is usually no deliberate intention. Consumers who buy cheaper imports do not do so with the intention of getting domestic manufacturing workers laid off. Rather, they are bent on saving money and stretching their household budget. Using the earlier distinction on behavior versus action, people's market activities are more accurately described as collective behavior, rather than as a collective moral action. And without such joint moral action, the community cannot be said to be a moral agent, at least not when it comes to market activity or economic life. How then should we treat collective responsibility? Are skeptics correct then in saying that it is merely the aggregation of individual responsibilities? Are we stuck with methodological individualism?

EMERGENTS AS A CONCEPTUAL SOLUTION

Aristotelean-Thomistic metaphysics can be used to argue for conglomerative responsibility. Aristotle claims that relations are not substances. However, Thomas Aquinas disagrees and provides the blessed Trinity as an example of a substantive relationality.[18] As a result, we have three persons in one God. Unfortunately, we cannot use this for human beings because God is pure act. It would be a very steep metaphysical hill to climb to argue in an analogical fashion how we also have substantive relationality for human beings. As a result, it would be extremely difficult to have conglomerated responsibility.

Herewith is where we can insert Finn's point on the use of sociology's critical realism in both theology and economics.[19] For the purpose of our chapter, critical realism's notion of emergents gives us a new way of looking at social structures, such as the marketplace. To begin with, a

---

18. Connor, "Relational Esse."
19. Finn, "What Is a Sinful Social Structure?," 147–54.

"transfactual" is a thing that is not perceptible to our senses but is nonetheless real, as in the case of gravity.[20] "The real includes not only everything that happens (all events, whether perceived or not) but also the causal forces—the powers or 'mechanisms' that bring about those events, including the relation between that Amazonian tree and the earth, a relation that generates the force of gravity that brings the tree down."[21] Applying such transfactuals to this chapter, we can say that the marketplace, often called the invisible hand, and its tight web of interdependencies and relations, while not perceptible by our senses, is nonetheless real.

Building further on the notion of transfactuals, Finn then underscores critical realism's notion of an emergent reality whereby "two or more 'lower level' elements combine to form a 'higher level' element that has different characteristics."[22] He cites water, formed out of hydrogen and oxygen, as an example. Water has completely distinct characteristics than either hydrogen or oxygen. It is the same phenomenon for social structures. Once again, take the invisible hand as an example. The marketplace is much touted for its ability to bring about allocative efficiency because of its price system that conveys timely information simultaneously across a multitude of people. The butcher, baker, and brewer do not exhibit any of these features.

Applying Finn's exposition of emergents and transfactuals on social structures, we are no longer stuck with having to choose either aggregative collectivity and its methodological individualism or a conglomerative collectivity. Collectives as transfactual emergents serve as the middle ground between aggregative and conglomerative collectivity. In other words, the marketplace is not merely an aggregation of market participants. It is a real entity, a social structure, formed out of the relations and interactions of its constituent participants.

Since our shared economic life is not a conglomerative collectivity, we cannot ascribe a collective moral agency to market participants as a group. Nevertheless, we can hold the community, as an emergent, to be jointly and morally responsible for the harmful processes and ill effects of its shared economic activities. In other words, even while it is not a moral agent in its own right as a conglomerative collectivity or a substantive relationality having a single will, the community as an emergent can nevertheless still be held praiseworthy or blameworthy for its acts of

---

20. Finn, "What Is a Sinful Social Structure?," 148–49.
21. Finn, "What Is a Sinful Social Structure?," 149.
22. Finn, "What Is a Sinful Social Structure?," 149.

commission or omission in economic life. It is a real entity. The notion of emergents as a conceptual tool allows us to make the following claims regarding collective responsibility that would not have been possible had we been limited to using only aggregative collectivity.

First, we can have group blameworthiness or praiseworthiness even in the absence of a proper collective moral agency because market participants possess the capacity for joint action. And it is a capacity that has been proven time and time again to be effective. Market exchange and collaborative economic life often arise spontaneously. Nevertheless, even with such spontaneity, aggregative collectivities can still be held to account for the harms they cause, whether directly or indirectly. Virginia Held notes that a "random collection of individuals" can still be held to account as a group because they can form themselves into an organized group and prevent harm.[23] This position is validated by empirical evidence.[24]

Held's argument applies even more so to markets because the market is more than just a random collection of individuals. It is undergirded, indeed, enabled by extra-market institutions. These enabling institutions are human creations. And while many of these are long-standing creations that took time to build and put in place (e.g., customs, law, usage), these are nevertheless subject to change and further development. Economic history is replete with many examples of the community's ability to modify institutions in an effort to mitigate or prevent economic harm. Nineteenth-century social legislation in response to the ill effects of the Industrial Revolution and contemporary grassroots clamor for safeguards in the wake of globalization illustrate the potency of aggregative collective response and action to economic harms. In other words, just because the community is not a moral agent on its own as a conglomerate collectivity or substantive relationality does not preclude it from being praised or blamed for its response or lack of response vis-à-vis problematic economic outcomes. It deserves praise or blame as an emergent that is capable of acting cohesively.

The case for treating market participants *jointly* as an emergent (the marketplace or the invisible hand) is strengthened even further by their obligation to organize themselves and jointly mitigate economic harm. This obligation becomes even more imperative because of their existing interpersonal relationships. Since market participants are already

---

23. Held, "Can a Random Collection?," 479.

24. See, for example, the works of 2009 Nobel laureate in Economics Elinor Ostrom, who has shown how groups do take action to avoid the tragedy of the commons.

engaged in cooperative specialization and the division of labor and are reaping enormous benefits from these, they can in a similar fashion also collaborate with one another in addressing market ills. Ties, bonds, and social infrastructure are already in place for them to use. All that is needed is a joint commitment and joint action. The marketplace as an emergent facilitates this. If they can work together to reap benefits, so can they in working jointly to address the unintended injuries (disexternalities) that arise from their pursuit of their joint benefits. Indeed, Virginia Held's argument holds even more for economic life.

A second contribution of emergents as a conceptual tool is that it helps us deal with the intertwining of individual and collective responsibility. The marketplace is a venue through which individuals pursue their economic activities jointly. This is particularly true in modern life in which there is greater interdependence whereby specialization and division of labor are the norms. Thus, the collective can indeed *enable* "individual blameworthy agents to perform harmful acts."[25] Such "harmful acts" include injurious market processes and outcomes that people leave unaddressed (acts of omission). The marketplace not only enables but sometimes even provides incentives for such harm-producing acts through its price mechanism or its (market) ethos. (Take the case of the market's underpricing of fossil fuels because it fails to consider the social cost that such fuels impose on ecology.)

Harms that are clearly known and are recurring become the object of economic responsibility both at the individual and collective level. Minimizing our modern lifestyle's carbon footprint is a simple example. The marketplace is amoral, that is, it does not launder consumer preferences, nor does it check the propriety of the exchanges that it facilitates. The marketplace consummates transactions for as long as there is consent on the part of both buyer and seller, and the buyer has the purchasing power to conduct the trade. The market does not even second guess whether such consent is flawed and whether the terms of exchange are fair. The market is simply not designed to do these tasks. Hence, through their participation in the marketplace, economic agents can be unwittingly party to wrongdoing or indirectly promote harm-producing economic activities. In these

---

25. Shockley, "Programming Collective Control," 442. For example, killing a neighbor may not merely be an act of murder, depending on its context. Such an act takes a completely different moral character if it occurs as part of a genocide, as in the case of Rwanda. The collective clearly enables and abets such an act. In economic life, an example of the collective enabling individual harmful activity is the rush to carve out farmland in the Amazonian rainforest or in the Indonesian hardwood forests.

examples, economic responsibility requires market participants to organize themselves in changing the formal and informal rules of the marketplace to restrict or even ban such injurious economic activities. Recall Virginia Held's earlier point. In other words, individuals cannot be held solely responsible for market ills because the marketplace, as an emergent, enables its participants to act in such a fashion. Individual responsibility is intertwined with collective responsibility. Recognizing the market as an emergent allows us to know exactly the obligor of that collective responsibility.

Third, individuals can be held to account because of the accumulative dynamic of the marketplace. The collective produces benefits or harms that its individual members could not have produced on their own.[26] Such an accumulative dynamic partly stems from specialization and the division of labor in economic life. Specialization and division of labor have demonstrated the potency of the collective in greatly multiplying an individual's economic impact on the rest of the community. Recall Adam Smith's invisible hand and the joint effect of the baker, brewer, and butcher's work. One could think of the invisible hand of the market as providing a multiplier effect to individual action, courtesy of the accumulative dynamic and division of labor of contemporary economic life. Steve Jobs would not have left such a legacy to the digital world had it not been for the army of innovators, designers, engineers, and many others in the electronics industry on whose shoulders he stood. Facebook, Google, and other major e-firms arose from the wide assortment of platforms and tools that had in turn emerged from the Internet. In fact, the Internet itself is an example of an accumulative benefit—the Internet as a whole is much greater than the sum of the individual technological and organizational innovations from which it was built.

Unfortunately, the same dynamic also produces market ills. The harmful impact of individual pornographers and pimps would not have been as severe as it is today had it not been for the infrastructure conveniently and unwittingly provided by the Internet-empowered marketplace. A globalized and a far more efficient marketplace has created a great demand for fish. Atlantic bluefin tuna caught in the Mediterranean find their way to the fish markets of Tokyo within a few hours. Similarly, other big fish species are traded halfway across the globe from where they are harvested. This more efficient and globalized trading in marine life has resulted in the decimation of fish stocks and coral resources. These are some

26. Smiley, "Collective Responsibility."

examples of accumulative harms. The actions of a single ocean-going fishing ship may not be harmful on its own, but it becomes devastating in its impact when replicated by hundreds or even thousands of like ships. Since market participants sustain and reinforce market processes, they can be held to account, as a group and as individuals, for the injurious effects of such accumulative harms. In sum, the notion of emergents allows us to make the claim that market participants can still be held accountable as a group, as an emergent, despite not being a conglomerate collectivity or a substantive relationality with a will of their own.

CONCLUSION

Daniel Finn has served both theology and economics well in bringing them into conversation with sociology. He recognized how critical realism's notion of emergents can be used to good effect in understanding the nature and dynamics of sinful social structures.

In this chapter, I argued that we could also use the notion of emergents in finding a solution to the long-standing debate among social philosophers on whether there is such a thing as collective responsibility. In the same way that critical realism's emergent challenges methodological individualism, we can also critique the claim that collective responsibility is nothing but aggregated individual responsibilities. Collective economic responsibility is not reducible only to the individual responsibility of market participants. Market participants, as a collective, can bear responsibilities and be praised or blamed not only individually but also collectively. This means that the invisible hand, that is, the market cannot be completely hands off when it comes to the processes and outcomes that it generates. Emergents show why individuating economic responsibility is not good enough because emergents themselves change the socioeconomic terrain. These changes are not merely an aggregation of individual contributions. As a real entity with powers and capabilities distinct from those of its market participants, the invisible hand is an emergent and consequently bears moral obligations for its resulting processes and outcomes.

BIBLIOGRAPHY

Bratman, Michael. "Dynamics of Sociality." *Midwest Studies in Philosophy* 30 (2006) 1–15.

———. "Shared Cooperative Activity." *Philosophical Review* 101 (1992) 327–42.
———. "Shared Intention." *Ethics* 104 (1993) 97–103.
Clark, John Maurice. "The Changing Basis of Economic Responsibility." *Journal of Political Economy* 24 (1916) 209–29.
Connor, Robert A. "Relational Esse and the Person." *Proceedings of the American Catholic Philosophical Association* 65 (1991) 253–67.
Corlett, J. Angelo. "Collective Moral Responsibility." *Journal of Social Philosophy* 32 (2001) 573–84.
Duff, R. A. "Responsibility." In *Routledge Encyclopedia of Philosophy*, edited by Edward Craig, 8:290–94. New York: Routledge, 1998.
Eshleman, Andrew. "Moral Responsibility." Stanford Encyclopedia of Philosophy, Jan. 6, 2001; revised Mar. 26, 2014. Edited by Edward N. Zalta. Fall 2019 ed. https://plato.stanford.edu/archives/fall2019/entries/moral-responsibility/.
Finn, Daniel, ed. *Moral Agency Within Social Structures and Culture: A Primer on Critical Realism for Christian Ethics*. Washington, DC: Georgetown University Press, 2020.
———. "What Is a Sinful Social Structure?" *Theological Studies* 77 (2016) 136–64.
French, Peter. *Collective and Corporate Responsibility*. New York: Columbia University Press, 1984.
———. *The Spectrum of Responsibility*. New York: St. Martin's, 1992.
Gilbert, Margaret. *On Social Facts*. New York: Routledge, 1989.
———. *Sociality and Responsibility: New Essays in Plural Subject Theory*. Lanham, MD: Rowman and Littlefield, 2000.
———. "Who's to Blame? Collective Moral Responsibility and Its Implications for Group Members." *Midwest Studies in Philosophy* 30 (2006) 94–114.
Haase, Michaela. "Economic Responsibility Revisited." In *Economic Responsibility: John Maurice Clark—a Classic on Economic Responsibility*, edited by Michaela Haase, 205–31. Ethical Economy, Studies in Economic Ethics and Philosophy 53. Cham, Switz.: Springer, 2017.
———. "John Maurice Clark's Approach to Economic Responsibility: A Reconstruction Based on the Classical Model of Responsibility." *Management Revue* 284 (2017) 461–86.
———. "Marketing Theory and the Concept of Responsibility: A Story of Three Interpretations." In *Handbook on Ethics and Marketing*, edited by Alexander Nill, 125–49. Cheltenham: Edward Elgar, 2015.
Held, Virginia. "Can a Random Collection of Individuals Be Responsible?" *Journal of Philosophy* 67 (1970) 471–81.
John XXIII. *Mater et Magistra*. Vatican, May 15, 1961. https://www.vatican.va/content/john-xxiii/en/encyclicals/documents/hf_j-xxiii_enc_15051961_mater.html.
Lewis, H. D. "Collective Responsibility." *Philosophy* 24 (1948) 3–18.
May, Larry. *The Morality of Groups*. Notre Dame, IN: University of Notre Dame Press, 1987.
———. "State Aggression, Collective Liability, and Individual Mens Rea." *Midwest Studies in Philosophy* 30 (2006) 309–24.
Narveson, Jan. "Collective Responsibility." *Journal of Ethics* 6 (2002) 179–98.
Paulson, S. L. "Hans Kelsen's Doctrine of Imputation." *Ratio Juris* 14 (2001) 47–63.
Shockley, Kenneth. "Programming Collective Control." *Journal of Social Philosophy* 36 (2007) 442–45.

Smiley, Marion. "Collective Responsibility." *Stanford Encyclopedia of Philosophy*, Aug. 8, 2005. Edited by Edward N. Zalta and Uri Nodelman. Fall 2010 ed. http://plato.stanford.edu/entries/collective-responsibility/.

———. "From Moral Agency to Collective Wrongs: Re-Thinking Collective Moral Responsibility." *Journal of Law and Policy* 19 (2010) 171–202.

Sosa, David. "What Is It Like to Be a Group?" *Social Philosophy and Policy* 26 (2009) 212–26.

Sverdlik, Stephen. "Collective Responsibility." *Philosophical Studies* 51 (1987) 61–76.

Tuomela, Raimo. "Actions by Collectives." *Philosophical Perspectives* 3 (1989) 471–96

———. "Joint Intention, We-Mode and I-Mode." *Midwest Studies in Philosophy* 30 (2006) 35–58.

———. "We-Intentions Revisited." *Philosophical Studies* 125 (2005) 327–69.

Velleman, J. D. "How to Share an Intention." *Philosophy and Phenomenological Research* 57 (1997) 29–50.

Watkins, J. W. N. "Methodological Individualism and Social Tendencies." *British Journal for the Philosophy of Science* 8 (1957) 104–17.

Weber, Karl, ed. *Food Inc.: A Participant Guide: How Industrial Food Is Making Us Sicker, Fatter, and Poorer—and What You Can Do About It*. New York: Public Affairs, 2009.

Weber, Max. *Economy and Society*. Vol. 1. Berkeley: University of California Press, 1978.

Wesley, John. "The Use of Money." Resource UMC, 1872. Edited by Thomas Jackson. Sermon 50. https://www.resourceumc.org/en/content/sermon-50-the-use-of-money.

Westerman, Claus. *Genesis 1–11*. Translated by John Scullion. Minneapolis: Augsburg, 1984.

Whalen, Jeanne. "Doctors Object to High Cancer-Drug Prices." *Wall Street Journal*, July 23, 2015.

Whiteman, Hilary. "Surrogate Mom Vows to Take Care of Ill Twin 'Abandoned' by Parents." CNN, Aug. 7, 2014. http://www.cnn.com/2014/08/04/world/asia/thailand-australia-surrogacy/.

Williams, C. "Obligation, Moral." *New Catholic Encyclopedia*, 2003. https://www.encyclopedia.com/religion/encyclopedias-almanacs-transcripts-and-maps/obligation-moral.

Williams, Oliver. "Can Business Ethics Be Theological? What Athens Can Learn from Jerusalem." *Journal of Business Ethics* 5 (1986) 473–84.

Worland, Stephen. Review of *The Legacy of Scholasticism in Economic Thought: Antecedents of Choice and Power*, by Odd Langholm. *Research in the History of Economic Thought and Methodology* 18A (2000) 285–92.

World Bank. *World Development Report 2015: Mind, Society, and Behavior*. Washington, DC: World Bank, 2015.

Wright, John. *The Order of the Universe in the Theology of St. Thomas Aquinas*. Analecta Gregoriana 89. Rome: Apud Aedes Universitatis Gregorianae, 1957.

Yergin, Daniel, and Joseph Stanislaw. *The Commanding Heights: The Battle Between Government and the Marketplace That Is Remaking the Modern World*. New York: Simon & Schuster, 2002.

Young, Iris Marion. *Responsibility for Justice*. New York: Oxford University Press, 2011.

Xu, Z. Y., et al. "Smoking, Air Pollution, and the High Rates of Lung Cancer in Shenyang, China." *Journal of the National Cancer Institute* 23 (1989) 1800–6.

Collective Action and Agency in Christian Ethics

Daniel J. Daly

On January 6, 2021, a group of President Donald Trump's supporters stormed the US Capitol Building to stop the certification of the 2020 election of President Joseph Biden. The insurrectionists smashed windows, raided the offices of representatives, threatened to kill elected officials, caused $2.7 million of losses, assaulted 140 officers, and caused the death of an officer.[1]

On November 23, 2023, a mob rioted in the heart of Dublin, Ireland. The anti-immigrant rioters responded to a knife attack on a woman and her children. Xenophobic rumors spread on the Internet after the attack, leading to the riot.[2]

These events raise questions of collective action and agency. To whom can and should we ascribe these events? To an organized group of Trump supporters or to individuals? To an anti-immigrant coalition or an Irish mob? Theological ethicists have recently become interested in such questions of collective agency. James Keenan has rightly noted that collective agency is "more presumed than examined."[3]

This chapter engages this emerging discourse by turning, in part, to the work of Daniel K. Finn. Finn's use of critical realist social theory

---

1. Select Committee, *Final Report*.
2. Specia, "Ireland's Riot Was Not a Surprise."
3. Keenan, "Recognizing Collectives," 102. Keenan contends that the church as a collective "is more presumed than examined." This is also true of other claims of collective agency and action, such as hospitals, universities, political parties, etc.

provides an explanatory framework for claiming that an action is committed by a collective or, more specifically, by an organization. This chapter is delimited to Finn's work on structures post-2012, which marked his adoption of critical realist social theory. It focuses exclusively on this part of Finn's work because it will likely be one of his most lasting contributions to the field.

In order to understand what a collective is, we will need an account of social structure. Finn's work provides the most lucid account of a social structure in theological ethics. Structures, and collectives as a kind of structure, are typically undertheorized in Christian ethics.[4] As Finn rather bluntly put it in 2016, "Catholic social thought has no coherent account of what a social structure is."[5]

This chapter has two goals. First, it delineates where Finn's work on social structures has innovated and influenced contemporary theological ethics. Second, it mines Finn's work to develop an account of collective or organizational action and agency. Organizational action and agency are emergent properties that are irreducible to the actions and agency of individual persons. Finn's innovative use of critical realist social theory helps to explain how organizations exercise agency and subsequently act.

FINN AND THE STRUCTURE-AGENCY MYSTERY

On Sunday morning at the Society of Christian Ethics in 2013, Finn presented a paper entitled "Social Causality and Market Complicity: Specifying the Causal Roles of Persons and Structures." Having just published an article on social structures, I was interested and attended the session. There, he discussed Christian Smith's *What Is a Person?*, now a classic text in critical realist literature. After the paper, I approached Finn and discussed Smith's book further. He invited me to lunch to continue the conversation. In retrospect, his paper birthed a subfield—critical realist Catholic social ethics. Over the next few years, Finn organized a group of scholars who were interested in critical realism. The group's conversations culminated in *Moral Agency Within Social Structures and Culture: A Primer on Critical Realism for Christian Ethics*, which he edited.

Finn turned to critical realism to more fully understand a vexing issue in Christian ethics: the relationship of structure and agency.

---

4. Daly, *Structures of Virtue and Vice*, ch. 2.
5. Finn, "What Is a Sinful Social Structure?," 138.

Sociologists sometimes refer to this as the structure-agency problem, but I more accurately call it the "structure-agency mystery." The existentialist philosopher Gabriel Marcel argued that a mystery involves a person intimately, whereas a problem can be solved. Marcel held that one should not degrade a mystery into a problem.[6] For Thomas Aquinas, mysteries about God and the person can be entered into and known more clearly, but they can never be comprehended.[7] The relationship between social structure and agency is, ultimately, not a problem that can be solved but a mystery that we can progressively understand but never finally exhaust. This is because moral agency, relationality, and membership in human communities are transcendent aspects of human personhood.

Although I and others have followed Finn's lead in adopting critical realism, one should not expect a single explanatory framework for the social world. Because the subject is the human person as she relates to society there is unlikely to be an analogue to Einstein's "unified field theory" regarding the structure-agency relationship. Our aim, therefore, is a best current account of the structure-agency relation.[8] Such an account should be tested and revisable.

Theological ethicists need the best current account of the structure-agency relationship because over the past fifty-plus years, beginning with liberation theology, they have discovered that structures influence moral character and social outcomes, such as poverty, racism, sexism, and environmental degradation. To describe the acts of a person without exploring the social forces that influence him is to under-explain human action. Likewise, focusing on individual actions without acknowledging social forces means under-explaining social outcomes such as poverty and disease. Therefore, the discipline needs greater insight into structure and agency.

Before Finn adopted critical realist social theory, most accounts of structure in theological ethics failed to adequately control the term or provide an account of the structure-agency relation.[9] There are a few exceptions to this rule. Some, like O'Keefe, Himes, Heyer, and myself, used Peter Berger and Tom Luckmann's dialectical account of structure and

---

6. Marcel, *Philosophy of Existentialism*, 19.
7. Aquinas, *Summa Theologiae*, I, q. 11–12.
8. Taylor, *Sources of the Self*, 7.
9. Daly, *Structures of Virtue and Vice*, ch. 2.

agency.[10] Others, such as Katie Grimes, turned to Bourdieu's habitus.[11] Ada Maria Isasi-Diaz drew upon Iris Marion Young's focus on rules, routines, and resources to explain how social structure influenced agency.[12]

Finn's use of critical realism is the most profound use of social theory in Catholic ethics to date. In 2014, he edited a landmark book on social and economic theory and Christian ethics, *Distant Markets, Distant Harms: Economic Complicity and Christian Ethics*. There, he brought together social theorists, economists, and ethicists because "Christian economic ethics has much to gain from a conversation with sociological colleagues."[13]

In his contribution to the volume, Finn critiqued Christian ethical accounts of structure and developed ethical analyses in light of a robust social theory. Finn's critical argument is prominent in his chapter in *Distant Markets*, where he argues that Christian economic ethics suffers from a deficient understanding of consumers' moral responsibilities.[14] The remedy to this problem is to turn to sociology and, specifically, critical realist social theory. Responding to the individualist approach to economic harms, Finn contends, "Personal virtue is necessary for a morally adequate market system, but it is not sufficient."[15]

His 2016 article in *Theological Studies*, "What Is a Sinful Social Structure?," contains his sharpest criticism of Christian ethical approaches to social structures. There, Finn laments that the concept of social sin has become "frustratingly multivalent."[16] Because the concept has no fixed definition, its capacity to name social pathologies is stunted. The concept's multivalence is due, in part, to the fact that "Catholic social thought has no coherent account of what a social structure is."[17] Because the "social" is undertheorized, by extension, so is the concept of social sin.

---

10. Berger and Luckmann, *Social Construction*; Daly, "Structures of Virtue and Vice"; O'Keefe, *What Are They Saying About Social Sin?*; Heyer, "Social Sin and Immigration"; Himes, "Social Sin."

11. Grimes, *Christ Divided*, 181.

12. Isasi-Diaz, "Spirituality and the Common Good."

13. Finn, introduction to *Distant Markets*, xi.

14. Finn, "Social Causality," 243.

15. Finn, "Social Causality," 258.

16. Finn, "What Is a Sinful Social Structure?," 137.

17. Finn, "What Is a Sinful Social Structure?," 138.

Finn's magnum opus in this area, *Consumer Ethics*, argues that a better account of the structure-agency relationship is needed because "a disproportionate emphasis in Christian ethics has been placed on personal virtue and action and too little attention has been paid to the character of the social forces that powerfully shape both moral agency and, over time, moral character."[18] Individualist accounts of action and social outcomes obscure how structures influence both realities. Finn identifies individualist explanatory frameworks as present (and deficient) in his other area of expertise, economics.

His constructive work begins in his chapter in *Distant Markets*. There, Finn claims that the critical realist school of sociology is the "most fruitful option" for Christian ethicists. He argues that critical realism's "epistemological and ontological assumptions" comport with those in Christian ethics.[19] As he did in *Distant Markets*, Finn endorses a critical realist approach in his *Theological Studies* article.

Finn's work on social structure further develops in *Consumer Ethics*. Finn follows Porpora's definition that social structures are "systems of human relations among social positions."[20] He regularly turns to the structure of American universities to illustrate what a structure is and how it shapes agency. American universities consist, in part, of the professor-student relation. Individuals inhabit academic positions and practice them in relation to the "restrictions, opportunities, and incentives" that the structures generate.[21] For example, students are restricted and penalized for the tardy submission of work and are rewarded for active participation in class discussions. These structurally embedded penalties and rewards causally influence the actions of students.

Finn develops what I consider to be a notion of "relational causality." In *Consumer Ethics*, he writes that "social structures exert causal impact by altering the decisions that persons within them make."[22] Later, he notes that "when we say a social structure causes this or that to happen, we mean that it does so by influencing persons to take actions causing those effects."[23] Causality in human actions is complex. Reason, will, and emotions are all engaged. However, Finn emphasizes an agent's social

18. Finn, *Consumer Ethics*, 143.
19. Finn, "Social Causality," 247.
20. Finn, "Social Structures," 30.
21. Finn, *Consumer Ethics*, 68.
22. Finn, *Consumer Ethics*, 43.
23. Finn, *Consumer Ethics*, 70.

setting. For instance, if a school bus driver arrives for work every morning at five a.m. we can say that she does so, in part, because of her relation to her boss. Her boss can terminate her if she arrives late. If asked, "Why do you wake up at four a.m. every day?" she would likely respond, "Because my boss might fire me if I don't!" Here, the bus driver retains her free moral agency, but her free action can only be fully understood or explained when we understand the structural relations that influence her to choose to arise before dawn. Finn recognizes that although the poor and vulnerable suffer more significant restrictions and severe penalties due to their social positions, all persons encounter constraints on their power through their relations to other position-holders.

The tenure system in American higher education provides another example of how structures exert relational causality. When one assumes the position of tenure-track professor, one meets a set of enablements, constraints, rewards, and punishments. Faculty are enabled to research, write, present conference papers, and (typically) teach courses in their area of interest. Constraints include the inability to take "days off" during the semester for leisure purposes, as well as avoiding certain acts like insulting students for wrong answers and skipping department meetings. A well-structured university enables professors to achieve the standards of excellence that the university rewards with tenure. If faculty are rewarded for publications, then the university should enable them to research and write by allocating time and resources for these activities.

Today, the reward of tenure is almost entirely predicated on publications. This is true even at small liberal arts colleges. Finn's account of what I am terming "relational causality" explains how tenure structures causally influence the agency and actions of tenure-track faculty. Individuals who hold faculty positions are incentivized to focus on research and publishing, sometimes at the expense of teaching and service to the community, in part because they know that the tenure committee will evaluate them on this aspect of their dossier. Here, an individual's participation in a relation among social positions (the tenure-track professor-tenure committee relation) causally influences her deliberations and actions. Ultimately, a person's assumption of the position of a tenure-line faculty member often influences her to "act differently than [she] would do otherwise."[24] Tenure-track faculty who desire to improve a course

---

24. Elder-Vass, *Causal Power*, 124.

over the summer often find themselves compelled to devote their time to research and writing to meet the institution's publication requirements.

In addition to influencing personal action, Finn contends that structures generate social outcomes. Finn demonstrates the power of social structures to influence social outcomes with the example of gerrymandering. He draws on recent examples in which both Republicans and Democrats respectively drew up zigzagged and pinwheel-shaped districts to protect their incumbent United States House representative. He notes that the party that gerrymanders state districts can win the majority of House seats even if the opposition party garners significantly more votes. Thus, one should not naively think that election results are the aggregate of the votes cast and instead should realize that structures causally influence who wins and loses elections. Finn contends that "interpreting election outcomes as simply the result of voting by individuals ('the people have spoken') conceals the causal impact of structural forces at play and far overstates the causal efficacy of individual voters."[25]

Finn also highlights the importance of structures in generating outcomes in the garment industry. In *Consumer Ethics* Finn argues that the poverty that Asian seamstresses suffer is a by-product of the clothing market. Seamstresses are poor, in large part, because of structures, not the ill will of consumers. Poverty wages result from a web of relations involving consumers, brand executives, factory owners, and legislators. No single factor causes some seamstresses in Bangladesh to make $113 per month.[26] Consumers' desire for cheap clothing and brand executives' and factory owners' desire for maximum profit conspire to create a web of market relations that depress wage rates for garment workers. Mindful of the structure's influence on the well-being of garment workers, Finn contends that "the moral character of my clothing purchase depends not simply on how the department store clerk and I treated each other but also on the moral character of the long chain of relationships connecting me to the Asian seamstress who sewed the shirt I am wearing."[27] Finn urges people of goodwill to transcend individualist ethics and develop moral sensitivities regarding one's participation in market structures.

> Personal virtue is necessary for a morally adequate market system, but it is not sufficient. Market pressures, information

---

25. Finn, *Consumer Ethics*, 18.
26. Associated Press, "Bangladesh Raises Monthly Minimum Wage."
27. Finn, "Social Causality," 259.

about which is delivered in the form of a change in prices, are responsible for a significant damage to human well-being, and market participants are responsible for the market relationships they enter into.[28]

Finn's account invites ethicists to morally scrutinize "market pressures" and the market participation of consumers. Both are needed for an adequate Christian social ethics.

Finn's insights into the causal nature of social structures on agency and outcomes yield several vital insights for Christian ethicists. First, critical realism enables Christian ethicists to go beyond individualistic ethical analyses or overly general structural analyses "to name more precisely what's going on and to suggest more specific paths to the transformation of contemporary economic life."[29] Critical realism enables Christian ethicists to assert that "our daily choices, made in freedom, are nonetheless profoundly shaped—for good or ill—by the social structures within which we live."[30] Second, because social structures shape agency, action, and outcomes, they have a moral character. Finn's work further supports those who claim that social structures are not morally neutral but can be categorized as virtuous or vicious.[31] Third, Finn's description of the long chain of relations between North American consumers and Asian garment workers enables consumers to understand their moral experience better. Many consumers feel that they play a causal role in the misery that garment workers suffer and experience moral guilt when buying inexpensive (and possibly sweatshop-made) clothing. Finn's deep understanding of how economic structures work and how consumers causally contribute to the suffering of garment workers validates consumers' moral intuitions. However, Finn avoids drawing moral equivalence between different agents. Although we all lead what Finn calls "indicted lives," not all lives are equally indicted.[32] Some, such as the sweatshop factory owner or CEO of the clothing brand, bear more moral culpability than the working-class parent who buys sweatshop-made clothing. Finally, because individualistic analyses abound in Christian ethics (and economics), Finn rightly argues that ethicists and persons of goodwill

---

28. Finn, "Social Causality," 258.
29. Finn, *Consumer Ethics*, 138.
30. Finn, "Social Structures," 40.
31. Daly: *Structures of Virtue and Vice*; and "Structures of Virtue and Vice."
32. Finn, *Consumer Ethics*, 140.

should increasingly focus on how consumers affect the lives of distant others.[33] In sum, Finn's work expands the agenda of Christian ethics.

COLLECTIVE ACTION AND AGENCY IN FINN AND KEENAN

I now turn to the topic of collective action and agency. Finn's work on the topic is the point of departure. The section then turns to James Keenan's account of collective agency. I consider collective action and then collective agency because the latter category is more contested, and some maintain that the former's existence is independent of the latter's.

Finn on Collective Action and Agency

Finn contends that collectives, such as corporations, can act. He notes that "while we can speak of Exxon or Facebook as corporations 'doing' something, all their decisions are made and announced by persons, typically corporate officers, who have taken on positions of authority within them."[34] In his 2015 book chapter, "Can an Organization Have a Conscience?," he argues that "organizations 'do' things and thus bear moral responsibility" because "the organization is making a judgment."[35] Notice that Finn's scare quotes in these passages indicate that organizations act differently than persons. Organizational action is analogous to personal action, not identical to it.

Finn's position on collective agency is more difficult to ascertain. In the aforementioned article, he claims that organizations can "make a judgment." Judgment is an exercise of agency. Later in the same article, he argues that "once we come to an adequate understanding of social structures," we find that organizations "can be characterized by a kind of collective agency, in that it is meaningful to speak of an organization doing something."[36] Because organizations act, Finn reasons they must possess a form of agency. Here, Finn endorses a qualified form of agency for collectives, similar to his analogous account of collective action.

33. Finn, *Consumer Ethics*, 134.
34. Finn, "Social Structures," 39.
35. Finn, "Can an Organization Have a Conscience?," 105.
36. Finn, "Can an Organization Have a Conscience?," 100.

However, in *Consumer Ethics*, he writes that "only persons are agents but that social structures exercise powerful influence on those agents."[37] Here, it seems that collective agency is not ontologically real; it is simply how structures organize the deliberations and actions of individuals acting in the name of the collective. Finally, Finn authored a chapter in *Moral Agency* that included a section entitled "Aside on Collective Agency." The section begins with the claim that "only persons are agents." He then offers two observations. The first is that there is a debate within critical realism regarding collective agency. The majority of critical realists contend that collectives act through their individual members. As in *Consumer Ethics*, Finn appears to side with that approach. He also notes that other critical realists maintain that "collective agency emerges from the interaction of such persons in authority" positions within the collective.[38] I return to this "emergentist" approach to collective agency below.

His second observation is that the question of collective agency is a "minor issue" for ethicists relative to the critical realist explanation of everyday actions of personal agents who are causally influenced by social structures.[39] He argues, "The summary statement that only persons are agents well describes 99.99 percent of the effects that structures have in our lives."[40] Here, Finn downplays the importance of collective agency and chooses not to develop a position on the issue. However, if, as Finn contends, "some of the world's most influential actors are large national or multinational organizations,"[41] collective agency is not a "minor issue" but a topic worth investigating for Christian social ethicists.

In sum, from 2015 to 2020, Finn's work moved away from an endorsement of even an analogous account of collective agency. As he increasingly integrated critical realist social theory into his thinking, he saw the collective as organizing the agency of the individuals who hold positions within the collective. Finn emphasizes that agency is personal but is causally influenced by the enablements and constraints that exist in the relations among the collective's positions.

---

37. Finn, *Consumer Ethics*, 39.
38. Finn, "Social Structures," 39.
39. Finn, "Social Structures," 39–40.
40. Finn, "Social Structures," 40.
41. Finn, "Social Structures," 39.

Keenan on Collective Action and Agency

In his 2024 *Theological Studies* article, "Recognizing Collectives as Moral Agents," James Keenan engages with Finn's work and develops his own account of collective moral agency. Keenan interprets Finn as rejecting collective agency when he cites Finn's claim that "only persons are agents."[42] Keenan agrees with Finn on this point, but then argues that "collectives are precisely of moral agents but that when we act collectively there are dynamics that are agential but complex and different from the agency of individual persons. And that when we act collectively, we are more than the sum of persons involved."[43] Even though he does not explicitly draw on critical realism, Keenan takes what I have termed an "emergentist" account of collective agency. Later, Keenan rhetorically asks: "But what happens when individual moral agents collectively organize and exercise their agency? Is not that collective moral agency?" Keenan summarizes his approach in a series of distinguishing marks of collective agency. Three are especially relevant to this chapter. First, he suggests that collectives must be organized and "express their agency with intentionality, power, and rationality."[44] Second, the virtue of solidarity must exist among the members of the collective.[45] Finally, like the African palaver method, collective agency is exercised only when all members are heard.[46]

AN EMERGENTIST ACCOUNT OF COLLECTIVE (ORGANIZATIONAL) ACTION AND AGENCY

Drawing on the work of Finn and Keenan, this chapter now makes a modest contribution to the development of an account of collective action and agency. It defends two claims. First, if collective action and agency are irreducible to individual agency, then they must be emergent properties. Second, *organizational* action and agency are the more accurate terms because only organizations can coordinate individuals so that they act as a collective.

---

42. Keenan, "Recognizing Collectives," 98, quoting Finn, "Social Structures," 39–40.
43. Keenan, "Recognizing Collectives," 98.
44. Keenan, "Recognizing Collectives," 122.
45. Keenan, "Recognizing Collectives," 108–15.
46. Keenan, "Recognizing Collectives," 108–9.

At the outset of this discussion it should be noted that the concepts of collective action and collective agency are related but distinct. Collective action occurs when an organized group acts as a coordinated body. Collective agency is expressed when an organized group deliberates and renders decisions that often causally influence collective action.

Collective Action

My account of collective action and agency depends on the concepts of emergence and organization. Emergence is "the process of constituting a new entity with its own particular characteristics through the interactive combination of other, different entities that are necessary to create the new entity but that do not contain the characteristics of the new entity."[47]

Finn often uses the example of water to explain emergence. Water emerges from the relationship of two hydrogen atoms with one oxygen atom. Although hydrogen and oxygen alone are flammable gases, H_2O is a liquid that extinguishes fire. In addition, moral habits, such as virtues and vices, emerge from the relation of a person's external actions, intentions, values, emotions, and reasoning.[48] It would be a mistake to reduce character traits to actions or intentions alone. These realities relate to create a reality—strong dispositions to action—that, as Finn writes, "cannot be explained by the characteristics of those elements that combine to create it."[49]

Collective action is always *organized*. Keenan suggests as much in his article. But what is an organization? Organizations are a type of social structure and, therefore, are composed of durable webs of relations among social positions. Organizations differ from mere assemblages or associations of people insofar as they "tend to be strongly structured by specialized *roles*; and second, they are marked by significant *authority* relations between at least some of these roles."[50] Organizations direct "coordinated interaction," which requires "role observance" within the organization. Organizations are capable of acting. Elder-Vass argues that organized collective entities, such as states, corporations, and trade unions, "always act through individual humans, but nevertheless in

---

47. Smith, *What Is a Person?*, 26.
48. Daly, *Structures of Virtue and Vice*, 140.
49. Finn, "What Is Critical Realism?," 20.
50. Elder-Vass, *Causal Power*, 152, emphasis in original.

causal terms we can say that when they do it is ultimately the larger social entity that is acting."[51]

Consider an orchestra. Elder-Vass contends that the orchestra as a whole produces the musical performance. Such a performance is impossible for a lone individual. "The ability to produce such a harmonized performance is therefore an emergent causal power of the group—the organization."[52] The orchestra's action is symphonic music. Symphonic music is a new entity that emerges from the relationship of the individual actions of the performers. The orchestra produces the harmonized performance precisely because it is an organization. It contains specified positions (viz., violin, trumpet, percussion), some of which possess authority over others (conductor). Organized collectives, such as orchestras, possess causal powers that go beyond their individual members. Here, the "productive capacity is a causal power of the organization and not of the workers."[53] Notice that a collective's action is an emergent causal power of the organization. Collective action emerges from a web of relations among social positions as individuals practice their positions. This is a specification of Keenan's claim that "when we act collectively, we are more than the sum of persons involved."[54]

Based on this account, the January 6, 2021, insurrection on the United States government is a vivid example of collective action. The January 6th Select Committee found that the

> Proud Boys led the attack, penetrated the Capitol, and led hundreds of others inside. Multiple Proud Boys reacted immediately to President Trump's December 19th tweet and began their planning. Immediately, Proud Boys leaders reorganized their hierarchy, with Enrique Tarrio, Joseph Biggs, and Ethan Nordean messaging groups of Proud Boys about what to expect on January 6th. Tarrio created a group chat known as the Ministry of Self-Defense for hand selected Proud Boys whom he wanted to "organize and direct" plans for January 6th. On social media, Tarrio referenced "revolt" and "[r]evolution," and conspicuously asked "What if we invade it?" on Telegram.[55]

---

51. Elder-Vass, *Causal Power*, 181.
52. Elder-Vass, *Causal Power*, 154.
53. Elder-Vass, *Causal Power*, 155.
54. Keenan, "Recognizing Collectives," 98.
55. Select Committee, *Final Report*, 56.

The report notes that the Proud Boys hierarchy directed the collective's actions on January 6, 2021. The coordinated effort of the Proud Boys organization enabled the group to exert greater causal power than unorganized individuals would have possessed.

Contrast the actions of the Proud Boys and their followers on January 6 with the mob who carried out the Dublin riots of November 2023. The Dublin rioters were an aggregate of individuals, each acting relatively independently of the others. The rioters lacked an authoritative leader and did not have specialized roles. Even though rioters were acting in spatial and temporal proximity to each other, the riots were not the act of an organized collective.

Collective Agency

The more difficult questions to answer are: Do collectives possess agency? Is collective agency, like collective action, an emergent causal power of an organization? According to Keenan (and the earlier Finn), collective agency is analogous to personal agency. Thus, in order to arrive at an account of collective agency, one must first describe personal agency. According to Thomas Aquinas, what we now call moral agency is exercised through an agent's understanding and voluntariness.[56] Moral agency involves intending an end and choosing the means through deliberations. Moral responsibility exists only when an agent performs an act with both knowledge of the action and free volition.

Deliberative processes within organizations are analogous to an individual's internal conversation regarding ends to pursue and the means to attain those ends.[57] Organizations, like individuals, can discern the end they desire to pursue, intend to achieve that end, seek counsel regarding how to attain the end, and choose the action that attains the end.[58] At each stage of the deliberation (discernment of end, intention of end, taking of counsel, choosing of action), organizations typically require groups of individuals to discuss and collectively decide upon the organization's direction. Knowledge and volition, the requirements of personal moral agency, are also analogously present in the organization's deliberation.

---

56. Aquinas, *Summa* I-II, q. 6. a. 1, ad 1.

57. On the notion of the "internal conversation," see Archer, *Structure, Agency, and the Internal Conversation*.

58. This account of moral deliberation is based on Aquinas, *Summa* I-II, q. 12–17.

The judgments that organizations make at each stage are emergent. They emerge from the structured collaboration among position holders in the organization. Judgments are rarely solely imputable to an individual agent within the organization. For example, a CEO must consult with the board about the annual goals of the organization. The final goals will emerge from within the conversation of the CEO and board members and may be quite different from the goals envisioned at the outset of the meeting. Exercises of organizational agency and action are emergent realities and, therefore, resist simplistic explanations. Collective agency is an emergent causal power of an organization and, therefore, is irreducible to the individuals who hold positions in the organization.

Because collective agency is necessarily organized, it is more accurate to refer to this social reality as "organizational agency." As Finn and Keenan suggest, organizational agency is analogous to personal agency. Personal agency is an apt analogy as it illumines more about collective agency than it obscures. Organizational agency is not merely the aggregated agency of individuals. A new form of agency exists when individuals perform their positions within an organization and collectively and deliberately make judgments.

Christian Organizational Ethics

Because organizations can act and exercise agency, ethicists should morally scrutinize them. However, Christian organizational ethics is undeveloped. Only Catholic healthcare ethics has developed a substantive discourse on organizational ethics.[59] The need for a robust Christian organizational ethics is pressing, given the enormous influence that organizations have on social outcomes and the moral formation of individuals. As demonstrated above, Finn has repeatedly implored the guild of ethicists to go beyond an individualist ethical paradigm and to evaluate structures, such as organizations.

Finn's and Keenan's work enables us to argue that organizations, like individuals, are morally responsible for their moral choices and actions. Organizational moral responsibility does not compete with or diminish individual moral responsibility. Instead, it widens the moral aperture of Christian ethics. As Finn suggested, structures, such as organizations,

59. Daly, "Virtuous Hospital." I summarize the discourse on Catholic organizational healthcare ethics and develop an account of organizational virtues that analyze an organization's structure.

"do 'things' and bear moral responsibility." The Proud Boys as an organization and their individual members bear responsibility for the suffering they collectively inflicted on January 6, 2021.

Christian ethicists should attend to two projects in organizational ethics. First, if, as Finn claims, organizations "do things," Christian ethicists need to develop methods of "organizational act analysis." This may involve the development of organizational moral norms, principles, and methods of virtue-based action guidance. A second research project pertains to individuals who hold positions within organizations. Such people need ethical tools to evaluate their contributions to organizational decisions and actions. Who of us has yet to participate in organizational decision-making and actions that we, at the time or subsequently, evaluated as morally wrong? How ought we morally assess our participation in organizational evil? Finn's work is helpful to this end as he rightly noted that although we all live "indicted lives," we are not all equally indicted. Organizations contain positions of authority, and those who inhabit those positions should (typically) garner more moral praise and blame for an organization's actions. Finn's work offers the guild of ethicists the sociological and ethical tools to develop the discourse in Christian organizational ethics further.

A GROWING EDGE OF CHRISTIAN ETHICS

In 2024, Finn noted that the study of collective action and agency should be a growing edge of Christian ethics.[60] This chapter has demonstrated that his work contributes considerably to the growth of this discourse. Finn's work on the ethics of social structures has raised the standards of excellence in addressing social realities within the practice of Christian social ethics.[61] Catholic social ethicists can no longer write of structures without controlling their usage of the term. Although one need not adopt a critical realist framework, Catholic social ethicists must now employ "structure" as a term of art in social theory.

Finn's incorporation of critical realist social theory in Christian ethics blazed new paths and innovated tools for others to continue exploring. Among the highest praise that one can give a scholar is that he or she

---

60. Finn wrote this in an email to the author in January 2024.

61. MacIntyre, *After Virtue*, 187. There, MacIntyre defines a practice. He notes that practitioners can "systematically extend" a practice by innovating its standards of excellence.

stimulated the thinking of others and contributed to their ideas. The first part of this essay shows how Finn innovated Christian ethics through his use of critical realism. Part 2 demonstrates how Finn's work continues to stimulate the work of others, such as Keenan and myself. This work is in its infancy because "beginning with the critical realist understanding of the social world leaves plenty of work for Christian ethicists to do."[62]

BIBLIOGRAPHY

Aquinas, Thomas. *Summa Theologiae*. Translated by Fathers of the English Dominicans Province. Allen, TX: Christian Classics, 1981.

Archer, Margaret. *Structure, Agency, and the Internal Conversation*. New York: Cambridge University Press, 2003.

Associated Press. "Bangladesh Raises Monthly Minimum Wage for Garment Workers to $113 Following Weeks of Protest." AP News, Nov. 7, 2023. https://apnews.com/article/bangladesh-garment-workers-wage-increase-5d55f9ba52ef2a156069e86dad665662.

Berger, Peter, and Thomas Luckmann. *The Social Construction of Reality: A Treatise in the Sociology of Knowledge*. New York: Doubleday, 1967.

Daly, Daniel J. "Structures of Virtue and Vice." *New Blackfriars* 92 (2011) 341–57.

———. *The Structures of Virtue and Vice*. Washington, DC: Georgetown University Press, 2021.

———. "The Virtuous Hospital: A Catholic Organizational Healthcare Ethics." *Journal of Healthcare Ethics and Administration* 8 (2022) 1–12.

Elder-Vass, Dave. *The Causal Power of Social Structures: Emergence, Structure and Agency*. New York: Cambridge University Press, 2010.

Finn, Daniel K. "Can an Organization Have a Conscience? Contributions from Social Science to Catholic Social Thought." In *Conscience and Catholicism: Rights, Responsibilities, and Institutional Responses*, edited by David E. Decosse and Kristen E. Heyer, 100–106. Maryknoll, NY: Orbis, 2015.

———. *Consumer Ethics in a Global Economy: How Buying Here Causes Injustice There*. Washington, DC: Georgetown University Press, 2019.

———. Introduction to *Distant Markets, Distant Harms: Economic Complicity and Christian Ethics*, xi–xvii. Edited by Daniel K. Finn. New York: Oxford University Press, 2014.

———, ed. *Moral Agency Within Social Structures and Culture: A Primer on Critical Realism for Christian Ethics*. Washington, DC: Georgetown University Press, 2020.

———. "Sin and the Social World." *Modern Theology* 39 (2023) 114–20.

———. "Social Causality and Market Complicity: Specifying the Causal Roles of Persons and Structures." In *Distant Markets, Distant Harms: Economic Complicity and Christian Ethics*, edited by Daniel K. Finn, 243–60. New York: Oxford University Press, 2014.

---

62. Finn, "Sin and the Social World," 120. I am grateful for the research and copyediting work of Joseph Pirone.

———. "Social Structures." In *Moral Agency Within Social Structures and Culture: A Primer on Critical Realism for Christian Ethics*, edited by Daniel K. Finn, 29–42. Washington, DC: Georgetown University Press, 2020.

———. "What Is a Sinful Social Structure?" *Theological Studies* 77 (2016) 136–64.

———. "What Is Critical Realism?" In *Moral Agency Within Social Structures and Culture: A Primer on Critical Realism for Christian Ethics*, edited by Daniel K. Finn, 19–27. Washington, DC: Georgetown University Press, 2020.

Grimes, Katie. *Christ Divided: Antiblackness as Corporate Vice*. Minneapolis: Fortress, 2017.

Heyer, Kristin. "Social Sin and Immigration: Good Fences Make Bad Neighbors." *Theological Studies* 71 (2010) 410–36.

Himes, Kenneth. "Social Sin and the Role of the Individual." *Annual of the Society of Christian Ethics* 6 (1986) 183–219.

Isasi-Diaz, Ada Maria. "Spirituality and the Common Good." In *Ethics and Spirituality*, edited by Charles E. Curran and Lisa A. Fullam, 249–57. Readings in Moral Theology 17. New York: Paulist, 2014.

Keenan, James, F. "Recognizing Collectives as Moral Agents." *Theological Studies* 85 (2024) 96–123.

MacIntyre, Alasdair. *After Virtue*. 2nd ed. Notre Dame, IN: University of Notre Dame Press, 1984.

Marcel, Gabriel. *The Philosophy of Existentialism*. New York: Citadel, 1995.

O'Keefe, Mark. *What Are They Saying About Social Sin?* New York: Paulist, 1990.

Select Committee to Investigate the January 6th Attack on the United States Capitol. *Final Report*. GovInfo, Dec. 22, 2022. 117th Congress Second Session: House Report 117-663. https://www.govinfo.gov/content/pkg/GPO-J6-REPORT/pdf/GPO-J6-REPORT.pdf.

Smith, Christian. *What Is a Person?* Chicago: University of Chicago Press, 2010.

Specia, Megan. "Ireland's Riot Was Not a Surprise to Those Who Watch the Far Right." *New York Times*, Dec. 7, 2023. https://www.nytimes.com/2023/12/07/world/europe/dublin-riot-far-right.html.

Taylor, Charles. *Sources of the Self: The Making of the Modern Identity*. New York: Cambridge University Press, 1989.

Sinful Social Structures and Political Polarization in the United States

Conor Kelly

ONE OF DANIEL FINN's seminal contributions to theological scholarship has been a more careful analysis of sinful social structures. In a choice emblematic of the interdisciplinary instincts that have defined his career, Finn responded to the fact that "Catholic social thought has no coherent account of what a social structure is" by turning to "the academic discipline that specializes in . . . [the] study [of social structures]: sociology."[1] His 2016 *Theological Studies* article assiduously defended an appeal to critical realist sociology for this purpose and used critical realism's nondeterministic account of the causal power of social structures to provide a notion of sinful social structures that could be used for theological reflection.[2] Recognizing the tremendous value of Finn's work in this area, this chapter adds to ongoing efforts in theological ethics to build on Finn's account of sinful social structures, turning here to the vexing problem of political polarization in the United States. The chapter argues that Finn's critical realist approach simultaneously helps reveal the causes underlying political polarization in the United States and points toward a more constructive response. This analysis provides further proof that Finn's work is particularly significant, and particularly useful, for his fellow ethicists.

---

1. Finn, "What Is a Sinful Social Structure?," 138, 142.
2. Finn, "What Is a Sinful Social Structure?," 147–55.

THE ROLE OF SINFUL SOCIAL STRUCTURES: FINN'S PROPOSAL

Those familiar with Finn's work are likely aware of his account of sinful social structures. Nevertheless, a brief recapitulation of the key claims in Finn's critical realist approach is crucial for further discussion of how his work can contribute to an examination of political polarization. In this context, the most important elements are Finn's clarification of the emergence of sinful social structures, his explanation of their nondeterministic "downward" causality, and his insistence on the corollary "upward" causality of individuals interacting with them.

With respect to emergence, Finn follows critical realist sociologists, such as Margaret Archer and Douglas Porpora, to argue that "social structures emerge from and are sustained by the actions of individual agents."[3] In practical terms, he explains that the way individuals interact with one another—"the relation between social positions" created by the overlapping roles (to borrow a more colloquial, albeit less precise, phrase) they adopt in society—introduce "restrictions, enablements, and incentives" that exert a causal influence on the decisions made by individual agents within this web of social connections.[4] Central to Finn's account is the idea that these restrictions, enablements, and incentives are real in an ontological sense. One may not immediately "see" them, but they are deeply embedded in the social relationships that define a person's day-to-day interactions.

Consider, for instance, the speed limit. I live in a small suburban village with an intentionally constrained speed limit of twenty-five mph, and the police in our village have a reputation for zealously enforcing this law. As a result, the relation between the preexisting social positions of citizen (driver) and police officer significantly shapes the way drivers behave in our village. It is not as though people drive slowly whenever they see a police officer (although they do typically slow down); rather, embedded in the relation between these particular social positions, people drive slowly throughout our town even when they cannot see a police car. There is a real structure that has emerged from the relation between two interrelated social positions, and people react to the restrictions, enablements, and incentives (or, in this case, *disincentives*) embedded in that

---

3. Finn, *Consumer Ethics*, 68.

4. Finn, "What Is a Sinful Social Structure?," 151. On the distinctions between positions and roles, see Finn, *Consumer Ethics*, 84.

relation in particular ways. Just because we cannot see a structure does not make it any less real.

The second point, about downward causality, helps elucidate how these "real" structures function. The key idea is that structures have a genuine power to shape the choices of the people who interact with them. We thus know they are real because we can see the results of their causal influence when "human persons make decisions in light of [a structure's] restrictions, enablements, and incentives—decisions that might be quite different" without them.[5] Finn calls this power "downward causality," because the influence on causality moves "down" from the larger web of social interconnections (the structure) to individual agents, shaping their decisions.[6] Crucially, while this downward form of power is indeed causal, because it directly shapes the choices made by the people interacting within the structure, it remains nondeterministic.[7] Moral agents retain their free will when interacting with(in) a structure, and thus must still choose how to act. Typically, however, agents make choices that align with the power of the structure because there are fewer costs and greater rewards for those who "go along" with the social structures they encounter.[8]

Once again, the case of speed limits can be illustrative. I can assure you that people drive differently in our village than they do in other parts of the metro area. While drivers happily travel at more than ten mph over the speed limit in other municipalities, brake lights flicker as soon as someone flirts with five mph beyond our statutory twenty-five. The speed limit does not *make* them do this—the fact that cars are pulled over by the police on a regular basis is evidence enough that drivers remain free agents who can, and sometimes do, choose to violate the speed limit. Nevertheless, the majority of drivers assiduously adheres to the speed limit in our village because the unique relationship between the social positions of driver and our municipality's officers of the law introduces a social and economic cost for ignoring the speed limit that is higher than most people want to pay. This is downward causality at work, for it is easier to go along, by driving more slowly than one does in other instances, than it is buck the trend and suffer the consequences.

Notably, although structures are real (emergence) and influence the choices people make (downward causality), they are not set in stone.

5. Finn, "What Is a Sinful Social Structure?," 151.
6. Finn, "Sin and the Social World," 115–16.
7. Finn, *Consumer Ethics*, 86.
8. Finn, "Social Structures," 31–32.

Structures can and do change over time, which is where the notion of "upward causality" enters the conversation. This causality, Finn explains, "runs from persons to structures" insofar as the decisions people make in response to a structure's restrictions, enablements, and incentives either reinforce that structure, allowing it to persist and strengthening its influence, or challenge that structure, eroding support for the structure's penalties and rewards and eventually changing the structure itself.[9] These changes can operate in one of two ways, which I categorize as insubordination and disruption.

The first, insubordination, occurs when individuals willfully violate the norms enshrined in a structure to call attention to a perceived injustice in its restrictions, enablements, and incentives. Acts of civil disobedience fall into this category, as people are prepared to pay the price to highlight problems in the way a structure operates. A sufficient amount of insubordination is designed to make a structure's restrictions, enablements, and incentives too costly to enforce, thereby changing its downward causality. To return to the speed limit, frustrated drivers could make a concerted effort to violate the speed limit in our village strategically, perhaps with a "drive for thirty-five" campaign. There would still be clear penalties to pay—at least initially—but if enough drivers participated, the police might realize the impossibility of detaining every driver exceeding the speed limit by just five mph. In response, the police might prioritize cars traveling ten mph or more over the speed limit, changing the restrictions, enablements, and incentives for drivers exceeding the limit by lower speeds. With this shift in downward causality, thirty becomes the new twenty-five, and people might drive just a little faster throughout the village.

While insubordination is a crucial way for those who find themselves at the mercy of a structure's downward causality to change its restrictions, enablements, and incentives, it is not the only means of upward causality. In some instances, people have a more direct influence over a structure's causal forces, allowing them to wield the power of disruption directly. The elected trustees of our village, for example, have the power to set the speed limit on village roads. They could replace the twenty-five mph signs with thirty mph signs, immediately implementing the change that a concerted campaign of insubordination might take months or even years to effect. This difference is significant, as it points to the fact that

---

9. Finn, "Sin and the Social World," 117.

the mechanisms of upward causality can vary depending on where one is positioned in a structure. Those with positions of authority can often exercise upward causality through disruption, while those in "lower" positions—the ones most directly impacted by a structure's downward causality—frequently need to rely on insubordination. Those who occupy overlapping positions, meanwhile, might have access to both levers of upward causality, as a driver who is also a voter can use insubordination in the car and disruption at the ballot box to challenge the speed limit. One task for those pursuing structural change, then, is to accurately identify where their specific social position(s) put them in relation to a given structure's mechanisms of downward causality, for this can determine whether insubordination or disruption will be more effective.

Taken together, these three elements of social structures—their real emergence, their downward causality, and their upward causality—provide a good picture of Finn's contributions to the theological discussion about what the Catholic Magisterium refers to as "structures of sin." Indeed, Finn's categories help to make sense of the Pontifical Council for Justice and Peace's claims that *"the consequences of sin perpetuate the structures of sin. These are rooted in personal sin and, therefore, are always connected to concrete acts of the individuals who commit them, consolidate them and make it difficult to remove."*[10] After all, the first part of this Vatican description, with its emphasis on consequences, speaks to emergence, while the second part, with its emphasis on the relationship between individual actions and these sinful social structures, captures the dynamics of structures' downward causality and agents' upward causality. In this sense, Finn's interdisciplinary work introduces the tools to interpret and apply these Catholic teachings more precisely.

Admittedly, the illustrations of Finn's categories introduced so far have been fairly benign. While the speed limit is useful for explaining the mechanisms of social structures, it is notable that ethicists are typically concerned with structures that have more nefarious effects than slowing down drivers on suburban streets. Finn's contributions are aimed at making sense of *sinful* social structures, for instance. For Finn, this designation applies "when a social structure penalizes morally virtuous choices or rewards evil choices (downward causality)," although he also cautions that while "it's likely that every social structure has some sinful restrictions . . . even social structures we may judge to be sinful are not

---

10. Pontifical Council for Justice and Peace, *Compendium*, no. 119, emphasis in original.

only sinful."[11] This admixture of good and bad in downward causality is helpful to remember, as it allows us to appreciate that a particular structure can have a negative impact even when it was not originally designed for evil ends—and may well have been created with the best of intentions.

In my own work building on Finn's categories, I have located the sinfulness of sinful social structures in their undermining of the common good.[12] John Paul II famously summarized the common good as "the good of all and of each individual," which helps to pinpoint the harms at stake in sinful social structures.[13] Their danger lies in exerting a downward causality that encourages the prioritization of the good of one individual—or some exclusive subset of individuals—over the good of all to the point that what would be best for everyone is sacrificed to achieve outcomes that are better just for a few. By applying Finn's categories of emergence, downward causality, and upward causality to structures that operate this way, it is possible to get a clearer sense of the structural root causes behind contemporary social problems and thus to develop more effective responses, as the case of political polarization illustrates.

SINFUL SOCIAL STRUCTURES IN ACTION: THE CASE OF POLITICAL POLARIZATION

Political polarization, the phenomenon of "increasingly harsh divides between opposing political camps and diminishing shared political ground," is not a new feature of the US political landscape (see: Civil War, 1861–65), but its modern manifestation is on the rise.[14] Particularly concerning is the development of "pernicious polarization," a term describing "the division of society into mutually distrustful political camps in which political identity becomes a social identity."[15] According to researchers, the United States has seen a measurable increase in political polarization since the early 2000s and has been in a "pernicious" state since 2015.[16] What the country has experienced in the last two decades represents a notable difference in degree if not in kind and deserves attention for this reason.

11. Finn, "Sin and the Social World," 117.
12. Kelly, "Nature and Operation of Structural Sin," 301, 309–12.
13. John Paul II, *Sollicitudo Rei Socialis*, no. 38.
14. Carothers and O'Donohue, introduction to *Democracies Divided*, 1, 4.
15. McCoy and Press, "What Happens?," para. 2.
16. McCoy and Press, "What Happens?"

Even more important than any quantitative shifts in the amount of polarization in US politics is pernicious polarization's disruptive social effects. Political scientists stress that polarization is not intrinsically harmful to democratic governance, as it can sometimes be a necessary resource for structural reforms that address injustices.[17] When polarization involves a sense of identity sorting around a single fault line, however, it becomes pernicious because it creates a cultural framing of us vs. them that makes even the possibility of engaging across the divide disappear.[18] Insofar as democracies require a degree of deliberation to function, this becomes a major obstacle to the simple operations of the government. Such a deterioration is especially problematic from a Catholic theological perspective, which presumes a social anthropology that makes both engaging with others and meaningful participation in society essential marks of human flourishing.[19] Hence, the US Catholic bishops have described a "contributive" form of justice that captures the duties individuals have to contribute to society in the manner appropriate to their specific roles and the corresponding responsibility society has "to enable [individuals] to participate in this way."[20] Democratic institutions provide a crucial means for fulfilling these obligations—on both sides of the equation—and pernicious polarization is therefore damaging for the reason and to the extent that it undermines the functioning of democratic governance itself. In other words, it operates as a threat to the common good.

Scholars who study political polarization argue that it is a multifactorial problem with no simple, or singular, root cause.[21] Polarization is therefore apt for analysis via Finn's account of sinful social structures because the problem is deeper than any isolated set of choices by independent individuals and instead emerges from the complicated interactions of people occupying varying social positions. Indeed, Finn's categories of upward and downward causality are particularly important, as researchers explain that polarization perpetuates itself (the upward causality of going along) in large part by "mak[ing] compromise, consensus, interaction, and tolerance increasingly costly and tenuous for individuals and political actors across the opposite sides of the polarization" (a form of

---

17. McCoy and Somer, "Pernicious Polarization," 235.
18. McCoy et al., "Polarization and the Global Crisis of Democracy," 18–19.
19. Pontifical Council for Justice and Peace, *Compendium*, nos. 149–51.
20. United States Catholic Bishops, *Economic Justice for All*, no. 71.
21. Van Prooijen, "Psychology of Political Polarization," 4–5.

downward causality).[22] By analyzing the underlying web of relations between social positions in civil society, then, we can see the restrictions, enablements, and incentives that emerge with real structural force to encourage the behaviors that create, perpetuate, and sustain polarization.

Admittedly, a full-scale analysis of the sinful social structures supporting pernicious polarization in the United States is beyond the scope of this brief chapter, but there is room to discuss one illustration of how Finn's categories help make sense of the precarious position of US democracy in this polarized moment. Think of the following discussion of gerrymandering and its sinful social structures therefore as a proof-of-concept test case and not just a simple analytic argument.

Gerrymandering and Political Polarization

Gerrymandering is the practice of establishing the boundaries of a legislative district—the geographic area that elects representatives for the state or federal government—in a manner that is intentionally designed to maximize the electoral results for one political party while minimizing the results for their opponents.[23] The practice is fairly common in the United States, where the Constitution requires a reconfiguration of legislative districts for the US House of Representatives every ten years to account for population shifts recorded in the decennial national census. Because the legal parameters for setting these districts are relatively sparse, whichever party controls a state's legislature at the time of redistricting tends to draw maps that tilt the electoral math in their favor.[24] They achieve this outcome by "packing" their opponent's voters into as few districts as possible, creating extra-large majorities that result in a lot of "wasted" votes beyond the minimal majority needed to win a district. The party can then simultaneously try "cracking" their own support, splitting their voters into as many districts as possible with just enough in each district to ensure a comfortable but not excessive victory.[25] These strategies maximize the total number of representatives elected from one's own party across all districts in a state.

---

22. McCoy et al., "Polarization and the Global Crisis of Democracy," 18.

23. Although there are multiple forms of gerrymandering, in this chapter I focus exclusively on partisan gerrymandering, given its connections to polarization. All references to gerrymandering herein are thus specific to partisan gerrymandering.

24. Kury, *Gerrymandering*, 13–23.

25. Legarde and Tomala, "Optimality," 10.

The scope of partisan gerrymandering is hard to measure, but one helpful tool for assessing its impact is the number of "competitive" districts, or places where the two parties' vote shares were within eight percentage points in the most recent presidential election. The absence of theses districts is indicative of gerrymandering because, when practiced effectively, gerrymandering has the effect of minimizing the number of districts that are genuinely competitive during the general election. After the most recent round of redistricting, the 2022 congressional election saw "fewer competitive districts than at any point in the last 52 years," bringing a steady decline to its newest nadir.[26]

The trend toward more noncompetitive districts not only suggests the extent of gerrymandering but also reveals its impact. These districts have a negative effect on participation, "because there's less incentive for voters to turn out in districts where one party dominates. Candidates from the minority party also have less incentive to run."[27] These shifts undercut the demands of contributive justice, making it harder for voters to participate in a meaningful way in the political process. Indeed, after the 2022 election, congressional representatives were elected by less than one quarter of the voting age population, a number that "reflects both low voter turnout and winners elected with a low share of the vote," two trends exacerbated by gerrymandering's ability to skew the impact of individual votes.[28] Furthermore, the decrease in competitive districts has an appreciable effect on polarization, as noncompetitive districts put all the pressure on the partisan primaries that select the candidates who will represent the dominant party in the general election campaign, when gerrymandering virtually guarantees their success. Because the primary electorate is more partisan, the shifting of competitiveness from the general election battle to the primary selection process encourages candidates to appeal to a party's base, which is ideologically more extreme than the general electorate.[29]

Gerrymandering as a Sinful Social Structure

By encouraging this process, gerrymandered districts represent an emergent social structure that places candidates for office in a unique

26. Li and Leaverton, "Gerrymandering Competitive Districts."
27. Fernandez, "Competitive Congressional Districts Decline."
28. FairVote, "Dubious Democracy 2022."
29. Troiano, *Primary Solution*, 11–14, 41–48.

relationship with a particular subset of citizens who occupy the social position of voters in a given (gerrymandered) district. This structure exercises its downward causality on candidates by incentivizing them to take more extreme positions to gain the support of the diehard partisans who move the needle in primary elections. Consequently, the structure places restrictions on bipartisanship and compromise by ensuring that representatives who buck their party's positions are defeated in a primary. Between the incentives on extreme positions and the disincentives on compromise, gerrymandering introduces two forms of downward causality that make polarizing positions more likely from elected representatives.[30]

Admittedly, these mechanisms of downward causality do not explain all aspects of the rise of polarization. Gerrymandered districts can only exert their downward causality on elected officials in the House of Representatives because senators are elected by the population of an entire state, whose boundaries cannot be reestablished every ten years for political gain. This distinction has caused some scholars to dismiss the causal impact of gerrymandering on partisan polarization, since the rise in polarization has affected both houses of Congress.[31] There are, however, two reasons to resist the argument that gerrymandering has nothing to do with the problem, both of which ultimately help to reveal gerrymandering's structural power.

First, there is evidence that a parallel kind of gerrymandering—or at least a similar form of packing and cracking—is happening on the state level in many parts of the country as voters choose to sort themselves geographically according to political affiliation, creating firmly "red" and firmly "blue" states where the most competitive portion of statewide elections has become the partisan primary contest.[32] As a result, there is a plausible explanation for the influence of the same form of downward causality (incentivizing extremism and restricting moderation) across different circumstances, reinforcing the idea that gerrymandering would affect polarization.

Second, Finn's description of the interrelationship between downward causality and upward causality reminds us that the influence of social structures is not linear, but cyclical. As a result, gerrymandering can have a meaningful impact on polarization beyond just its effects on

---

30. For more details on these mechanisms, see Mulroy, "Great Unskewing," 106–9.
31. McCarty, "What We Know," 6.
32. Mulroy, "Great Unskewing," 105–6.

the people connected through gerrymandered districts when its incentives, restrictions, and enablements affect the way people act beyond the confines of their district. The cyclical nature of partisan polarization suggests that this is precisely what happens, because party elites (e.g., elected officials) respond to the incentives that reward extremism by staking out more fringe positions and these positions then become identified with the party itself. This, in turn, prompts the voters who identify as members of that party to promote the fringe positions, making it necessary for other candidates to adopt these positions in order to win their party's support even when those candidates are not running for gerrymandered seats, including statewide positions.[33]

At this point, Finn's categories have shown how gerrymandered districts contribute to polarization through the downward causality they exert on elected representatives, who, "as single-minded seekers of reelection," respond in kind.[34] What still needs to be established, however, is the sinful nature of this structure, which again is defined by the promotion of some narrow form of self-interest(s) at the expense of the common good. Gerrymandering embodies this flaw on multiple levels.

To begin, by creating clear reelection risks and rewards, gerrymandering encourages representatives to act in pursuit of their own self-interest (of reelection) rather than in defense of the good of their constituents as a whole. This is especially true when one considers the fact that elected officials from gerrymandered districts have little accountability to the constituents in their district who are aligned with the opposing party. By allowing representatives to categorically dismiss the concerns of this group in the name of a candidate's personal reelection fortunes, gerrymandering does not abide by the Catholic vision of the common good as the good of all *and* of each individual.

Further, by creating an incentive structure that makes a representative beholden to the most extreme elements of one political party, gerrymandering undermines compromise. While this is not inherently a bad thing, because compromise is not an intrinsic good (consider how the "Three-Fifths Compromise" denied the personhood and dignity of enslaved Black persons during the crafting of the Constitution), the lack of compromise in recent years has had consequences that are at odds with the common good. To give but one example, wide popular majorities in

---

33. Merrill et al., *How Polarization Begets Polarization*.
34. Mayhew, *Congress*, 5.

the United States support a number of "commonsense" policies to address gun violence—the most popular proposal (with nearly 90 percent support) is for universal background checks—but politicians, especially at the federal level, have been loath to act in no small part due to the incentives created by gerrymandered districts.[35] In general, this disconnect between the will of the people and the actions of their representatives would suggest a violation of the demands of contributive justice and a breach of public trust, which is itself part of the common good the government is supposed to protect.[36] In the specific case of gun laws, where universal background checks have an appreciable difference on the number of people killed by gun violence, the inaction is a direct threat to "the sum of those conditions of social life which allow social groups and their individual members relatively thorough and ready access to their own fulfillment," which is how the Second Vatican Council defined the common good.[37] Consequently, gerrymandering's ability to forestall commonsense reforms by prioritizing the self-interest of a candidate's reelection and the group self-interest of their party means that it pits the "good" of a few against the common good of all, making it a sinful social structure.

Responding to Gerrymandering

If, in light of this analysis, gerrymandering can be identified as a sinful social structure, the next obvious question is what to do about it. Here, Finn's understanding of upward causality is vital. Again, this concept refers to the power individuals have to shape the restrictions, enablements, and incentives that give sinful social structures their ability to promote damaging outcomes. In the case of gerrymandering, the notion of upward causality helps to demonstrate that the people who have an ability to make a difference are the ones who typically describe themselves as especially powerless in the face of polarization: the voters.

To appreciate how voters have a say in the structural power of gerrymandering, one must remember that the downward causality of gerrymandered districts runs through the partisan primaries that make reelection contingent upon satisfying the concerns of one party's flank.

---

35. Tausanovitch et al., "Partisan Gerrymandering."

36. Hollenbach, *Common Good*, 190–202.

37. Second Vatican Council, *Gaudium et Spes*, no. 26. See also Siegel et al., "Impact of State Firearm Laws."

Within this structure, candidates respond to incentives that are "paid out" in the currency of votes, which means that *voters* are the ones who hold the power. This point is often obscured in colloquial complaints about gerrymandering, because most people think of the state legislature—which has the authority to establish a district's boundaries—as the key source of the problem. Certainly, the state legislature does have power over gerrymandering, and thus must be a crucial part of any genuine structural reforms. As long as gerrymandered districts are in place, however, voters must not abdicate their power too quickly, for they (collectively) determine the force of the incentives and restrictions created by any gerrymandered district.

The easiest way to see this power is to think about insubordination. Within the structure of a gerrymandered district, the ones who can interrupt the structure through insubordination are the candidates themselves, because they are the ones who will bear the cost of refusing to abide by the incentives built into the system—namely, they risk losing votes as a result of compromises that do not promote the narrow interests of their party's base. The real question, then, is what will happen if a representative counters the trend by pursuing a compromise that serves the common good rather than their own or their party's self-interest. In gerrymandered districts, these insubordinate candidates typically face their voters and lose their primaries, which sends a clear message to future candidates that the pathway to job security is to defer to the most extreme voices in their party. This is how the structure "reproduces" itself through upward causality.[38]

Voters could, however, exercise their power differently. Those who are frustrated by partisan polarization could make a point of proactively voting for a candidate who has chosen to defy their party in the name of bipartisan solutions, rewarding rather than punishing this behavior. Doing this most effectively might require voting against one's own partisan allegiances, but as Cathleen Kaveny has astutely noted, voters in the United States cast their ballots for candidates and not parties, so there is more to be gained from supporting a brave candidate from the opposing party who is willing to work for bipartisan solutions than there is from championing a candidate who has near total loyalty to one's preferred party, because the latter will only reinforce polarization.[39] Notably, such a shift in thinking aligns with the first of two mechanisms theologians propose

---

38. Finn, "Social Structures," 30.
39. Kaveny, *Law's Virtues*, 198–200.

to counteract sinful social structures, representing a kind of "conversion" at the personal level that can help erode the strength of the structure.[40] Indeed, if more voters were to embrace this conversion and ignore partisanship in order to reward candidates who employ insubordination in the face of gerrymandered districts, they would chip away at the structure's downward causality, giving gerrymandering itself a lesser hold.

Alongside these efforts at supporting healthy forms of insubordination, voters can and should pursue strategies of targeted disruption in an effort to remove the sinful social structure of gerrymandering altogether. Such strategies are crucial, because structural reform is an essential complement to personal conversion in the theological response to sinful social structures.[41] On this level, voters would either need to pressure their state legislatures to change the redistricting rules to prevent partisan gerrymandering or pursue changes to the voting system through their state constitutions. Critics of gerrymandering have proposed a variety of these structural solutions, often through means like nonpartisan redistricting commissions that take the power of crafting individual districts out of politicians' hands altogether. Such commissions have had mixed success, however, with some becoming so mired in political polarization themselves that they cannot issue any new maps![42] Some of the most meaningful structural reforms are therefore ones like multimember districts with proportionate representation, or a ranked choice voting system, that remove the influence of partisan primaries and make general election races more competitive.[43] Regardless of the specific policies voters pursue, the goal should be to disrupt the incentives that encourage candidates' fealty to the most extreme elements of one political party, and instead to create new incentives that support moderation for the common good.

CONCLUSION

This discussion of gerrymandering through the lens of Finn's contributions to the notion of sinful social structures is far from a comprehensive analysis of all the features that have led to increases in partisan polarization in the United States. The discussion has shown, however, that much

---

40. Heyer, "Social Sin and Immigration," 413.
41. Heyer, "Social Sin and Immigration."
42. Mulroy, "Great Unskewing," 117–21.
43. Mulroy, "Great Unskewing," 103.

can be uncovered by using Finn's categories to make sense of a complex social problem like polarization. Finn's careful delineation of the emergence, downward causality, and upward causality of social structures, alongside the benchmark of the common good, provide the tools to pinpoint the sinful elements of a social structure like gerrymandering that puts the benefits of the few ahead of the needs of the many. At the same time, these resources also indicate the places where targeted changes will have the highest likelihood of success, making Finn's work valuable for both its diagnostic precision and its prescriptive vision.

BIBLIOGRAPHY

Carothers, Thomas, and Andrew O'Donohue. Introduction to *Democracies Divided: The Global Challenge of Political Polarization*, edited by Thomas Carothers and Andrew O'Donohue, 1–13. Washington, DC: Brookings Institution, 2019.

FairVote. "Dubious Democracy 2022." FairVote, 2023. https://fairvote.org/report/dubious-democracy-2022/.

Fernandez, Madison. "Competitive Congressional Districts Decline." *Politico*, Feb. 27, 2023. https://www.politico.com/newsletters/weekly-score/2023/02/27/competitive-congressional-districts-decline-00084506.

Finn, Daniel K. *Consumer Ethics in a Global Age: How Buying Here Causes Injustice There*. Washington, DC: Georgetown University Press, 2019.

———. "Sin and the Social World." *Modern Theology* 39 (2023) 114–20.

———. "Social Structures." In *Moral Agency Within Social Structures and Culture: A Primer on Critical Realism for Christian Ethics*, edited by Daniel K. Finn, 29–42. Washington, DC: Georgetown University Press, 2020.

———. "What Is a Sinful Social Structure?" *Theological Studies* 77 (2016) 136–64.

Heyer, Kristin E. "Social Sin and Immigration: Good Fences Make Bad Neighbors." *Theological Studies* 71 (2010) 410–36.

Hollenbach, David. *The Common Good and Christian Ethics*. Cambridge: Cambridge University Press, 2002.

John Paul II. *Sollicitudo Rei Socialis*. Vatican, Dec. 30, 1987. https://www.vatican.va/content/john-paul-ii/en/encyclicals/documents/hf_jp-ii_enc_30121987_sollicitudo-rei-socialis.html.

Kaveny, Cathleen. *Law's Virtues: Fostering Autonomy and Solidarity in American Society*. Washington, DC: Georgetown University Press, 2012.

Kelly, Conor M. "The Nature and Operation of Structural Sin: Additional Insights from Theology and Moral Psychology." *Theological Studies* 80 (2019) 293–327.

Kury, Franklin L. *Gerrymandering: A Guide to Congressional Redistricting, Dark Money, and the U.S. Supreme Court*. Lanham, MD: Hamilton, 2018.

Legarde, Antoine, and Tristan Tomala. "Optimality and Fairness of Partisan Gerrymandering." *Mathematical Programming* 203 (2024) 9–45.

Li, Michael, and Chris Leaverton. "Gerrymandering Competitive Districts into Extinction." Brennan Center for Justice, Aug. 11, 2022. https://www.brennan

center.org/our-work/analysis-opinion/gerrymandering-competitive-districts-near-extinction.

Mayhew, David R. *Congress: The Electoral Connection.* 2nd ed. New Haven, CT: Yale University Press, 2004.

McCarty, Nolan. "What We Know and Do Not Know About Our Polarized Politics." In *Political Polarization in American Politics*, edited by Daniel J. Hopkins and John Sides, 1–8. Monkey Cage. New York: Bloomsbury Academic, 2015.

McCoy, Jennifer, and Benjamin Press. "What Happens When Democracies Become Perniciously Polarized?" Carnegie Endowment for International Peace, Jan. 18, 2022. https://carnegieendowment.org/research/2022/01/what-happens-when-democracies-become-perniciously-polarized?lang=en.

McCoy, Jennifer, and Murat Somer. "Toward a Theory of Pernicious Polarization and How It Harms Democracies: Comparative Evidence and Possible Remedies." *ANNALS of the American Academy of Political and Social Sciences* 681 (2019) 234–71.

McCoy, Jennifer, et al. "Polarization and the Global Crisis of Democracy: Common Patterns, Dynamics, and Pernicious Consequences for Democratic Polities." *American Behavioral Scientist* 62 (2018) 16–42.

Merrill, Samuel, III, et al. *How Polarization Begets Polarization: Ideological Extremism in the US Congress.* New York: Oxford University Press, 2024.

Mulroy, Steven J. "The Great Unskewing: Remedying Structural Bias in U.S. Elections." *University of Louisville Law Review* 58 (2019) 101–46.

Pontifical Council for Justice and Peace. *Compendium of the Social Doctrine of the Church.* Washington, DC: United States Conference of Catholic Bishops, 2004.

Second Vatican Council. *Gaudium et Spes.* Vatican, Dec. 7, 1965. https://www.vatican.va/archive/hist_councils/ii_vatican_council/documents/vat-ii_const_19651207_gaudium-et-spes_en.html.

Siegel, Michael, et al. "The Impact of State Firearm Laws on Homicide and Suicide Deaths in the USA, 1991–2016: A Panel Study." *Journal of General Internal Medicine* 34 (2019) 2021–28.

Tausanovitch, Alex, et al. "How Partisan Gerrymandering Prevents Legislative Action on Gun Violence." Center for American Progress, Dec. 17, 2019. https://www.americanprogress.org/article/partisan-gerrymandering-prevents-legislative-action-gun-violence/.

Troiano, Nick. *The Primary Solution: Rescuing Our Democracy from the Fringes.* New York: Simon and Schuster, 2024.

United States Catholic Bishops. *Economic Justice for All: Pastoral Letter on Catholic Social Teaching and the U.S. Economy.* Washington, DC: National Conference of Catholic Bishops, 1986.

Van Prooijen, Jan-Willem. "The Psychology of Political Polarization: An Introduction." In *The Psychology of Political Polarization*, edited by Jan-Willem van Prooijen, 1–13. Current Issues in Social Psychology. New York: Routledge, 2021.

Daniel Finn
An Engaged Catholic Intellectual

James L. Heft, SM

I WELCOME THE INVITATION to contribute the epilogue to this Festschrift in honor of Dan Finn. I have had the privilege of knowing him for nearly twenty years and benefitted for fifteen of those years from his wisdom and collaboration as a member of the board of trustees of the Institute for Advanced Catholic Studies. I have admired who he is: a Catholic intellectual, an engaged moral theologian, and a scholar of Catholic social teaching. He is a person of courage and prudence who has promoted Catholic social thought and not hesitated to address controversial issues in ways that decrease misunderstanding, so needed in our time when ideological differences intensify divisions, not only in our country, but also in our church. There are many reasons to admire and celebrate Dan.

Dan and I had many similar experiences at similar times in our lives. In his college years, he thought seriously about becoming a priest. He attended a seminary but decided that the priesthood was not his calling, while I was ordained a Marianist priest but never attended a seminary. After graduating from college, we both taught for a while in Catholic high schools. Dan devoted himself to working with African American migrant laborers and marginal farm families when I was directing retreats for young adults, and was actively involved in the civil rights and anti–Vietnam War movements. We both finished our doctorates in 1977 and found faculty positions at Catholic universities. Both of us share a deep commitment to the Catholic faith's intellectual, moral, and spiritual traditions. We have devoted our lives to Catholic education, he mainly as a scholar and professor of theology and economics at the College of St.

Benedict and St. John's University. I have served as a teacher and mainly as an administrator and creator of innovative ways to strengthen Catholic higher education, first at the University of Dayton and then for nearly twenty years through the Institute for Advanced Catholic Studies at the University of Southern California, devoted to interdisciplinary and interreligious research on major issues affecting the church and the world. Our scholarly work has taken slightly different but complementary paths: he has specialized in economics and Catholic social thought while I have focused on the history and educational significance of the Catholic intellectual tradition at both the secondary and university levels. In this Festschrift, I will defer to other distinguished contributors to comment on Dan's professional and academic contributions to ethics, economics, and Catholic social thought.

It was only over the past fifteen years that I have had the privilege of knowing and working with Dan as a member of the board of trustees of the Institute for Advanced Catholic Studies. I have come to a deeper appreciation of the significance not only of his professional contributions, but also his ability to offer wise advice to me and to the leaders and supporters of the institute. We have worked together in building and strengthening this unique research institution at the University of Southern California, a private non-religiously affiliated research university. The institute is committed to the development and deepening of multiple disciplinary approaches in sustained and substantive conversation with the Catholic intellectual and moral traditions. He was kind enough to invite me to be a part of the important institute research series that he directed, The True Wealth of Nations, which has published six excellent volumes of scholarship over fifteen years on economics and Catholic social teaching. Dan not only facilitated the outstanding seminar-style conferences but also served as a very active editor of all the volumes. Thus, the volumes exhibit an internal coherence and sustained trajectory of development that is very rare for volumes of collected essays.[1]

---

1. The first four volumes are published by Oxford University Press: *The True Wealth of Nations: Catholic Social Thought and Economic Life* (2010); *The Moral Dynamics of Economic Life: An Extension and Critique of* Caritas in Veritate (2012); *Distant Markets, Distant Harms: Market Complicity and Christian Ethics* (2014); *Empirical Foundations of the Common Good: What Theology Can Learn from Social Science* (2017). The last two volumes are published by Georgetown University Press: *Business Ethics and Catholic Social Thought* (2021); and *Rethinking Justice in Catholic Social Thought* (2025).

CATHOLIC INTELLECTUALS IN CHANGING TIMES

Since Dan and I experienced the ups and downs of post–Vatican II Catholic life and Catholic education in the United States, I think it would be helpful at the beginning of these reflections to describe briefly some of what we both experienced in the Catholic community over those sixty years. The current situation of Catholic higher education and the life of the church in the United States is, I want to suggest, different from that of any earlier period in our lives.

The years immediately following Vatican II were filled with confidence in the Council's documents and the spirit of renewal. Those documents, rooted as they were in the biblical and patristic sources, expressed a fresh and bold rethinking of the church's mission in the modern world. It was the first church council to recognize officially that the Catholic Church had entered into a post-Christendom era, one that required collegiality among its hierarchy, dialogue with members of other religions by its laity and theologians, a renewed search for unity among Christians, and an official welcome of a faith-based use of the historical and critical studies of Scripture. For those who had lived during the years after the end of World War II, during part of what Jesuit historian John O'Malley called the "Long Nineteenth Century," the changes introduced by Vatican II were not only extensive, but for many often head-spinning.

The late sixties, however, were also especially turbulent in the United States. The Vatican II euphoria began to dissipate quickly. Student protests rose up against the Vietnam War. In 1968, Martin Luther King and Robert F. Kennedy were assassinated, and outside the Democratic National Convention violent protests erupted. The religious orders that had founded 90 percent of the Catholic colleges and universities in the United States began losing many of their members, and since then fewer young people have decided to enter them. The number of lay faculty rapidly increased and called for greater roles in governance and leadership. Tenure systems were established and academic freedom affirmed. Members of the founding religious orders established lay boards of trustees. Different interpretations of Vatican II competed for attention and influence. Women's voices among the laity and in religious orders challenged the way that bishops exercised their authority, especially the ways in which it excluded them from positions of influence and leadership.

Since Vatican II, some laity, disenchanted with what they perceive as a liberal drift among long-established Catholic colleges and universities, have established an increasing number of small Catholic colleges dedicated mainly to the liberal arts. They embody a more traditional form of Catholicism marked by a strong focus on a traditional Catholic identity and clear expectations for virtuous living among both their students and faculty. In recent years, public confidence in university education has decreased, and some political and even episcopal figures criticize their "woke," meaning liberal, tendencies. Social media has sharpened divisions among Catholics, and more bishops disagree in public. Not surprisingly, many young adults no longer participate in parish life. The political tone has shifted to the right.

In recent times, the rapid developments in US culture and among Catholics in the United States bring out clearly that Dan's special gifts are a blessing for professional theologians and lay leadership in the church. What follows is a brief description of those developments. In the northeast and upper middle west where religious orders had established most of the Catholic colleges and universities, the situation has changed dramatically. Instead of enjoying the burgeoning enrollments of the late sixties, student enrollments have dropped, and some smaller Catholic colleges have merged with bigger ones to avoid closure. Especially since the 2020 pandemic, many Catholic colleges and universities face increased financial stress, and ten smaller ones have had to shut their doors. Few of them had adequate endowments. The handful of well-endowed Catholic universities and colleges have weathered these difficult financial times and have little difficulty enrolling students, but some continue to debate, sometimes sharply, whether their financial security and prestige might have also weakened a more prophetic version of their mission, diminishing their ability to serve poorer student populations and promote Catholic social teaching. Faculty in the few doctoral programs in theology have also had to come to grips with the fact that their graduates have a difficult time finding academic positions.

Most of these trends have been widely reported in the media. There are, however, other recent developments, and I think ones especially important for the American Catholic community, that have received less attention. Dioceses and mainly lay Catholics have started to create academies and schools to educate devout Catholic graduates from both public and Catholic universities to prepare them to become skilled in evangelization. For more than twenty years, thousands of generous and idealistic college graduates have joined the FOCUS missionaries (Fellowship of Catholic University Students). They devote two years of their lives evangelizing students on college campuses, including some Catholic campuses. They emphasize Bible studies, adoration, confession, and one-on-one mentoring. They spread the gospel in an evangelical manner and invite students to accept Jesus as their Lord and Savior. They also foster religious and priestly vocations.

In recent years, I have heard an increasing number of professors, especially theologians, in long established Catholic colleges and universities, criticize these initiatives as forming young adults in a conservative and evangelical form of Catholicism absent of emphasis on Catholic social teachings. They attract, however, an increasing number of Catholic college graduates. Some of these graduates have told me that they enroll in these programs to learn what they feel they did not learn in the Catholic universities they attended: a deep love for Catholicism and a passion for evangelization.

Most of these new academic initiatives offer certificates, not degrees. They do not seek academic accreditation. They hire committed Catholics to teach, some with PhDs, but do not offer tenure or salaries competitive with established Catholic universities. Typically, their faculty are not required to do research or publish in refereed journals; those who publish books rarely publish them in academic presses. They receive considerable support from the Napa Institute, Word on Fire, and *First Things*. Those young adults who join FOCUS go through a short but intensive summer formation program that emphasizes personal holiness and skills for evangelizing college students to bring them back to the Catholic Church.

What bothers some faculty at major Catholic universities is that these new initiatives present a conservative form of Catholicism, emphasize a narrow understanding of doctrinal fidelity and personal morality, encourage adoration of the Blessed Sacrament, and create an alternative to "liberal" forms of Catholicism. They teach little about the importance of ecumenism, interfaith dialogue, the significance of religious freedom, and the primacy of conscience, and rarely explore the different degrees of teaching authority in the church or Catholic social thought.

There are also other recently founded "independent" centers for religious and Catholic intellectual formation that have grown up. They are not conservative but more centrist and seek to deepen the commitments of their participants to an active and theologically informed commitment and participation in the Catholic faith. For example, the Nova Forum at the University of Southern California started with initial funding from the Institute for Advanced Catholic Studies. It creates opportunities for students and scholars of the Catholic intellectual tradition to study texts and read books, all of which illuminate the dynamic intellectual and spiritual resources of Catholicism. Many of these programs are located at major secular universities. Their purpose is to expose students to the richness and breadth of Catholicism, intellectually, aesthetically, and spiritually.

The June 2024 newsletter of the Lumen Christi Institute in Chicago featured several initiatives located not just in Chicago but also in Milwaukee.[2] Participants described how these initiatives offer a broad vision for promoting and teaching the Catholic intellectual tradition, one that is "outside the traditional bounds of the academy yet still engaged with it." Another participant expressed gratitude that it increased "a love for robust study and teaching of the Church's intellectual tradition in a manner unbeholden to the expectations and priorities of the academic world today." One scholar added that these initiatives helped him to find better ways of learning that could "serve the Church through continuing intellectual formation in non-traditional ways, set apart from a formal teaching position in a university." A graduate from Duke University discovered in these initiatives a context in which "theology can be done with both intellectual rigor and confessional faithfulness—theology with and for the Church." He had found his university context "dissatisfying, in part because of its increasing separation from the life of the Church."

These two examples of new initiatives not part of Catholic higher education, one of a more evangelical character and the other a more scholarly character, share a critique of the limitations of how theology is done in the typical university context. Perhaps what some of the faculty in our Catholic universities are not sufficiently aware of is that these types of programs are filling a real need that too many of our Catholic colleges and universities do not address adequately: developing a love of the church, personal holiness, and public witness to the faith. If these needs are being met, it is usually in and through campus ministry programs that often emphasize service, community, and the sacraments. At a number of our Catholic colleges and universities, campus ministry leaders and faculty do little collaboratively, resulting in campus ministry programs that do not relate to the academic mission of the university and faculty who do not pay sufficient attention to the pastoral dimensions of their subjects and the spiritual needs of their students.

---

2. Accessible at Lumen Christi Institute, *Beacon*.

In a recent article, Catholic moral theologian and seminary professor Charles Camosy encouraged Catholic seminaries to form seminarians so that they would join these new educational initiatives in evangelization, which he described as "an explosion of creativity in Catholic education."[3] Though he mentioned the Catholic University of America and University of Dallas, he did not suggest that Catholic higher education in general should also support these initiatives.

I think that these movements call for a course correction in many of our Catholic universities. I think that there is a real need in many of our Catholic universities to link more intimately the academic and the pastoral dimensions, the study of theology with growth in the spiritual life, and the understanding of basic doctrines on Catholicism as the distinctive framework for understanding the church. There should be greater collaboration between theologians and campus ministers. Too often theologians who have rightly fought hard for the professionalization of their discipline have overlooked the importance of joining the critical evaluation of the tradition with a love for it, a love strong enough to help students come to love it in such depth that they will want to share it with others.

Many challenges make that synthesis difficult. A widespread suspicion in secular higher education in the United States has made it impossible to teach theology except in schools of ministry separate from the rest of the university. Even in some Catholic universities, some faculty think theologians indoctrinate their students. While it is very acceptable for biology or social science professors to want their students to fall in love with their subjects, they think that theologians who want their students to fall in love with God engage in advocacy not education, indoctrination and not critical thinking.

Several serious challenges face theologians who want to integrate the intellectual and the pastoral dimensions of the Christian faith. There is first the growing number of students in Catholic universities who are not Catholic, not to mention the increasing number of Catholic students who no longer affiliate with the church. Social media and secular culture have left many students without much understanding of any religious tradition. Few students are familiar or at ease with religious language. How to balance explanation and love of the Catholic intellectual tradition with continuing responsible critique of it, and how to bring together an emphasis on the salvific value of being a Catholic without marginalizing

---

3. Camosy, "How Seminaries Can Serve."

others in our classrooms who are not Catholic, is not easy. We need, I believe, to discover the important connection between teaching and witness, expressed so well by Pope Paul VI when he wrote in his encyclical *Evangelii Nuntiandi*, "People listen to witnesses more than teachers; but they listen most of all to teachers who are witnesses."[4]

FILLING THE GAP:
THE ROLE OF CATHOLIC INTELLECTUALS

When I think of Dan, I think of someone who understands well these recent developments in the American Catholic Church. I also think of him as a Catholic intellectual, not just as a Catholic academic. Catholic intellectuals at Catholic colleges and universities recognize and fill the gap between the academic and the pastoral by teaching a fuller sense of the Catholic tradition, and do so in ways that move students to dedicate their lives to living and sharing their faith with others. These faculty recognize the important role of campus ministry programs but do not exclude a pastoral emphasis and application from the courses they teach. Dan is both a teacher and a witness.

I think of Dan as a Catholic intellectual more than a Catholic academic. Over the years, I have become more and more aware of the limitations that many of us academics have. Typically, too many of us focus only on our academic discipline and share our research and publications mainly with other academics. Even as dedicated teachers, we are most concerned that our students understand what we teach and become competent professionals, and that upon graduation be gainfully employed. These concerns are, of course, appropriate, even admirable. However, for Catholic intellectuals, though necessary, they are not sufficient.

When I think of Catholic intellectuals, I think of someone whose intellectual interests are grounded in an ever-deepening search for truth, never confined to a single discipline, but still respectful of the research done by scholars in other disciplines. An existential preoccupation drives Catholic intellectuals. They do not hesitate to ask their students "So what?" and ask themselves, "What difference do I make in the lives of my students in my teaching and research?" Catholic intellectuals realize that at the deepest levels, they have a calling: to be not just Christian teachers but also witnesses to the gospel. Catholic intellectuals do not hesitate to

---

4. Paul VI, *Evangelii Nuntiandi*, no. 41.

speak about the truth of the gospel. However, most academics feel more comfortable speaking about knowledge and data. Academics fear, and with some reason, that religious people who think they possess the truth are likely to impose it on others. Catholic intellectuals, however, realize that in seeking truth, they never own or master it. The deeper they enter into it, the greater is their insight and the more mysterious the character of it becomes. As Flannery O'Connor wrote: "Mystery isn't something that is gradually evaporating: it grows along with knowledge."[5]

Dan is, in my opinion, a Catholic intellectual who humbly witnesses to the presence and power of Christ, the teacher and advocate for the poor. I realize that the kind of language I am using to describe Dan is likely to embarrass—even put off—many academics, even those who are Catholics. What I have written might even embarrass Dan, especially if he thinks that I think he is a saint. He and I know each other well enough to know better than even to suggest that. In my appreciation of Dan, however, I want to describe why I admire him, what drives him, and how he has devoted his life to being a Catholic intellectual.

CATHOLIC SOCIAL TEACHING

Over the past one hundred and fifty years, one of the most remarkable developments in Catholic thinking has been the growth and sophistication of Catholic social teaching (CST). Put simply, CST seeks to understand and articulate the social consequences and applications of a Catholic vision of the common good. It assumes that Catholics have a moral obligation to care for everyone's human and spiritual good, not just for that of Catholics, but for all people of all religions or none.

In my opinion, few Catholic intellectuals understand as well as Dan does the importance and challenges of implementing Catholic social teaching, especially as it relates to economics and social justice. One of the great things about Catholic social teaching is that it helps prevent the privatization of the faith, the mistake of limiting being a good Catholic only to a "personal relationship" with Jesus Christ, or to how one raises one's family or serves in the local parish—all of which are, of course, important. At the last judgment (Matt 25:31–46) we will be asked whether we have fed the hungry, sheltered the homeless, visited those in prison,

---

5. Gooch, *Flannery*, 348.

and clothed the naked. These are not just moral and theological matters, but inevitably also political and legal matters.

I have said that CST spells out the social responsibilities that flow from the teachings and life of Jesus and the doctrinal affirmations of Christianity. In the United States, the political allegiances of many Catholics shape their understanding of Catholicism more than their Catholicism shapes their political priorities. Sadly, many Catholics hear little from the pulpit about Catholic social thought. This is true also of the general public, which knows about the church's teachings on birth control, the ordination of women, and abortion. In 2015, Pope Francis published *Laudato Si'*, an encyclical on the environment. The following year, when I was at USC, I invited an environmental biologist, an environmental engineer, and a political scientist, none of whom were Catholic, to read the encyclical and be part of a panel sharing their reflections on it. They were all literally amazed that the leader of the Catholic Church could write such a document. They were very impressed with the encyclical. Most people, and that includes even Catholic academics, have heard little about Catholic social teaching and rarely read encyclicals.

That same year, I arranged a lunch with a well-to-do Catholic with the hope that I would be able to raise money for the Institute for Advanced Catholic Studies. Even before we ordered anything to eat, he began to rail against the "socialist" pope and his encyclical on the environment. "Why does the pope get into politics? Why does he address such a divisive political issue? He should stick to writing about the Catholic faith and the importance of the family and sexual morality!" I asked him, "Have you read the encyclical?" He replied that he had not. I asked him if he would be willing to read it if I sent him a copy. He said he would. We continued our lunch but did not discuss the encyclical again. I mailed him a copy of the encyclical and, three months later, arranged a second lunch with him. Again, right away, he started criticizing the "leftist" Pope Francis. I asked him if he read the encyclical I had sent to him. He said no. I suggested that we talk about other things. He also never gave any money to the institute.

One of the major challenges of understanding and implementing CST in the United States is the hyper-politicization of nearly everything, fostered by many media outlets, both left and right. Even if my friend had read the encyclical, I doubt that he would have recognized that it is based on the theological doctrine of creation. At the beginning of the creed, Catholics profess that they believe that God is the "Creator of heaven and earth." Therefore, the earth is not only good, but also a gift. That means that we are not landlords, but tenants. We have a moral obligation to accept God's gifts with gratitude and treat them with care. Dan always makes explicit the integral relationship between the fundamental doctrines of the church and their social ramifications. The encyclical urged all people of goodwill, even those with no religious faith, to enter into a dialogue about our environment, one informed by science and by a recognition of the suffering of many poor people who are most vulnerable to the threats of pollution and extreme weather.

Besides separating CST from its theological foundations, something the secular left too readily does, a second challenge of CST is its idealistic character. Early in his life, Dan worked as a community organizer. That experience made it clear to Dan how difficult it is to bring about better and more just structures in society. It takes a lot of time, persistence, patience, and prudence. While it is true most US Catholics, especially the more affluent ones, have heard little about CST, only those who have heard of it and tried to implement it know how difficult it is to bring about social change. I have often wondered how many professors who teach Catholic social thought have ever tried to organize people to implement it.

There are two additional challenges in implementing Catholic social thought. The CST teachings issued by the Vatican usually remain very general, and usually present only basic principles: the dignity of the human person, subsidiarity, solidarity, the common good, etc. How those principles should be implemented for people in Laos compared to South Africa, or people in Maine compared to those in Brazil, is complicated. Its implementation requires both understanding the needs of the people living in a particular country and then adapting the general principles to that local situation for implementation. To do that requires, in the case of economics, an understanding of how the economy operates in a local situation and only then being in a position to design the most appropriate forms of implementation. Dan has spoken and consulted in over twenty countries, a global exposure that has deepened his ability to understand that Catholic social teachings need local adaptation, perseverance, and patience for successful implementation.

During the 2024 spring semester, the University of Dayton's school of business invited Dan to give presentations to the faculty and the students about Catholic social teaching. He gave presentations tailored to each group. I attended both. In each case, he clearly described not only the principles of CST but also how the culture and economic structures of the United States needed to be taken into account for the implementation of CST. He used PowerPoint in both of his presentations, avoided overly long texts, but simply underscored key points that he wanted to dwell on and explain further by giving additional concrete examples. He also made clear how difficult it is to change existing cultural and economic structures and made a compelling case to both audiences why Christianity calls for the difficult work of organizing, especially if we really want to benefit the poor and exploited. In short, besides being a fine scholar of Catholic social thought, Dan is also an excellent teacher.

MEMBER OF THE INSTITUTE'S BOARD

In the late 1990s, with the help of many people, I was engaged in the early stages of conceptualizing and planning for the establishment of what eventually became the Institute for Advanced Catholic Studies at the University of Southern California. It was at that time that Jesuit David Toolan introduced me to Paul Caron, a business entrepreneur who had recently retired from overseeing much of J. P. Morgan's operations in Europe and the Middle East. A Georgetown graduate and then living in Europe, Caron combined extensive knowledge of financing and investments with a genuine interest in Catholic social teaching, especially as it applied to economics. He soon became a member of the institute's board. Caron told me about reading some articles written by Dan. He thought they reflected a sophisticated understanding of capitalism and Catholic social teachings. A series of conversations between Caron, Dan, and me, and then with the board, led to the board inviting Dan to become a member. He accepted.

Early on, we realized that when putting together the board of trustees for this unique research institute, we needed three types of people. First, people who could bring financial expertise and support to the board. Second, academics who understood the Catholic intellectual tradition and valued interdisciplinary and interreligious research. Third, "amphibians," that is, leaders in Catholic higher education, including presidents and provosts, skilled at mediating conversations between business leaders and academics. Dan is unusual in that he is not only an excellent Catholic thinker; he is also someone who understands the business world much better than most academics. Dan built bridges of understanding.

Over the years, fewer and fewer members of our two political parties talk with each other. We have board members of the institute who identify as both Republicans and Democrats. On several occasions, Dan could reassure politically conservative members of the board of the value and importance of Catholic social teaching. Instead of immediately talking about the political value of CST, he drew on his theological background to show how CST is rooted in the Gospels and fundamental theological teachings of the church. In still another way, his background in economics allowed him to speak credibly to the business members of the board about the complexity and trade-offs that are inevitably present in the implementation of Catholic social teaching. To the more liberal members of the board, Dan often pointed out the complexities of social change and described the trade-offs that so often accompanied the implementation of Catholic social teaching.

As a board member, Dan actually served as both a scholar and as an amphibian, an unusual and important form of that Catholic "both/and." At these meetings, he regularly explained the distinctive character and appropriate application of Catholic social thought. He did not hesitate to express an opinion that was different than someone else's, but did so in ways that others respected what he said even when they continued to disagree. His passion for the institute's mission and willingness to devote considerable time to editing and producing the impressive TWN series, as well as organizing, at the invitation of the Vatican, several international meetings in Rome, has been a major gift to the institute.

PRUDENT AND FORTHRIGHT LEADER

During the pontificates of St. John Paul II and Benedict, tensions between theologians and the Vatican increased. In 2007, Dan served as the president of the Catholic Theological Society of America (CTSA). He devoted his presidential address to the issue of power, especially how power can and ought to be exercised by theologians and bishops. One prominent US cardinal had described the CTSA as an "association of advocacy for theological dissent," and as a "wasteland." In the midst of these heightened tensions with the bishops, Dan recommended in his presidential address that the CTSA stop publishing statements that defended the organization and theologians from Vatican investigations and condemnations. He did not disagree with these statements, but said that they ended up hurting the organization when they are misunderstood. He pointed out that one of their consequences was further division and mutual misunderstanding between conservative and liberal theologians in the United States, who increasingly attend their own meetings, read their own journals, and talk mostly to one another.[6] He favored more dialogue among theologians, especially among conservative and liberal ones.

A second example of his leadership with the wider Catholic community has been his willingness to write widely accessible articles about difficult issues that not only divide theologians and bishops but also confuse ordinary Catholics. For example, in his 2012 *Commonweal* article, "Dear Prudence: Translating Moral Principles into Public Policy," he affirmed that while at their ordination bishops received a charism that promised the Holy Spirit in witnessing to the Word of God, he did not hesitate to say that the charism did not guarantee that they will always teach prudently. He went on to stress the importance of prudential judgment. He also warned against the use of "intrinsic evil" in moral statements in such a way that it becomes the litmus test for what is truly important.

My third and final example of Dan's forthright and prudent way of engaging in civil public dialogue was his 2008 *Commonweal* article, "Libertarian Heresy: The Fundamentalism of Free-Market Theology." In it, he criticized neoconservative Catholic thinkers Michael Novak and Fr. Robert Sirico. This led Sirico to write a letter to the editors of *Commonweal* that took issue with Dan's analysis. The editors invited Dan to respond to Sirico. Dan began by mentioning three of Sirico's points with which he agreed. Then he proceeded to spell out three areas of disagreement—forthrightly and prudently. At the end of his letter, Sirico had accused Dan of inaccurately and unfairly describing his position. In response to that accusation, Dan wrote a sentence that I think captures well his life-long dedication to honest and civil dialogue: "In my view of intellectual discourse, that is the most serious charge he [Sirico] makes, since the distortion of others' viewpoints not only is unjust to them, but is an acid that eats away at the common good and undermines the civility so badly needed in the Church and the world."[7] Needless to say, Dan had not distorted Sirico's views.

---

6. Finn, "Power and Public Presence."
7. Finn, "Author Replies," final para.

MENTOR AND HONEST FRIEND

In conclusion, I think that Dan is a true Catholic intellectual, one whose interdisciplinary instincts have helped him address major theological and ethical issues in credible and measured ways. For decades, he has closed the gap between the academic and the intellectual, the roles of teacher and witness. In short, his way of thinking and manner of speaking addressed well many of the most recent challenging developments in the church in the United States. I have been enriched not only by his contributions to Catholic intellectual life, his blend of academic rigor and pastoral sensitivity, and his wise counsel as a board member of the institute, but above all by his friendship and witness to the gospel.

BIBLIOGRAPHY

Camosy, Charles. "How Seminaries Can Serve the Creative Explosion in US Catholic Education." *National Catholic Reporter*, July 9, 2024. https://www.ncronline.org/opinion/guest-voices/how-seminaries-can-serve-creative-explosion-us-catholic-education.

Finn, Daniel K. "The Author Replies." *Commonweal*, Nov. 17, 2008. https://www.commonwealmagazine.org/catholicism-capitalism-joblessness-sir-thomas.

———. "Dear Prudence: Translating Moral Principles into Public Policy." *Commonweal*, Oct. 10, 2012. https://www.commonwealmagazine.org/dear-prudence.

———. "Libertarian Heresy: The Fundamentalism of Free Market Theology." *Commonweal*, Sept. 22, 2008. https://www.commonwealmagazine.org/libertarian-heresy.

———. "Power and Public Presence in Catholic Social Thought, the Church, and the CTSA." *Proceedings of the Catholic Theological Society of America* 62 (2007) 62–77.

Gooch, Brad. *Flannery: A Life of Flannery O'Connor*. New York: Little, Brown, and Co., 2008.

Lumen Christi Institute. *Beacon*. Spring 2024. https://lumenchristi.org/wp-content/uploads/2024/10/2024-Spring-Beacon-Website-Version.pdf.

Paul VI. *Evangelii Nuntiandi*. Vatican, Dec. 8, 1975. https://www.vatican.va/content/paul-vi/en/apost_exhortations/documents/hf_p-vi_exh_19751208_evangelii-nuntiandi.html.

www.ingramcontent.com/pod-product-compliance
Lightning Source LLC
Chambersburg PA
CBHW051055230426
43667CB00013B/2312